Dear Martha,

Love + Light,

Barbara Yudell

Discovering
Soul
Connections

by

Barbara Yudell

ROBERT D. REED PUBLISHERS • SAN FRANCISCO, CA

Robert D. Reed Publishers
750 La Playa Street, Suite 647
San Francisco, CA 94121
Phone: 650/994-6570 • Fax: -6579
E-mail: 4bobreed@msn.com
www.rdrpublishers.com

Book Design by Marilyn Yasmine Nadel
Cover Design by Julia Gaskill

ISBN: 1-931741-03-4
Library of Congress Control Number: 2001118499
Printed in Canada

This book is dedicated to my father's spirit and to all of the loving spirit guides, in the non-physical dimension, who have helped me to attain and to communicate my personal spiritual enlightenment.

I would also like to thank my husband and soulmate, Marvin, whose loyal support has helped to facilitate the writing of this book.

"The greatest mystery in the world is its comprehensibility."

—Albert Einstein

Table of Contents

Introduction 1

Chapter I
Dorothy, You Are Not in Kansas Anymore 5

Chapter II
The First Steps on the Yellow Brick Road 40

Chapter III
Glinda, the Good Witch 50

Chapter IV
Ruby Slippers on the Yellow Brick Road 67

Chapter V
Meeting the Scarecrow, the Lion, and the Tin Man 75

Chapter VI
Glinda, the Good Witch,
Speeds Up My Journey on the Yellow Brick Road 89

Chapter VII
Meditating Upon My Spiritual Journey 112

Chapter VIII
The Illuminated Yellow Brick Road 152

Chapter IX
Closer to Her Spiritual Oz 177

Chapter X
Understanding My Mission on the Yellow Brick Road 194

Chapter XI
The Wizard of Oz 205

Chapter XII
The Wizard Within 225

Epilogue 246

Acknowledgments

I would like to thank Sonya Lugo, Gloria Fleischner, Bernie Wagner and Ina Werthman for helping to smooth my way on the personal spiritual journey that is described in this book.

My sincere thanks also go to Darnella Cordier, Adele Altabet, Bernice Greenwald and Hillary Arenstein who helped with the editing of *Discovering Soul Connections*.

Finally, I am extremely grateful for the loyal friends who helped to turn a computer illiterate into a computer literate: Betty Wagner, Ed Cohen, Paul Schneider, Roy Brown and Howard Sapossnek.

Introduction

The spiritual seed, from which this book has sprung forth, was fertilized when my father died in 1975. This quiet, kind and hard working man, a virtual atheist when he walked the Earth, became one of my staunchest spiritual mentors when he transitioned to the other side. When my father left the physical plane, I frequently felt the presence of his spirit. It did not take me too long to recognize that his desire to protect me, to keep me safe and to guide me had survived his journey from our dense dimension into the more ethereal dimension of the spirit.

At the time of this writing, almost twenty-six years have passed since my father's death. The amazing things that have happened to me during this relatively short period of time are what motivated me to write this book. With a gentle and resolute hand, my father's spirit has led me in the direction of spiritual growth. This other worldly guidance combined with my own unquenchable desire for sacred knowledge has led me to remarkable discoveries about my immortal soul. Years of reading, study and delving deeply into the core of my very being have brought me priceless information about who I really am under this disposable suit of flesh, which I call my physical body.

The psychic journal, which I call my Lucid Notebook, that I started a number of years ago, has provided me with the material for this book. As I recorded every spiritual discovery that I was lucky enough to make and every bit of information about my immortal soul that came my way, I ultimately recognized that I was obligated to share the sacred knowledge that I was accumulating with others.

Many of my spiritual discoveries were stimulated by books that I read, many by the courses in Metaphysics and Parapsychology, which I took and even more by the wonderful spirit guides who reached out to me from another dimension. My Higher Self, that part of my soul that still resides in the invisible dimension, has also been of great assistance to me in gathering information for this book. The many 4:00 A.M. and early morning hypnagogic sessions, when my Higher Self inundated my consciousness with information about my immortal self, were also of utmost importance in furnishing the material for this book.

When I finally sat down to write this introduction, and while I was mulling over the things that were responsible for the writing of this book, I recognized that the most important factor was my insatiable curiosity. For as long as I can remember, I have always been curious about who I really was and what made me what I am today.

Even though I have never been a religious person in the traditional sense, I have always felt spiritually connected to the other side. I have always known that this physical world where we spend so much of our time is not all that there is. I have always believed in a benevolent God. It has also always been very clear to me that we are not alone on our journey through this school of hard knocks called physical life. Learning about the spiritual journey, which I consider myself to be so privileged to be on, has proven to me that I was always right. We are always connected. We are connected to God. We are connected to our Higher Selves. We are connected to our past and future lives. We are connected to dead relatives and helpful spirit guides in the more ethereal dimension where we once lived and to which we shall some day return. We are also connected to everyone else who is walking around in a cumbersome body suit of human flesh at the same time that we are.

My sincere hope is that this book that I have written

because it was evident that I had to share what I have learned about these sacred connections, will help you to connect to the love, the guidance and the spiritual assistance that are always there for you. If even one person who reads this book discovers his or her spiritual connections, I will feel that my mission has been successfully accomplished.

My background as a teacher has helped me to write a book that I hope is educational as well as interesting. When you finish the reading of this book, I hope that you will walk away with some helpful spiritual information. I hope that you will have a better understanding of how you can bring about the opening of your third eye chakra and, therefore, reach spiritual enlightenment. My desire is that my book will also help you to understand what happens in the human body to bring enlightenment about, and the various clues that lead to an understanding of your immortal soul that you can connect with on a daily basis. With this outcome in mind, I have included examples of my experiences with past life regression, numerology, synchronicities, after-death communications, near death experiences and how I learned to understand the messages from the non-physical dimension. You will also learn how I determined the symbols by which my immortal soul is known.

Writing a book about my personal spiritual story has been an education in itself. I do not think that I would ever have delved as deeply into the essence of who I really am if it were not for the writing of this book. My desire to share what I have learned about my immortal soul has also helped me to gain a better perspective of my soul's total spiritual journey. It has helped me to better understand my phobias, my strengths, my weaknesses, and my aspirations. The most important gift that I have received from the spiritual explorations that I undertook in order to gather information for this book, was a profound understanding of my soul's missions through time. Exploring many of my past lives and taking a look at the successes in my present life have helped me to recognize that my soul's most important mission has been, and still is, that of being a communicator. As a communicator, I have spent many lifetimes trying to connect others to knowledge of who they truly are under their cumbersome suits of flesh. I now recognize that this has been the driving force behind the writing of *Discovering Soul Connections*. It is my fervent hope that what I have diligently tried to communicate to you, will have as profound an effect on you, as it has had on me.

CHAPTER I

Dorothy, You Are Not in Kansas Anymore

There is a non-physical world that reveals itself
if we are ready to pay attention to it.

Have you ever wondered how you became who you are
today? I have always wondered how I became so
strong and disciplined. Where did my insatiable curiosity
come from? How did I develop my natural talents for writing
poetry and for dancing? Why have I always been afraid of
elevators? Why was I terrified of knives when I was a child
and why do I have a persistent fear of sudden violent death?

Traditional psychotherapy provided me with answers to
some of these perplexing questions, but did not totally sat-
isfy my thirst for personal knowledge. The majority of the
questions about how I became who I am were not answered
through acceptable scientific means. The most satisfying
answers about myself that I have received have come to me
not through my five physical senses, but rather through my
sixth sense. Accessing this information was not an easy
process because I had been brain washed by our rational
and scientific society. I had been very effectively taught that
if I could not see it, or hear it, or in any way prove that
something existed with my five physical senses, and
through acceptable scientific means, it did not exist.

Accepting the reality of my non-physical senses put me
on the path of personal enlightenment and answered more
questions than psychotherapy could ever answer. As I
became more at home with my sixth sense and with the
information that it was connecting me to, I began to realize
that we limit ourselves when we accept the belief that it

takes only one lifetime to mold us into who we are. This new way of thinking helped me to accept a concept, which is a part of the spiritual teachings of a majority of our planet's population, the theory of reincarnation.

Many people who have been brought up in the rational and scientific western world find the theory of reincarnation very hard to accept. They believe, as I once did, that when you are dead, you are dead. When I speak to people who hold this belief, I try to explain the theory of reincarnation in the terms that I used when I taught elementary science in grade school. I compare reincarnation to the rain cycle.

I explain that the water on our planet evaporates and in its new gaseous form turns into clouds in the sky. Then, under the right conditions, it turns into water again and descends upon the Earth in the form of raindrops. These little drops of water find their way into rivers, lakes and oceans and ultimately change into gaseous form again in order to go back up into the sky. I compare this rain cycle to what I call the cycle of souls. If we think of our individual souls as raindrops, we can then understand that when we are in gaseous form in the clouds, we are part of our soul group. It is then much easier to understand that when we turn back into raindrops and descend back to Earth, that we have individualized and are ready to have another experience in physical form. Our soul energy never disappears. It merely changes from one density into another. Just as water is water, whether it is in its liquid state, its gaseous state or in its densest state as ice, our souls are still our souls whether they inhabit a body of flesh or return to the lighter more ethereal form of the non-physical dimension. When a soul decides to return to the physical dimension and to inhabit a dense suit of flesh, it will have another human experience. When that particular lifetime is completed it leaves its dense suit of flesh and returns to its lighter more ethereal body in the non-physical dimension. Every lifetime teaches the soul important lessons and brings it closer to perfection.

Past life regression, or the accessing of past lives in an altered state, has helped me to understand who I am today.

These empowering regressions have taught me that I have lived some lifetimes as a man and others as a woman. I have been rich and I have been poor. I have been light skinned and I have been dark skinned. My past life experiences have been in just about every walk of life.

After accessing about twenty-five or thirty past lives, I came to realize that when a past life occurred was of no particular consequence. In fact, my study of Metaphysics and Parapsychology has taught me that in the non-physical realm everything happens at once. Our many lifetimes can be compared to a television set. Many television programs are aired at the same time. When we turn on our television, we tune in to one program. We can gain much information by having our attention focused on this one program. If instead, we were allowed to view fifty or one hundred shows at the same time on a giant television screen we would probably reach a point of exasperation and turn off our television. Being aware of one lifetime at a time helps us to learn from each and every one of our many incarnations. Every experience that I have had in my numerous past lives has been like a raindrop. All of these raindrops have filled up the reservoir of my soul and has increased my knowledge of myself.

One of the most interesting and influential lifetimes that I have accessed in the past few years was one that I discovered through a spontaneous past life regression on a trip to Vienna and Budapest in 1998. My husband, Marvin, and I took this trip because both his mother and my father had been born in Vienna at just about the same time. We went in 1998 because my intuition told me that this was the year to go.

Through a series of events, which I will describe later on in this book, I discovered that I had been Empress Elisabeth of Austria. As Sisi, as I was affectionately called, I was the wife of Emperor Franz Joseph, the ruler of the Austro-Hungarian Empire during the last half of the nineteenth century. I was assassinated in 1898. Traveling to Vienna and Budapest in 1998 was very fortuitous because the Austrians and the Hungarians were celebrating the one-hundredth anniversary of my assassination at this time.

What made this lifetime stand out from all the other incarnations that I have been fortunate enough to connect to, was the fact that many of my relatives in my present lifetime were in my Sisi lifetime too. My husband in my present lifetime, Marvin, was also my husband, Franz Joseph, when I was Empress Elisabeth and my older son, Jay, was my only son, Rudolph. Also my mother-in-law and my father in my lifetime as Barbara Yudell were my mother and my cousin respectively in my lifetime as Empress Elisabeth. Finally, my husband Marvin's sister, Arlene, played a significant role in this important incarnation.

As confusing as all of the above relationships may appear, they are a wonderful illustration of a very important principle of reincarnation. The truism that is revealed is that members of the same soul group reincarnate together. Before a soul is reborn, it decides when and where it will come down to Earth. Then it meets with the rest of the souls in its soul group in order to determine who among them will accompany the soul on its journey back to physical life. I think of this process as a casting call in a dramatic repertory group. The members of such a group appear in all or most of the plays that are produced by it. Different plays find the same actors and actresses assuming different parts. The only difference between reincarnation and a repertory theater group is that when we return to physical life with members of our own soul group, we do so for the lessons that we all can learn.

The story of how I got in touch with my sixth sense and learned about my immortal soul started in 1975 when my father died. Up until January of 1975, my life was very much like Dorothy's life in *The Wizard of Oz*. My feet were firmly planted on the ground and my mind was content to believe that life, as I knew it, was the only reality. I was busy with what many American housewives and mothers were doing at this time, working part-time while running a home and taking care of a husband and two young children. Then, without any warning, a metaphorical tornado swept into my life and changed my concept of reality forever.

I had spoken to my semi-retired parents in Florida on New Year's Day. My mind was at rest because everything seemed to be going well in their lives. My father was working part-time in a butcher shop and my mother was enjoying the benefits of living in a retirement community in the sunny south. Nothing in our telephone conversation gave me cause for alarm.

A few days after I spoke to my parents in Florida, for an unknown reason, I became obsessed with the concept of death. My husband, Marvin, and I had taken our two young sons, Jay and David, on a day trip to West Point. Immediately after entering the academy's military museum, I was gripped with the sensation that this was a museum of death. Breath knocked out of me and terrified that I might faint; I immediately ran outside and stood, gasping in the fresh air. My husband found me pale and shaken, with no rational explanation for what had just happened. This totally unexpected experience left me feeling confused and emotionally raw. My confusion compelled me to share this unusual experience with everyone I encountered during the next few days. My fervent hope was that someone would shed some light on what had happened to me among the cannons and artillery in the West Point Military Museum.

A week after this mysterious experience, I was called to do some substitute teaching in a middle school in New York City. During my lunch period, the principal of the school walked into the teacher's cafeteria and sat down to have lunch with me. Pleased that I had another opportunity to share something that I was having difficulty understanding, I explained what had happened at West Point and the strange obsession with the concept of death that had been haunting me all week. Despite her obviously sympathetic response to my unusual and disturbing experience, this educated and intelligent woman had no better explanation for the cause of this uncomfortable occurrence than I had.

After lunch I resumed teaching, putting all thoughts of this depressing obsession out of my mind. My attention shifted to keeping the students in my classes interested in the lesson plan for the day. An hour after I had shared my unexplainable experience with the principal, a secretary came to the door of my classroom to tell me that there was an emergency telephone call for me. When I put the receiver to my ear, my brother-in-law delivered the shattering news that my father had just died suddenly while working at his part-time job in Florida. I was in a state of shock, even more confused than I had been all week. There had been absolutely no time for me to prepare myself for this trauma. Questions whirled around in my mind. Was it possible that I had somehow picked up the knowledge of my father's impending death through a vehicle other than my five physical senses? I numbly put this puzzling question on the back burner and went about making the appropriate funeral arrangements. The principal of the school where I had been teaching when I received the news of my father's sudden death came to his funeral. She threw her arms around me and asked, "Do you remember what we were discussing just a short time before you received the news of your father's death?" As I nodded numbly she informed me that I had just had a decidedly mystical experience.

The allegorical tornado that this supernatural experience produced in my uneventful everyday life swept away all of my preconceived ideas of reality and of the concepts of life and death. Everything that had been drummed into my head for the first thirty-six years of my life had lost its veracity in the light of the otherworldly event that I had just experienced. Nothing made sense anymore. Like Dorothy, I had been swept from one reality into another with no real preparation. But, unlike Dorothy, I was alone in "Oz," without Toto, the Cowardly Lion, the Scarecrow or the Tin Man. My husband, a kind and supportive man, had never experienced anything like this himself, and found it hard to relate to what I had just gone through. I found myself floundering and desperately trying to rely upon my own inner resources to get myself onto the Yellow Brick Road leading to the Emerald City of understanding. This was particularly difficult because I didn't even have Dorothy's magical ruby slippers to assist me in my attempt to locate the mystical road to enlightenment.

The information about my father's death that had come to me through my sixth sense, had made it apparent to me that there were forces out there that I could not see with my physical eyes or hear with my physical ears. It was obvious that they were influencing me nonetheless. Since I was alone in my personal "Oz" and had no one who could help me to understand my strange premonition, I had no choice but to fall back on the companions that had helped and supported me through my life so far, books. I went to the library and took out books on death, the after-life and spirituality in general. Reading these books seemed to pose more questions than answers. I did not let this discourage me because I was determined to find out why my reality had shifted.

Time and life went on and I continued to have sporadic episodes of extrasensory perception. But, unfortunately, I had no better understanding of why this was happening than I had when I foresaw my father's death in 1975. In 1979, another, much more traumatic tornado, that would ultimately turn my reality upside-down, came swooping into my life. The tornado of 1979 came in the form of two gunmen, who shot up our house in Paramus, New Jersey with a high powered rifle, in an attempt to extort money from us. These two felons targeted us because we lived across from a county park, where families from poor inner city neighborhoods often held picnics. The two men who shot up our house were unemployed and were at a family picnic in the county park. They saw our home from the park. Our house, in an upscale development, was in the middle of a cul-de-sac. If the gunmen had gone too far into this cul-de-sac, they could be trapped. If they chose a house that was near the entry to the cul-de-sac, they took the chance of being seen from the main road. The unfortunate placement of our house was not the only reason that these two felons selected us for their attempt at extortion. They saw our eight-year-old son and his many friends running around on our front lawn. We learned later that this was the catalyst that sparked the extortion attempt.

Overnight, my life became a frightening and not very well written grade B movie, complete with stakeouts, police chases, and sloppily written extortion notes. We were asked to vacate our home. After we packed our suitcases and moved in with Marvin's sister and brother-in-law, detectives from the Paramus Police department moved into our master bedroom for what seemed like the longest week of my life. While I waited for the two gunmen to return with an extortion note, an obsessive thought kept running through my mind. I kept torturing myself by thinking that things like this happen to other people, not to my family. At the end of this fear filled, trauma-ridden week, the two felons who had shot up our quiet home and had fractured our sense of peace and security were apprehended on a date that changed my life forever, September 14, 1979, my 41st birthday. They had come back to hand deliver an extortion note that demanded that we give them $25,000 or our son would get the next bullet. In retrospect, I realize that there was spiritual significance to the fact that this traumatic event occurred on my birthday. This stressful event was actually a catalyst for many future metaphysical and spiritual lessons.

The stress and the fear that these two felons had maliciously foisted upon my family did not begin to disintegrate for another two years. During this time, the two gunmen walked around free on bail. At the end of this period, they were sentenced to five years in prison. The one stroke of good fortune that came my way during this hellish time was contained in the fact that my family did not have to go through the stress of a court trial. The guilt and subsequent sentencing of the two criminals who had shattered my equanimity was determined by plea-bargaining. But, despite this one lucky break, the unrelenting day in and day out stress of worrying about my family's safety and physical and emotional well being, took its toll on me as severe physical symptoms. The emotional upheaval that I had undergone during this time had depressed my immune system and had allowed a Candida Albicans infection to take hold in my body. This stubborn fungus, which causes annoying and uncomfortable vaginal yeast infections, was also the cause of severe food and chemical allergies. Not only did I have strange reactions to things like the vinyl upholstery on chairs and to household cleaning products, but I also found myself unable to eat most of the common foods found in supermarkets. This new physical problem made it almost impossible for me to lead a normal life. I couldn't even walk into a department store because the chemicals, which evaporated into the air from clothing and cosmetics made my brain swell and caused almost total disorientation. These cerebral allergies made driving home from the mall one of the greatest challenges of my life.

I was again wracked with fear and despair. How was I going to be able to raise my children and take care of my husband and my home if I couldn't function in the twentieth century world? Thankfully, my very strong survivor's instinct, and my strength of will, kicked in and made me determined to lick this problem as I had every other problem that had ever come my way. I obtained the name of a highly recommended nutritionist. Marvin and I drove to northwestern Connecticut for a consultation with her. I will forever be grateful to this woman for asking me if I had ever had a vaginal yeast infection. When I answered in the affirmative, she told me that I had a Candida Albicans infection. She then helped me to develop a strict program of low carbohydrate diet, natural, yeast free, food supplements, exercise, colon cleansing and chiropractic treatment. Digging up every little bit of fortitude and strength of will that I had developed over this lifetime helped me to stay on this rigid program for seven years. Having a kind and supportive husband also made it possible for me to stay on this strict regimen. Marvin's only wish was that I get well. He did what he had to do to make this possible. He even got me involved in what turned out to be a highly successful, home-based nutrition and natural, biodegradable products business.

Even more important than the monetary benefits that this business gave to me, was the satisfying benefit of helping other people to detoxify and to lead healthier lives, while I regained my health.

In retrospect, I see that another side benefit of what I call my "healing crisis" was a heightening of my psychic ability and a sharpening of my spiritual sensibilities. I recognize that one of the reasons that this occurred was that when ever I had a severe allergic reaction, the heart pounding fear that this engendered, forced me to adopt a regimen of breathing exercises. This new system of breathing helped to calm me, to lower my blood pressure, and to slow down my heart rate. It wasn't until much later that I realized that these breathing exercises were actually my first meditative experiences and were responsible for much of my subsequent spiritual growth.

Looking back from a more spiritually evolved perspective has also helped me to recognize that having a home-based business was also of great help to me in my progression up my spiritual path. Being my own boss afforded me the luxury of remaining in bed for a while after awakening in the morning, instead of flying out of bed in order to get to work. Since I did not have to be a prisoner of an alarm clock or a nine to five job, I often allowed my answering machine to pick up incoming calls until I was ready to get out of bed and to start my day. I can see that these daily exercises of doing nothing but enjoying my inner world were also responsible for the gradual heightening of my spiritual sensibilities. This insight came to me much later, after I learned that going within can help one to connect to, and to communicate with God and with our many spiritual helpers in another, invisible dimension.

When I think back to this time of tremendous spiritual and psychic transformation, I realize that I was connected to otherworldly help and guidance all along. I am absolutely sure that I would never have been able to stay on the Spartan-like natural health program, that I had developed for myself, without some kind of heavenly help. One incident

in particular stands out as an illustration of just how stren-
uous this regimen was. While I was getting well, and in
order to break the monotony of being at home so much, I
suggested to my husband that we take a family trip to
Quebec City in Quebec, Canada. Marvin and I and our two
children walked into and out of seven restaurants until we
found one that could offer me a meal that I could eat.
Despite any inconveniences that my strict regimen placed
upon my family and myself, I stayed on my program
because getting well was the most important motivation in
my life. My aim was to rebuild my immune system and my
health so that I could be the kind of wife and mother that I
so desperately wanted to be. It took the perspective of time
for me to recognize that while I was living through this
nightmare, I was also rebuilding myself psychically and
spiritually.

During this extremely difficult time, I found that doing
word puzzles was very therapeutic. I started to purchase
puzzle magazines and before long Marvin was complaining
about the stockpiles of these books that were springing up
all over the house. I went from crossword puzzles to acros-
tic puzzles and then to code words and then to logic problems.
From my present perspective, I see that while I was lifting
my spirits and occupying my mind with these engrossing
puzzles, I was also developing a skill, which would eventually help me in my spiritual transformation. This seemingly
innocuous hobby was helping me to see the connection
between things. Becoming more expert at connecting letters
and syllables to form words sharpened my observational
skills and helped me to see how our souls are connected to
each other and to entities in the non-physical dimension. I
was also learning to function effectively in a world of symbols. These puzzles were very much like a psychic corre-
spondence course sent to me by unseen mystical mentors
from another realm of reality. The fact that I followed my
inner voice and did things that made me feel better made me
understand that I have always been in touch with my intuition. Looking back at my life has convinced me that I have

always followed my gut feelings and not my logical left-brain. By following what my less logical and more psychic right brain wanted me to do, I was helped to become more aware of spiritual connections, which would ultimately be the material for this book.

The next spiritual tornado that swept into my life and succeeded in hastening my sacred transformation occurred in September of 1993. At about 4:00 A.M. on a Saturday in the early part of the month, I suddenly awoke from a deep sleep because I was extremely thirsty and needed a glass of water. Since my natural health program did not allow me to drink tap water, I had to go downstairs to the kitchen where there was a reverse osmosis water filter attached to the sink. While I was drinking this purified water, I noticed that the florescent light bulb above my head was flashing off and on. What happened next was, and still is one of the most unusual and awe inspiring experiences of my life. As I was wondering why the light above my head was flashing, I saw something paranormal. In the far corner of my long country kitchen, I saw an elongated oval green light, which was surrounded by a golden halo, floating in the air. Since this experience was so alien to me, I was sure that I was losing my mind. Marvin was still upstairs in our bedroom, fast asleep. In a state of near panic, I shut out the kitchen lights and made a beeline upstairs to the safety of my sleeping husband, and my waiting bed. Still shivering with fear from an episode that I did not understand, I decided that I would not tell anyone about this incident for fear that they would not understand.

I swiftly escaped from the memory of this eerie phenomenon by sinking into a deep protective sleep. About five hours later, Marvin awakened me with some troubling news. He had just received a phone call informing him that my best friend, Sandy's mother had died during the night. I had known Edith for almost as long as I had known her daughter. We had always enjoyed each others company when ever we were together at gatherings in Sandy and her husband, Stan's home. Marvin and I attended Edith's funeral with great sadness. At the funeral, we found Sandy, an only child, overwhelmed with pain, guilt and recriminations. She was convinced that she had failed as a daughter and she was doing a good job of beating herself up because of this. When we went to Sandy and Stan's house after the funeral, I did the best that I could do to console my distraught friend and to convince her that she had been a good daughter and that her mother had known that her only child really loved her.

I did not make the connection between Edith's death and the mysterious green and golden light that I had seen in my kitchen until the next day. As soon as I recognized that there was a connection between these two events, I picked up my telephone with much trepidation and placed a call to Sandy. When I asked my friend when her mother had died, she informed me that her mother had passed away at about 4:00 A.M., the same time that I had seen the strange green light in my kitchen. As Sandy shared this information with me, I could feel gooseflesh running up and down my arms. Despite my emotionally charged reaction, I took a deep breath and said, "Sandy, I saw a strange oval green light surrounded by a golden halo floating in the air in my kitchen at about the same time that your mother died. I feel very strongly that there is a connection between this light and your mother's death. Maybe your mother's spirit was trying to tell me something?" Sandy's response sent icicles through the telephone wires. In an attempt to placate me, she did not say that I was crazy, but made it quite obvious that she really did not believe me. Still choking on what I had just shared with my friend, I decided not to push my luck and changed the topic. Since Sandy seemed to be in a little less pain, it occurred to me that the ethereal green light was really Edith's way of asking me to help her daughter to overcome the needless recriminations that she was torturing herself with. I asked myself whether what I had said to Sandy on the day of the funeral had helped her to shed some of this guilt. It did not take long for me to find out that my thinking was right. A thank-you for a job well done came the very next night. When I went downstairs for another drink of water in the early morning hours, I had the strangest feeling that someone was rubbing my arm, as if to express their appreciation for something that I had done for them. I actually felt that Edith's spirit was in the room with me and that she was expressing her gratitude for the help that I had given her only child. This time I was not afraid.

About two or three days later, I received an excited phone call from Sandy. As her breathless words tumbled through the telephone wires, I learned that her daughter, Nina, was returning home from teaching in the local high school and saw the same glowing green and gold light that I had seen in my kitchen when her grandmother died. During the two or three weeks following this affirming telephone call, Edith's spirit seemed to be popping up all over the place. Sandy woke up in the middle of the night to the sight of a glowing green light right over her head. Then Sandy's oldest daughter, Cindy, told us that her young daughter had seen and waved to her great-grandmother, Edith. Even Edith's younger sister, Ruth, reported a contact from her older sister's spirit. Edith, certainly not a comedienne in life, became a source of glee and enjoyment after her death. We all enjoyed the vigorous way in which she let us know that she was still around. I found it very whimsical that this quiet and self-effacing woman had become such a marvelous communicator when she passed over to the other side.

Life went on and so did my spiritual and metaphysical reading. The experience that I had just had with Edith's spirit made me eager to understand the dynamics by which Sandy's dead mother could project from a more heavenly realm into our physical world.

Sandy called me again about two weeks later to tell me to turn on my television to the Montel Williams' talk show. I did. There was a pediatrician named Dr. Melvin Morse on this show speaking about near death experiences in children. I was totally engrossed in what this articulate physician had to say. Dr. Morse related what children who had been brought back from clinical death reported seeing, hearing and experiencing on the other side. I watched this show with rapt attention. It seemed to speak to an inner knowing deep within my soul. I decided that I certainly was going to buy Dr. Morse's book.

By the next morning, I had completely forgotten about Dr. Morse and his book. After breakfast, I made all of my business calls and put incoming orders together for delivery. Then, because my Spartan health regimen had completely healed my immune system, I drove to a local department store to buy a gift. I had to walk through the book department on the way to the area where the gift that I wanted to purchase was located. Before I left the book department, I almost bumped headfirst into a huge display of Dr. Melvin Morse's latest publication. I purchased the book and started to read it as soon as I returned home. In retrospect, I recognize that this was not an accident. Since I had forgotten about Dr. Morse's book and my walk through the book department was meant to get me to the gift department, I now realize that a higher power constructed this scenario so that I would purchase a much-needed book.

As I read this book on near death experiences in children, I was filled with a sense of amazement and awe. Dr. Morse had succeeded in putting several pieces of my spiritual puzzle together by connecting me to the awareness that I had had a near death experience when I was three-years-old. The family story was that I was riding on a tricycle with a large lollipop in my mouth. For some unexplained reason the tricycle tipped over and the lollipop was shoved down my throat. I am only alive today because my mother was nearby. If she hadn't gotten to me in time and pulled the lollipop out of my throat, I would not be in my present physical form.

This unexpected discovery came to me because there were vivid memories of this traumatic occurrence planted firmly in my conscious mind. The most outstanding memory I retained from this disturbing experience was actually a mental picture of my little body stretched out on the pavement next to the toppled tricycle. I now recognize that this mental image was from a vantage point well above the ground. In retrospect, I now understand that I have retained this mental image up until the present day because my soul actually left my body during this time, giving me an out of body experience. Obviously, this out of body experience became an in body experience when the lollipop was wrenched from my throat and my soul returned to its physical home.

I could hardly control the excitement that this new discovery brought into my life. The telephone lines buzzed as I told everyone that I knew what I had just realized. The more that I shared my recent discovery with others, the more childhood memories came crashing into my conscious mind. The first corroborating memories were of a recurrent dream, which plagued me throughout my childhood. This upsetting dream always found me in a scary dark elevator, which was racing toward the roof of an apartment building. This elevator, which emitted a strange whirring sound, proceeded to go through the roof of the building, soaring into the full moonlit and starry night. This frightening memory seemed to burst within my skull, bringing me the startling realization that this dark and speeding elevator was symbolic of the tunnel experience reported by so many people who return from death. In retrospect, it only makes sense that a child of three would equate a tunnel with an elevator. I instantly recognized that this recurrent dream was my soul's way of trying to get me to understand that I had had a near death experience at age three. My intuition then connected me to the knowledge that the full moon and the myriad stars that I saw in my dream, when the elevator speeded through the roof and into the sky, were symbolic of the peaceful and loving light that people who return from clinical death see at the end of the tunnel. The last memory that corroborated my unexpected discovery that I had had a near death experience at the tender age of three was a clear mental picture of majestic looking beings who were dressed in white robes and who exuded love, understanding and acceptance. I was sure that these were the welcoming beings of light that near death experiencers so often report seeing before they return to their physical bodies. I had never realized that these memories were connected to each other. Now that I saw that they were, I was filled with great joy because I now knew that I had had an experience with the divine when I was quite young.

This totally unexpected knowledge that I had had a near death experience as a child, answered many questions that had plagued me during my entire lifetime. Now I finally understood why I was having paranormal experiences. Reading Dr. Morse's eye opening book taught me that near death experiences very often activate the right frontal lobe of the brain. This is the part of the brain that is responsible for bringing in psychic, spiritual and paranormal experiences. Learning that children who have near death experiences often show an appreciable increase in intelligence also explained my high I.Q. I was in a greatly accelerated academic program in junior high school and then graduated from the Bronx High School of Science, a school for youngsters with high I.Q.'s, when I was sixteen-years-old. It also explained my constant desire to help others. I had even had my nose broken when I was ten years old, while defending my best friend who was being beaten by the neighborhood bully. My family was always a little puzzled by the missions that I set up for myself. Dr. Morse's book showed me that this was a trait that was shared by many who had nearly died and then had returned to life transformed by their near death experiences. Everything that I learned in his book caused a huge sigh of awareness and relief to come up from the very recesses of my being.

Learning that I had had a near death experience at a very young age seemed to open a door to another world. I became an even more voracious reader of spiritual and metaphysical books than I had ever been before. Every question that these books answered led to two or three more questions. I became a regular at the library and at our local bookstore and consumed New Age and spiritual books like a child left in a sweet shop consumes candy. The books that I read at this time were mostly about near death experiences and reincarnation. They were very healing because they corroborated what my recent experiences were teaching me; there was an after-life. My reading taught me that souls in the after-life could influence and affect us and helped us to get the most out of our human experience. I also learned that we all have spirit guides and guardian angels, many of whom have had human incarnations, who counsel and protect us at all times. As I recognized that we are never alone during our stay in Earth School, my entire philosophy of life and spirituality changed. If becoming more spiritual was what New Age people meant by ascending, that was exactly what I knew that I was doing.

Not long after the life-altering discovery of my childhood near death experience, my husband and I decided that it was time to retire. Something way down deep inside of me wanted desperately to move to Florida. I rationalized that this desire stemmed from my dislike of northern winters and my predilection for sunlight, but the yearning seemed to run deeper than this. After doing some research, we bought a house in Boynton Beach, Florida and put our house in the northeast up for sale. Trying to sell a house while running a thriving home based business and taking care of a home and a family, turned out to be more than I had bargained for. Since time was at a premium and something had to give, my spiritual reading came to an abrupt halt. I now see that this was extremely detrimental, because spirituality would have helped me to cope with the stress that selling a house always creates.

The stress of selling our house intensified from week to week. Since my nutrition business was home based, I found myself juggling clients, real estate agents and prospective house buyers. Some of the stress came from the fact that my business grew by leaps and bounds because some of the agents and some of the people who came to see our house decided that they needed my products and became steady customers. It seems ironic that at a time when I could have benefited from spiritual reading the most, I had absolutely no time to do it.

After about eight or nine months of living in what seemed like a madhouse, I awakened one morning wondering silently why our house would not sell. This silent question came to me while I was still lying in bed in a semi-meditative or hypnagogic state. As soon as I mentally asked this question, a thought, which I now realize, was either from my Higher Self or from one of my spirit guides or guardian angels, flashed through my mind, "You stopped your spiritual reading. Read about pyramids." This thought startled me and I immediately jumped out of bed. The use of the word "you" confirmed my absolute certainty that this thought did not stem from my own conscious mind. Even though I was not sure at the time from where this advice came, I decided not to question it. After a shower and a quick breakfast, Marvin, at home because it was Saturday, and I took off in our car for the local bookstore, following the advice I received that morning. I felt like a knight in King Arthur's court, off on a quest for the Holy Grail. I still do not know if Marvin actually believed me at this point, or if he was merely trying to placate me. What I do know is that he was as desperate to sell our house as I was.

When we entered the bookstore, I really had no idea of what book I was looking for. Thankfully, I had learned to rely on my intuition. I had learned that when in doubt, I should trust my right brain. What happened next is something that has happened many times since then and has become a metaphysical tool, which I use quite frequently. I merely stood in front of the New Age bookshelves, and let my eyes wander over the titles. One book in particular, *The Celestine Prophecy*, jumped out at me because it seemed to be glowing with a sort of spiritual luminosity. I had heard very briefly about this book on the "Oprah Winfrey Show" one day while I was surfing television channels with our remote control. I took this book off the shelf and purchased it because I intuitively knew that its luminosity meant that it contained guidance from the non-physical dimension. I was not about to question this.

I recognize, in retrospect, that this book was exactly what I needed at this particular time in my spiritual evolution. I will never again question the adage, "When the student is ready, the teacher will appear." Time has taught me that this is true and that the teacher can be a book or a human being, a magazine, a movie, a television program, a spirit guide, or even an animal.

Deciding that there was no time to waste because our house in Florida was almost finished and it was imperative that we sell our New Jersey house, I started to read *The Celestine Prophecy*, as soon as we returned home. One of the most important things that this book taught me was that a Higher Power often sends us messages in the form of meaningful coincidences or synchronicities. When I did some research on synchronicities I discovered that the Swiss psychiatrist Carl Jung coined the word "synchronicity." Jung described a synchronicity as a meaningful coincidence that does not rely on cause and effect. My continued study of these meaningful coincidences or synchronicities and my tremendous experience with them has taught me that they are random coincidences that carry a spiritual message from the other side with them. Though others insist that there must be several occurrences of the same coincidence in one or two days to make it a synchronicity, I have found that one random coincidence can also carry a spiritual message. The experience of going to the bookstore and having just the book that I needed at the time almost jump off the shelf into my waiting arms was an example of a synchronicity. I have subsequently found that these meaningful coincidences have been and continue to be very prevalent in my life. Synchronicities are a wonderful form of guidance because if we truly believe in them and follow them, they invariably lead us to spiritual truths.

As I ravenously devoured the book that I knew had been sent to me from another realm of reality, I also learned that we can transfer a positive or a negative energy field, to another person in our vicinity. Now I knew why a Higher Power had sent me this book. My intuition told me that this was exactly the knowledge that I needed at this time to help us to sell our house.

At this point, my intuition alerted me that resuming and learning from my spiritual reading was going to make something important happen. I knew with utmost certainty that God was now going to send us just the right couple for our house. I was prepared to share my positive energy with them to make sure that they actually bought the house. I did not have to wait too long to find out that my intuition was right. Two days later, a real estate broker who had just brought a young couple to see our home called to let us know that they wanted to see it again. They returned the very next day. After they inspected our house again, we all sat down in the living room. While Marvin and I were answering questions, I made a conscious effort to transfer as much positive energy as I could to these young perspective buyers. With positive thoughts running through my mind, I mentally directed the good energy that these thoughts engendered to these interested people. Since I had never done anything like this before and was not completely sure that it would work, I could feel my heart nervously pounding against the wall of my chest. I could also feel little droplets of perspiration sliding down my back. After about an hour, the real estate broker and her two clients decided that it was time to leave. About thirty minutes after they departed, something told me to look out of our dining room window. I was surprised to see that the two interested young people were still sitting in their parked car in front of our house. They remained in their car, probably discussing our house, for more than an hour. I wondered whether I had pumped out too much positive energy and had somehow spiritually glued them to the house.

The following morning, the telephone rang and before I could even pick up the receiver, an inner voice told me that we had sold our house. When I hung up the phone, I tried to determine whether my happiness came from an almost certain house sale or from the fact that I was becoming more psychic. The very next day our real estate brokers met at our house and after about an hour of negotiations we were told that the interested couple was ready to sign a contract and purchase our home. This experience left me with the feeling that I had achieved a closer connection to the non-physical dimension. I had received celestial guidance and I had followed it. A feeling of accomplishment pervaded my entire being. I felt like I had many years before this, when I was in school and I received an A on a difficult assignment. It seemed to me that selling our house so soon after resuming my spiritual reading was a reward for following other-worldly guidance. I had tested the concept of transferring positive energy from one person to another and it had worked. This wonderful feeling of accomplishment and success was reinforced the following morning when, upon awakening, I realized that the new owner's last name was a synonym for the word "light". Since the word light is used in spiritual circles as a synonym for God, I knew that this was a message from the non-physical dimension that I was moving in the right sacred direction. I was communicating with Higher Powers. In retrospect, this was also probably the very first time that I consciously knew and accepted the fact that I was a light worker, an immortal soul, in bodily form, whose mission was to connect heavenly light to the physical world.

Thankful that my heavenly helpers had assisted me in solving one problem, I had perfect trust that they would continue to aid me in orchestrating the rest of our move to Florida. My intuition had been encouraging me to make this move for the last few years. Deep in my heart I knew that Florida, a place of sunshine and light, was where my spiritual journey would move into high gear.

The very next problem to be tackled was to find a professional who would organize and run a tag sale for us, so that we could sell belongings that we did not want to take to Florida with us. With this in mind, I opened up our town newspaper to the business section and started to call tag sale professionals. I left messages on answer machines and went on with the rest of my day.

My secretary, Nancy, arrived bright and early the following morning, and after some small talk, we both became absorbed with running my nutrition business. The first telephone call of the day was from one of the tag sale people that I had contacted the day before. As I spoke to her, I could see that Nancy realized that I was talking to someone who ran tag sales. She reached into her handbag, dug out a business card and handed it to me. My mouth dropped open when I looked at the card. I found it hard to believe that the person whose name was on the business card was the person I was talking to on the phone. This was obviously a synchronicity, containing some kind of spiritual guidance from the other side. Deciding to follow this synchronicity to see where it would lead me, I hired the person who I was talking to on the phone. When I hung up the receiver, I excitedly told Nancy "Heaven just sent me a little spiritual hint in the form of a synchronicity and I'm going to follow this clue to see where it leads me." I added that I was now firmly convinced that heaven was indeed supporting our move to Florida.

A few days before the sale was to begin, three people showed up to appraise and tag the articles to be sold. One of the three people was a man, Frank, whose back so disabled him, that he was receiving social security payments from the government. He was a friend of the woman who ran the tag sale and was going to assist her by doing non-physical jobs. My husband was so impressed by this man's affability and organizational skills that he hired him to help us to organize and clean out our garage and basement workroom after the tag sale was over.

Frank arrived on the agreed upon day, walked into the open garage and shocked me by greeting me with this statement, "Barbara, I had an operation on my back. I was given morphine and had a very strange reaction. I went up a long dark tunnel toward a bright light. There was organ music playing in the background while all of this was happening. Then my past, my present and my future were shown to me all at the same time." I had no idea what had compelled this friendly and unassuming man to blurt such personal information out to an almost total stranger. Was this what the synchronicity involving the business card, which Nancy had given me, was all about? I immediately told Frank that he had had a near death experience. I added that I had also had what is often referred to as an NDE when I was only three-years-old. When I asked him if he knew what I was talking about, he said that he had seen someone talking about this on a television talk show. I told him that I owned many books and a videotape on the subject that he could borrow, which pleased him tremendously.

Frank started to sort through the junk in our garage and I went into the house to get the promised videotape. When I returned to the garage with this tape, I found Marvin standing with Frank and listening to his story. As I walked toward the two of them, I could hardly believe what I heard. Marvin was telling Frank, "I had a similar experience when I was almost ten years old. I had a very bad case of chicken pox and was running an extremely high fever. As my mother was trying to lower my temperature, I could see a long tunnel with a bright light at the end of it." I was so dumbfounded by what I had just heard that I could not respond right away. By the very next day, after I had processed what I had just learned, I was composed enough to ask my husband why he had never told me about this occurrence, especially after he had found out that I had had an NDE. I still find it hard to accept the explanation that it never occurred to him to tell me about his own near death experience. It seems to me now, from the perspective of time, that he probably thought that I was a little wacky at the time that all of this was happening. He might have also felt more secure in opening up about this when another man corroborated the authenticity of having a near death experience. In retrospect, this confidence should not have shocked me. After having read the profile of someone who has been transformed by a near death experience, I had actually told one of my friends that I thought that my husband fit into this category too. Was a Higher Power tapping me on the shoulder and telling me that my instincts and my intuitions were right on target and that I should never doubt them again?

I was certainly very grateful to this Higher Power for connecting me to the knowledge that my husband, Marvin, had also had a near death experience. Even though I knew that this was definitely a synchronicity, an intuitive feeling told me that there was more to this meaningful coincidence than what appeared on the surface. A small voice within me told me that my husband's NDE might have happened at about the same time that I had my near death experience. I think that I felt this way because Marvin is almost seven years older than I am and was almost ten years old when I turned three. I asked him if he could remember when he had his near death experience and he told me that it was during October of 1941. Hearing this was extremely exciting because I was almost certain that this was the same month that my tricycle had tipped over, the lollipop had gone down my throat, and I had had a near death experience. I decided to call my mother in Florida, in order to determine whether my memory of the date of this traumatic event was correct. Thankfully, it was easy for my mother to remember this incident because she had been pregnant with my twin sisters at the time. The answer was just the one that I had expected; I had also had my NDE in October of 1941. This corroboration of something that I intuitively knew to be true was making me feel like an intuitive detective. I was uncovering little bits and pieces of spiritual information that I hoped would eventually complete the total picture of my spiritual story. Over the years, my metaphysical reading and my personal experiences have taught me that all synchronicities contain messages from the non-physical dimension. These meaningful coincidences are like a bridge connecting the physical dimension, where we live our earthly lives, to the non-physical dimension, where we go after we die. The synchronicity of Marvin and I both having had near death experiences in October of 1941, decades before we met, was not the only meaningful coincidence that connected us to each other. When I look back over our lives together, I recognize that our meeting, courtship and our marriage consisted of a series of synchronicities.

The first of these outstanding synchronicities starts with the fact that I was actually not even supposed to be in

Miami Beach, Florida, in April 1963, when Marvin and I met in the Boom Boom Room in the Fontainebleau Hotel. I was really supposed to be back in Queens, New York taking the oral part of an entrance examination for a free Master's Degree in Administration and Supervision at Queens College Graduate School of Education. I already possessed both a Bachelor's and a Master's Degree in Education from this school, but had been recommended to take the examination for this additional program by the principal of the elementary school in Ozone Park, Queens where I had been teaching since I graduated from college. Flattered by this recommendation, I took and passed the written part of the test and was scheduled to take the oral part during our annual Spring Break.

Despite the prestigious benefits that passing an exam such as this would have given me, when my friend, Sylvia, asked me if I would like to fly down to Florida with her during this time for a much-needed vacation, I immediately said yes. There is no rational reason for why I blithely threw away an opportunity that thousands of teachers would have been more than thrilled to receive. The only motivation for my behavior that makes any sense to me was that I was following my intuition when I made this life altering decision to accompany Sylvia to Florida in lieu of taking the scheduled examination. Deep within me, where my soul resides, I am sure that I knew that my destiny did not lie in the administration and supervision of an elementary school. I feel this way because I left elementary school teaching as soon as I was able to do so, when my children were partially grown, and went into the nutrition business. Instead of following the path of Elementary School Supervision and Administration, I followed the path that my soul wanted me to take and went to Miami Beach to meet my husband to be.

This trip was particularly exciting to me because at twenty-four I had not done much traveling yet, and this was my first visit to Florida. It was also the very first time that I had ever flown in an airplane. After an uneventful ride in a jet plane, Sylvia and I checked into a small hotel on Collins Avenue in Miami Beach and lolled the hours away by soaking up the wonderful Florida sunshine. I was thoroughly enjoying being young and relatively free of responsibilities. Someone at the hotel's pool had told us about the Boom Boom Room at the Fontainebleau Hotel. We were told that there was a very good band playing every night and that for the price of one drink we could sit and enjoy the music for as long as we wanted. That evening, Sylvia and I and another woman we had met at poolside, shared a cab to the Fontainebleau. We settled ourselves at the bar, ordered drinks and enjoyed the marvelous Latin music that I have always been passionate about. While I was enjoying what the band was playing, a rather youngish looking man approached me and asked me to dance. After he joined me in a pretty decent Pachanga, I let him know that I thought that I was much older than he was. He laughed as he showed me his driver's license. He was thirty-one and not twenty-one, which he looked like to me.

When he told me that his name was Marvin Yudell, I had the strangest feeling that I knew him. When we compared notes, we decided that even though we had grown up about a ten or fifteen minute car ride from each other in the Bronx, New York, we had never crossed paths. Besides teaching music in a middle school in the Bronx, where he still lived, he was also a professional musician. He played the trumpet on the weekend and never had the time to attend parties and singles dances. Marvin bought me a drink and we talked for the rest of the evening. We discovered that besides having teaching in common, we both came from middle-class Jewish backgrounds and that we both loved Latin music and music in general. In fact, his love of Latin music was what brought him to the Boom Boom Room in the first place. He had come to visit a friend who was playing in the band.

After a few more dances, Marvin escorted me back to my hotel and asked me out to dinner for the following evening. I accepted the invitation and excitedly told Sylvia about it when I got back to our room. She was not happy about me going out with a total stranger. I told her that I felt very comfortable with this man, as if I had known him forever.

The next day found me at the pool soaking up some more of the beautiful Florida sunshine. To my surprise, Marvin showed up in his bathing suit and asked me to go into the water with him. We spent the next few hours learning about each other and before he went back to his hotel to dress for dinner, he proposed to me. He seemed so sincere that I was not the least bit shocked by this proposal. My answer to him was that I was looking forward to our dinner date that evening. Something like this had never happened to me before. I had always been very popular and had dated quite a bit but no relationship had ever felt right. This felt right from the very beginning. From the start, we both knew that we belonged together.

The sense of warmth and familiarity that our dinner date left me with only increased my intuitive feeling that this virtual stranger and I were destined to spend the rest of our lives together. During dinner, Marvin told me that he had to leave Florida before the end of Spring Break because he had to play his trumpet at some weddings and Bar Mitzvahs over the weekend. Disappointed that we would not be able to spend more time together enjoying the beautiful Florida weather, I gave him my telephone number at my apartment, which I shared with two friends in Jackson Heights, Queens. We kissed good-bye and he promised to call me after I returned home to New York. When I returned to my room and told Sylvia that I was going to marry a man who I had just met, her answer to me was, "You are definitely crazy and should have your head examined." She found it very hard to understand how I could be so sure after such a short period of time that this was the person that I wanted to live with for the rest of my life. My answer to her was, " I wish I could help you understand but I have no rational answer for the way that I feel. The only thing that I can tell you is that I am sure that I have found Mr. Right. This certainty comes from a gut feeling. It is not rational and well thought out."

As soon as I returned home, Marvin and I started dating. Each date brought us closer to the realization that it was fated that we eventually would meet. Conversation led us to the discovery that one of Marvin's friends was my parent's neighbor in their attached two family house, in Kew Gardens Hills, Queens. He had been trying to introduce us for two or three years prior to the time that we finally met in Florida. Marvin had resisted because he did not like blind dates. But, fate is tenacious and ultimately found a way to get the two of us together. Call it fate or karma; no one can resist the inevitable.

Happily, the reality of everyday life did not change the way we felt about each other. Eleven months after we met in Florida, we were married in the Bayside Jewish Center in Queens, New York. After our honeymoon, we settled into a little house in New Jersey. I soon discovered that the synchronicity of how we met was not the only meaningful coincidence in our lives.

We both had large families in Jerusalem, Israel. Marvin's father was born in Palestine in 1899. His family, the Judelevitz's, had been in what is now Israel, for the last three hundred years. They are in the history books and were among the pioneers who built Israel into what it is today. My grandmother's family went to Palestine from Poland in 1900 and also helped to build that country. She was the only one that settled in the United States with her husband and children. I was fascinated by the fact that two young Jewish people who had met in Miami Beach should both have such illustrious families in their people's homeland.

This significant meaningful coincidence led to an even more outstanding synchronicity when we finally traveled to Israel in 1982 and in 1985. On our very first trip to Israel in 1982, our tour bus dropped us off at a store that sold ethnic jewelry and religious articles in a section of Jerusalem inhabited by a sect of religious Jews. This store, in Mea Shearim, was called B. Cohen's. As soon as I descended from the bus, I was immediately overcome by an intense feeling that the people who owned this shop were members of my family. This unexpected feeling had nothing to do with the fact that my grandmother's maiden name was Cohen. Cohen is the most common surname among Jews. When I shared this feeling with Marvin, he said, "The name Cohen is as common as Smith. Forget about this nonsense. It's crazy. You'll make a fool out of yourself if you share this with the people who own this store." Since I had no rational proof that the people who owned this store were my family, and since Marvin was so adamant that I not pursue this gut feeling, I sadly decided not to pursue my intuition.

When we returned to the United States, I decided that I would start saving money for a return trip to Israel when our older son, Jay, graduated from high school. The feeling that I had missed the opportunity to meet the Israeli part of our family plagued me. As time went by, I was even more convinced than I had been in Israel that the people who owned B. Cohen's in Jerusalem were these long lost relatives. Part of the reason that the Israeli branch of our family and the American branch had not maintained better contact was the difference in our religious observance. Very often, extremely religious Jews do not consider more secular Jews to be part of their religion and limit their contact with them. This was not going to deter me. I was beginning to feel like someone who was adopted at birth and was determined to find her birth parents. As I saved my money and planned our next trip to Israel, I decided that when we were there this time I would take the chance of making a fool out of myself by asking total strangers if they were my family.

Three years later our son, Jay, graduated from high school and we took off for Israel again. We rented an apartment in Jerusalem for a month so that we could show our two sons the land where their strongest roots were planted. We also rented a car with the anticipation of locating as many of our relatives as we could in such a short period of time. The excitement of discovering and connecting to our Israeli roots had been building up for the past three years and had now reached a crescendo. Just being on Israeli soil made me feel that all of the sacrifices that I had made in order to make this trip possible were completely worthwhile.

Even though we had located some of our more secular relatives on our first trip to Israel and even some of Marvin's more religious relatives, I still had the need to follow my intuition to where I thought some of my own religious relatives were. The desire to meet and to get to know these relatives had been intensifying for the past three years. As soon as we had settled into our rented apartment and had unpacked, I suggested that we go to B. Cohen's in order to do some shopping.

As soon as we entered the store, I headed directly to the counter. I waited patiently for the man behind the counter, who was speaking English, to finish waiting on another American customer. When the transaction was finished and the customer left the store, I immediately started to tell this total stranger my family history. The words came tumbling out of my mouth. "My grandmother's name was Liba. During the 1920's, she went from Bialystok, Poland, where she was born and raised, to the United States. Her parents and sisters and brothers went from Poland to Palestine in about 1900. After a short arranged marriage, she got a Jewish divorce in Poland. Then she married my grandfather, a widower with two small children. They had six more children. My mother was the oldest of this six." As I spoke, I became even more excited because I could see that I was capturing his attention. He asked me if my grandmother was also known by another name. I quickly blurted out, "Yes, she was also known as Alte because she almost died when she was a baby." He nodded his head when I told him this. He understood that by renaming my grandmother Alte, or old one, her parents were hoping to protect her by fooling the angel of death.

This obviously orthodox man seemed even more interested than he had been before. He asked me to continue to give him more information about my grandmother. Finding it difficult to control the excitement that was welling up in my chest, I continued, "My grandmother had two brothers named Alte (another survivor) and Yeshua. She also had two sisters, Sorah and Rachumka." As I said the word, Rachumka, I could see the light of recognition in this stranger's eyes. Rachumka, a name as uncommon as Rumplestilskin, had done the trick. This unusual name had also belonged to his great-grandmother. I could feel my heart beating faster and my palms getting sweaty as I realized that my strong intuitive feeling might very well be right. This man was probably my cousin! Almost as excited as I was, he immediately called his mother, who graciously came down to the store to meet us. She was overjoyed to make our acquaintance and informed us that she had been quite friendly with my mother when she lived in Palestine for two years after leaving Poland and before immigrating to the United States. My newly found relative wanted to obtain as much information as she could about my grandmother's life and death. She also wanted to know how her relatives had fared in the far away country of America, which she had never visited. We enjoyed sharing our family's genealogy.

After a joyful visit with my grandmother's one remaining sibling, my great-uncle Alte, we returned to the store where I had been privileged to meet the religious branch of my family. Marvin, who had been caught up in the same excitement that I was feeling, decided to jump on the familial bandwagon. He told my relatives about his illustrious family, the Judelevitzes. He explained with pride that his family had walked from Russia to Palestine over three hundred years ago. He added that they were a family of great rabbis. Our mutual joy and excitement was intensified when we were told that Marvin's family, the Judelevitzes, and my family, the Cohen's, lived next door to each other in Jerusalem and that they were the best of friends. When I heard this, I asked, "Did one of the Cohens ever marry a Judelevitz?" I was told, "Yes. A woman in our family actually did marry a Judelevitz." I chuckled when we were told that this Judelevitz was a musician who played at weddings and Bar Mitzvahs, just like my husband.

When we finally left B. Cohen's and returned to our apartment, I took some time to mull over the incredible happenings and discoveries that we had made on this auspicious day. It occurred to me that had I not had the perseverance and the courage to follow my intuition, I would never have had connected to this amazing synchronicity. This was actually the first time that I recognized the incredible order in the Universe. It was becoming clear to me that there was a meaningful connectedness between each of us and the Universe in which we all live. I could almost sense imaginary blinders being removed from my five senses as I began to believe what the ancient mystics have been telling us for centuries: there is unity in all things. The only way that I can communicate how I actually felt after making these astounding discoveries was that I felt like Sir Isaac Newton must have felt when he discovered the Law of Gravity. In retrospect, I now realize that it was at this point that I decided to pursue this new observation in order to find out other ways that this Universal Law of Unity in all things manifested itself in my life.

LESSONS FROM CHAPTER I

* A near death experience can occur when an individual brushes death, comes close to death, or is pronounced clinically dead and then revives or is resuscitated.

* It is estimated that about 15 million Americans have had near death experiences.

* Many near death experiencers report out of body experiences. They report that they were up on the ceiling, looking down on their bodies.

* A loving presence or dead relatives come to greet many near death experiencers.

* Many near death experiencers report that they hear organ music or a whirring sound.

* Near death experiencers often have a past life review, when they see everything that they have ever felt and done in their lifetime pass in front of them at the same time.

* Some experiencers report that they were in majestic crystal cities with halls of judgment and huge libraries or in beautiful gardens and pastures.

* Some people report meetings with religious figures and angels.

* Many people who report having an NDE report talking with loved ones or playing with former pets.

* Some people report seeing a very bright light that they refer to as a "being of light."

* Many people report that they were sucked back into their bodies after they were told that it was not their time to go.

* People who return from these experiences often report that their lives have been changed for the better and that they have lost their fear of death.

* Many near death experiencers report that this experience has made them psychic.

* Others report that an NDE has made them more eager to help other people.

* There are reports that such an experience fosters a belief in the after-life.

* There is a greater acceptance of the fact that we all have immortal souls among near death experiencers.

* Most near death experiencers accept the concept of death as part of our experience of life.

* Those who come back from this mystical experience tell us that they were surrounded by the most beautiful unconditional love.

* This love has been described as the kind of love that most people have for their children.

* It is important that we learn from these reports of near death experiencers by practicing unconditional love and forgiveness in our everyday lives.

* By practicing unconditional love and forgiveness we will not allow others to "live rent free in our heads."

* A synchronicity is a meaningful coincidence.

* Cause and effect do not connect the things that are connected in a synchronicity.

* Synchronicities are connected in a random fashion.

* When two things that do not emanate from the same source happen at just about the same time, we have a synchronicity.

* Following the path that the synchronicity is setting out for you will ultimately lead you to necessary spiritual guidance.

* You can create your own synchronicities by asking the Higher Power to send one as a verification of a personal spiritual discovery.

CHAPTER II

The First Steps on the Yellow Brick Road

Our very own Yellow Brick Road is always sprinkled with spiritual symbols, signs, synchronicities and celestial clues.

After being blown out of my everyday reality or what I call my Kansas, I started out on a journey up the Yellow Brick Road of an ever-expanding new concept of what reality really is. Like Dorothy, in *The Wizard of Oz*, I had never asked to be put on this path, but was skipping up it in my imaginary ruby red slippers nonetheless. It seems to me now, from a perspective created by years and experiences, that I had been subconsciously preparing for this excursion into a newly defined concept of reality for a very long time. It is obvious to me now that my spirit guides and mystical mentors were firmly convinced of my readiness for enlightenment. The revelations of our essential oneness and our connection to the afterlife, our deceased love ones, and the realm of the spirit always came to me at just the right time. I always seemed to be ready for the newest enlightenment and I was always given enough time to understand it and to digest it before the next spiritual discovery came my way. My otherworldly guides and mentors most certainly functioned by the old metaphysical adage that when the student is ready the teacher will appear.

When my husband retired in 1994 and our house was sold, we immediately moved to Boynton Beach, Florida. I thought of this move as starting out on Dorothy's Yellow Brick Road to Oz, because I was aware that this move was being motivated by my intuition and not by my logical left-brain. Deep within my heart, I knew that Florida was where

I had to be for the remainder of my spiritual journey in this physical incarnation. If I was going to get even closer to God, I knew that I had to be in the Sunshine State.

As if adjusting to my husband's retirement and moving to a new house in a new state were not stressful enough, doubts about whether I should continue to operate my home based nutrition and biodegradable product business began to creep into my mind. Our new retirement home was considerably smaller than the one that we had just left behind in New Jersey and storing products and maintaining a home based business office was becoming a considerable problem. The UPS back in New Jersey was now shipping our products to us. We were also using this shipping company to ship the majority of our client's product orders back to them. Our stress was intensified when the UPS depot in Boynton Beach closed down just a few months after we had settled in our new house. Marvin had to drag large boxes three towns away to Deerfield Beach for shipping. Even receiving orders consisting of ten to fifteen large cartons became a problem; since home based businesses were strictly forbidden in our community. As if all of this was not enough, many of the distributors who I had so lovingly trained to run their businesses while I was living in New Jersey, decided that since I was no longer around, that they did not have to pay me what they owed me. Some of them also decided to switch to local distributors, which made my business dwindle. I was beginning to wonder if all of this was happening for a reason that I did not quite understand. The stresses began to accumulate and were intensified by the fact that I knew that this situation was holding back my spiritual development.

As life became more and more stressful, a feeling that perhaps I was veering off the Yellow Brick Road began to nag at me. One day, in desperation, I walked into a metaphysical bookstore because something in the back of my mind was telling me that the answer to my dilemma would be found in this New Age shop. After browsing through the bookshelves for several minutes, I decided to let my intuition guide me and reached for a book. This book was designed as a divination tool. All that I had to do was to keep a question in my mind while I opened to a page at random in order to receive the appropriate insight. Even though the use of divination tools was quite new to me, I intuitively knew that this was going to be the next step in my spiritual development. Hoping beyond hope that this would work, I kept the question of whether or not I should continue to operate my home based business in my mind, and then opened to a page at random. This randomly selected page instructed me to be patient and trusting because a solution to my problem would be occurring very soon. My intuition told me to take this advice very seriously. An answer did not take long in coming.

In retrospect, it was probably no accident that my answer came during Chanukah, also known as the Festival of Lights, because my decision actually brought much more light into my life. Marvin and I were at home, celebrating the holiday with our children. Our older son, Jay, was living with us while his new house in Boca Raton was being built. Our younger son, David, had flown down from New York with his future wife, Tracy. My family was enjoying opening their gifts while I was at the stove, frying traditional holiday potato latkes. I was reveling in the joy of having my entire immediate family together for this warm holiday reunion. But, my joy was quickly dispelled by one simple ring of our telephone. It was one of my more troublesome distributors from up north. Before I could even say hello, she started to yell and to scream and to hurl invectives at me. Even the knowledge that she was interrupting a family holiday party did not stop her. I valiantly tried to remind her, "I am sure that you know that the company, for which we distribute, was built by a minister and was founded on the Golden rule, 'Do unto others as you would have others do unto you.'" But, she obviously was not going to buy any of this and continued to demonstrate an incredibly ego driven selfishness. This turned out to be only the first of many equally stressful telephone calls, which convinced me that I would have to give up this business if I was going to maintain my physical, emotional and spiritual health. Marvin supported my decision because the stress was affecting him as well. Thankfully, the pension that he had worked so hard and long to obtain was large enough to support both of us decently and to allow me the freedom to work on my spiritual development. As soon as the holidays were over, I liquidated my products and retired.

This turn of events gave me an incredible feeling of relief. I had followed my intuition and had made a decision, which would free me for what I really wanted to do with the rest of my life. I now realize that this decision marked the beginning of the most exciting part of my spiritual journey. My mind was cleared of mundane worries and concerns and was, therefore, in a better position to pick up more spiritual communications.

A spiritual explosion seemed to occur almost immediately after I gave up my business. It was almost as if my spirit guides, mystical mentors, and my Higher Self were actually waiting for me to free my mind before they could fill it again with more spiritual material. I can almost envision all of my unseen spiritual helpers holding a little otherworldly meeting and deciding that it was time for Barbara Yudell to be assisted in an accelerated spiritual evolution. This assistance came and I began to see the little celestial clues that a Higher Power and my Higher Self were dropping in my path like the bits of bread on the forest path in the fable of *Hansel and Gretel.* Spiritual symbols, signs and synchronicities came flooding in on a daily basis. With the trust of a child following a loving parent, I started to identify and to understand these cosmic clues. Starting to follow the celestial clues, which were being sprinkled on my spiritual Yellow Brick Road, was the beginning of my quest for ultimate understanding of my soul's sacred mission in the physical dimension. It also helped me to gain knowledge of my immortal spiritual journey through time.

From my present vantage point, I can see that my strong desire to understand my soul's spiritual path, combined with the seven-year healing crisis that cleansed my body and my mind, opened the pathway to sacred understanding. It is also quite clear to me that the many word puzzles and word games, which I felt compelled to do as I got well, also sharpened my observational skills and helped me to see what others could not or would not see. I, like no one else that I know, have trained myself to observe and to record things that seem insignificant to others. It is also possible that all of my new observations occurred simply because it was time for me to open my eyes and to see what was going on around me. I now see, with crystal clarity, that all of the mystical experiences, which I have had from the time of my father's death to the time that we moved to Florida, were responsible for my strong faith and willingness to accept communication from the invisible spiritual realm. This understanding brings me great joy because observing and accepting information and clues from a dimension, which we cannot access with our five physical senses is certainly a gift that should not be taken lightly.

My early morning hypnagogic respites were also a blessing because this time spent in silence between sleep and wakefulness also opened spiritual doors. Emptying my mind of its daily senseless chatter helped me to achieve a greater closeness to God and to all of my spiritual helpers. All of the puzzles in the world could not have opened the gateways to the spiritual dimension as efficiently as these daily meditative sessions. By shutting out the mundane physical world, I received the blessing of being allowed to come closer to the realm of the immortal soul.

In thinking about the progression of my spiritual odyssey and my slowly growing awareness of my spiritual connections, I often wonder when I first recognized the importance of the ever-present number "twenty-six (26)" as a directional signal in the supernatural vehicle, which was propelling me up the path of sacred understanding. It seems totally unbelievable that I was blind for so long to the significance of this ever-present number. If I were a gambler, I might have been more aware that the odds were astronomical that so many twenty-sixes could occur at random in my life. In retrospect, I recognize that my oblivion to the spiritual significance of this ubiquitous numerical symbol was testimony to the power of our society's left brain training. When my right brain, the part responsible for psychic awareness and intuition, finally woke up and snapped to attention, I was shocked at how many twenty-sixes had always existed in my life.

The first twenty-six that I can remember is actually a sum of eighteen and eight. Most of my growing up years were spent in an apartment house on a street in the Bronx, New York. The number on this building was 1808. There may have been many twenty-sixes before this, but since I moved to this address at the tender age of five, my recollection of any earlier occurrences of this spiritual numerical symbol have unfortunately been lost. The next occurrence of this number came when I was sixteen-years-old and my family moved to an apartment building on 26th Avenue in Queens, New York. After Marvin and I married, we moved to a house in New Jersey, which had 26 in its address. We also lived at 26 Brown Circle when we lived in New Jersey. After our older son, Jay, was born, we bought a piece of land in Royal Palm Beach, Florida, that just happened to be located in section J26.

As I think back, it occurs to me that learning about the existence and meaning of synchronicities may have helped bring me to the awareness of the significance of the preponderance of twenty-sixes in my life. After I realized that these twenty-sixes were not just random occurrences, I became aware of even more twenty-sixes in the roadmap of my soul's sojourn in this physical incarnation. One example of this is that my birthday is on September 14th and that Marvin's birthday is on the 12th of December. With the use of simple arithmetic we can verify the synchronicity of twelve and fourteen adding up to twenty-six.

When we finally moved to Boynton Beach, Florida, my new address confused me. Where was the number twenty-six? This puzzling question was answered shortly after we moved into our retirement home. While riding around our new community on my bicycle, I made the discovery that there was a large green metal telephone box with a big 26 on it located almost directly behind our house. Soon after I made this discovery, my son, Jay, called me from his dental office to share the observation that we were now living on the 26th parallel. I mulled this new discovery over and wondered whether this was why I had felt so compelled to move Marvin and myself lock, stock and barrel down to this part of Florida. Only time and continued observation would tell me if living on the 26th parallel was a significant unconscious consideration in our move.

Incredible as it may seem, as more twenty-sixes popped up in my life, I began to realize that this ubiquitous number was even more deeply ingrained in the warp and weave of my life than I had originally suspected. For example, when I started teaching in 1959, I taught second grade for six years and then I taught sixth grade for two years. This insight was followed by the observation that when my son, Jay, was six years old, his younger brother, David, was two years old.

At just about the same time that I began to see the proliferation of twenty-sixes in my life, Marvin and I decided to attend classes at the Kabbalah Center in Boca Raton to learn about the fascinating subject of ancient Jewish mysticism. When Marvin and I attended the free introductory lecture at the Kabbalah Center, I was fascinated that so many aspects of New Age thinking were actually derived from this four thousand-year-old Jewish mystical system. Even one of the most frequently used divination tools used by psychics and New Age aficionados, the tarot cards, came from the Torah, one of the holiest books in Judaism. Firmly convinced of the merits of studying the Kabbalah, Marvin and I signed up to study numerology, astrology, reincarnation and general mysticism. My chief motivation in taking these classes was to learn how I could strengthen the link between the physical dimension where we live our earthly lives and the far larger, invisible dimension where our immortal souls go after our physical bodies die.

While we were at the Kabbalah Center for the free introductory lecture, I purchased two paperback books on the fascinating subject of ancient Jewish mysticism. Allowing my intuition to guide me, I selected these two titles from a display of about twenty or thirty books. I was so excited about discovering this whole new twist on Metaphysics and Parapsychology that I started to read one of these books as soon as I returned home. After quickly finishing this book, I immediately started to read the second book. Marvin and I started to attend classes in Kabbalah the very next week. The teacher, an Israeli biologist who was trained at the Kabbalah Center in Tel-Aviv, Israel, started the first session of this new class by holding up two books, which he strongly suggested that we read in order to enhance our beginning studies of the Kabbalah. To my astonishment, these were the exact books that I had purchased at random the week before. I had even read these two starter books in the order that the teacher had suggested. This simple occurrence strengthened my growing realization of how strong my connection to otherworldly guidance was becoming. It also served to strengthen my eagerness to learn about this ancient system of mysticism, which was originated by Abraham, the father of monotheism.

I found the study of Kabbalah to be very exciting and I eagerly awaited every session. At long last the time to study Kabalistic numerology, or gematria, finally came. We learned that every Hebrew letter has a numerical value and that the most important numbers in the Kabbalah and in Judaism are seven, thirteen, eighteen and twenty-six. I can only explain the way that I felt as being in a state of extreme awe when the instructor wrote the four holiest letters in Judaism, Yud-Hay-Vov-Hay, on the chalkboard. This feeling was produced by the explanation that Yud-Hay-Vov-Hay is the holiest name of God in Judaism. It was added that it is so holy that it may never be spoken aloud. The final information about Yud-Hay-Vov-Hay that we received was that it added up to the number twenty-six in gematria. When the instructor added that these four holy letters have sometimes been erroneously pronounced as Yahweh and have been mistakenly interpreted as Jehovah, I was overwhelmed by a torrent of questions that came flooding into my consciousness. Was there a connection between the twenty-six in Yud-Hay-Vov-Hay and my personal twenty-six? If this were so, would it explain why I had always had so many Jehovah's Witnesses as clients when I ran my nutrition and biodegradable product business in my home in New Jersey? Since nothing ever happens by accident, I had no choice but to feel that God or the Light was guiding me on my spiritual journey and I was determined to stay on my designated sacred path.

My thirst for metaphysical and spiritual enlightenment was so strong that, besides taking courses at the Kabbalah Center, Marvin and I took two courses in reincarnation and past life regression with a rabbi-psychologist. We drove to North Miami and Hollywood every week because I was becoming firmly convinced that I had lived before and would certainly live again. It was becoming clearer and clearer to me that the deja-vus that we all experience from time to time and the many talents, affinities and inclinations that we are born with were indeed proof of reincarnation. How else could I explain the nightmares of being chased by ferocious Native American braves that I had had as a child? Or the glimpses of lifetimes on an island in the South Pacific, that had also appeared to me in my childhood dreams? Everything that I read about reincarnation convinced me further that not only was this wheel of the soul a reality, but that it was indeed a necessity. It was dawning on me that it would certainly take more than one lifetime for me to learn all of my spiritual lessons and to accomplish my soul's sacred mission. The fact that reincarnation was an important part of the Kabbalah and was accepted by the majority of the inhabitants of our planet was also strong proof of its existence to me.

LESSONS FROM CHAPTER II

* There are spiritual numbers that follow individuals and families.

* Try keeping a journal of what is going on in your life. If you see the same number repeating itself you might want to investigate what it means.

* There are some numbers that are more spiritual than others are. Three is a very spiritual number. It is the trinity. Seven and eleven are also very spiritual numbers. Thirteen, eighteen and twenty-six are also considered to be sacred numbers in the Kabbalah and in Judaism.

* To find out what your birth number is, write down the day, month and year of your birth. Add these numbers up and then reduce to a single digit. For example, the date December 28, 1945 would translate to 1+2+2+8+1+9+4+5=32. We then add 3+2 and get 5. The birth number for this date is 5. Kabbalah and New Age numerology will provide explanations of the significance of each number.

* Reincarnation is a very important part of metaphysical and spiritual thinking.

* We have all lived before and will live again. It takes more than one lifetime to learn all of our spiritual lessons and to fulfill our spiritual missions.

* The majority of the inhabitants of our planet believe in reincarnation.

CHAPTER III

Glinda, The Good Witch

As spiritual beings journeying on a voyage of discovery,
we are always accompanied by a retinue of
invisible sacred companions.

ife seemed to be getting more and more exciting and
certainly more fulfilling. I enjoyed the meditations that
we were learning how to do at the Kabbalah Center and in
the Past life Regression classes that we were taking with the
rabbi-psychologist. Since every book on metaphysics and
parapsychology that I read stressed the importance of meditation in the search for enlightenment, I decided that I
would enroll myself in a lunchtime meditation seminar in
the Jewish Community Center in the neighboring town of
Delray Beach. In my excitement about possibly expanding
my recently acquired ability to meditate and always eager to
share the new experiences that occurred in my life, I told
some of the students in my reincarnation class at the
Kabbalah Center about the meditation seminar during a
break. As I spoke, a woman who was sitting in the front row
of the classroom got up and walked toward me. When she
reached the chair next to mine she sat down and proceeded
to tell me that she was the instructor of the upcoming meditation seminar. Her name was Gloria Fleischner and she
had recently moved to Florida from New Jersey. She had
taught at the Metaphysical Society in New Jersey. I told her
a little bit about my background and my aspirations in the
field of her expertise. We connected to each other instantaneously and when she told me, "When the student is ready,
the teacher will appear," I knew that I had finally found a
metaphysical mentor. After attending Gloria's powerful med-

itation seminar, we exchanged telephone numbers. I asked her to put my name on the top of the list of perspective students for her upcoming classes.

Adding almost daily meditation into my schedule seemed to bring even more magical spiritual discoveries into my life. On September 17, 1996, shortly after I met Gloria, I made one of these discoveries. The first revelation was that on the 26th of the month or on a date that added up to 26, spiritual information would flood into my consciousness. September 17th fit into this category because September is the ninth month of the year and nine and seventeen add up to twenty-six.

Around dinnertime on this date, I went to the bookshelves in my breakfast area to get a cookbook. When I opened the cookbook, two sheets of paper fluttered to the floor. I stooped down to pick these papers up and instantly recognized the poetry that was typed on them. A strong feeling of nostalgia flooded through me as I read the poems, which I had written on a cross-country trip to California that Marvin and I had taken in 1966. Grateful that I had connected to some very good memories of the past, I put these rediscovered papers back in the cookbook so that I could prepare dinner. At about three o'clock in the morning my eyes snapped open and I was filled with the intuitive knowledge that one of the rediscovered poems had twenty-six words in it and must, therefore, contain spiritual content. Knowing that sleep would not return until I checked this surprising insight out, I quietly crept out of bed, walked into the dinette and removed the two pieces of paper from the cookbook. Trusting my intuition had paid off again. The poem that I had written about the Grand Canyon had exactly twenty-six words in it. As I reread this poem, its spiritual content virtually leapt out at me. A careful second rereading brought me to the realization that this poem was an allegory for the sacred journey of the immortal part of my being. Finding this poem twenty-six years after the 1970 date on the paper further reinforced it spiritual content.

Grand Canyon

Deeper, deeper cuts the Colorado,

Canyon walls marking its trail.

For the brave and the willing to follow.

For the meek and the heartless to fail.

How awesome! I had written a poem about my soul's spiritual journey even before I was consciously aware that the immortal part of myself was actually on such a sacred trip. Now that I was aware of this originally innocuous poem's spiritual content I began to analyze it. When these four short lines were dissected in this new ethereal or heavenly light, I could see that "the Colorado River" was a symbol for my immortal soul. In this metaphorical sacred journey, my soul was cutting deeper and deeper to the core of my being to form a spiritual canyon of understanding that was indeed as grand as the Grand Canyon. It was also quite clear to me that my soul was trying to tell me that pursuing my sacred dream of spiritual discovery and understanding was not a task to be taken lightly. This poem communicated to me the spiritual truth that the less brave would always back away from this task. They would prefer to distract themselves with the trials and tribulations of daily life and the rise and fall of the stock market than to look within and, therefore, grow and transform.

These stunning revelations prevented me from getting any more sleep that night. My mind was revving like a well-tuned engine. I instinctively knew that if one of these miraculously rediscovered poems was inherently spiritual, the others must be too. Since sleep was eluding me, I began to reread and to analyze the other poems. I read *September Sea*. I remember writing it on a windy day in September while sitting on the sand and staring out at the ocean.

September Sea

I love the shore in September,
    when the sea is windy and free,

For the rise and fall of the crashing waves
    brings inner peace to me.

There my soul rides on the seagull's wings out
    to the foaming crests,

And then circles back to the sweeping dunes
    to light for a sunlit rest.

Oh, I love the sky with its drifting clouds,

And the sea with its wavy foam.

For here I know where I belong,

For here my heart's at home.

When I read this poem, I recognized that I was right; this simple bit of poetry contained personal spiritual content. This was actually an allegory of my very early near death experience. My subconscious mind had filtered this information into my conscious mind in a way that was acceptable to it. Rereading this verse with my spiritual eyes open brought me the awareness that I had used the sea as a metaphor for heaven. I then realized that my word picture of the seagull majestically flying out over the ocean symbolized my soul leaving my body for a short while to soar above the spiritual sea of eternity. My sacred self, in the form of the seagull, then swooped back to the shore to land on the wind swept dunes, which I could then see, symbolized physical life. I spent a little time digesting this poem before I read the next poem.

As the clock ticked toward dawn, I picked up the rest of these enlightening poems and read the very next one, which was about Mount Rushmore.

Mount Rushmore

Granite faces, washed by heavenly tears,

Eyes unseeing, ears that do not hear.

Silent voices, reminding those below,

That injustice, greed and hatred,

Are our country's greatest foes.

After reading this poem two or three times in a completely different light, created by my new awareness, I could see that it too had spiritual content. I recognized that this poem was a communication from my guardian angels and spirit guides. My mystical mentors were letting me know that they were around. They were also trying to reinforce heavenly standards of behavior. This awareness filled me with a warm and wonderful feeling of connectedness and security. This feeling underscored something that I had known for a very long time; we are never alone. We, as spiritual beings journeying on a voyage of discovery in a vehicle made of physical flesh, are always accompanied by a retinue of invisible sacred companions. These omnipresent heavenly helpers are always trying to encourage us to behave better and to be kinder. Their greatest rewards come from helping us to do our spiritual homework.

The next poem in my homegrown anthology of poems was a simple verse entitled *Welcome*.

Welcome

Rolled out, extended, a welcome mat of green.

With dipping hills and miles of road,

And swiftly changing scenes.

A land of beauty, highs and lows,

And towns both large and small,

And all its people beckoning, come out and pay a call.

I sat quietly for a long time after reading this poem. What had seemed like a simple and unassuming verse when first written, now took on a much greater significance. Studying Metaphysics, Parapsychology and Spirituality had taught me that green was the color of healing, love and the subconscious mind. Recalling this important piece of spiritual information stimulated my intuition and helped me to recognize that the welcome mat of green in this poem was symbolic of God's loving guidance. This loving guidance is essential to us in our spiritual journeys from lifetime to lifetime; on a path of reincarnation that helps us to learn the sacred lessons for ascension, our upward progression to the perfection of God. Rereading this poem helped me to see that the dipping hills and the highs and lows in this verse stand for the many experiences, which I have had in these lifetimes. The beckoning people were obviously the personalities from my past lives who had helped me to learn much-needed lessons. From the present perspective I then understood that the people that we meet in all of our lives and the experiences that we undergo help us to purify our souls and ultimately bring us closer to God.

Dawn was over and the sun was shining brightly. Thinking about *Welcome*, led me to decide that it was time that I continue to explore my personal journey from lifetime to lifetime by getting involved in some past life regression. Again, the old adage that "when the student is ready, the teacher will appear" manifested itself in my life. I opened the local newspaper and was immediately attracted to an advertisement about an upcoming seminar on reincarnation to be held in Fort Lauderdale. The seminar was going to be facilitated by Dr. Brian Weiss, a local psychiatrist and the author of a very informative book on reincarnation and past life regressions. I was immediately filled with excitement. I enrolled in the seminar because I thought that if I were lucky, it would connect me to more knowledge and insights that would help me to understand my sacred self and its spiritual journey through the millennia.

On the Saturday morning of Dr. Weiss' all-day workshop, I awoke filled with excited anticipation. When I walked into the seminar, I was comforted by the observation that there were three hundred and fifty other spiritual seekers in the room. It was reassuring to discover that there were so many other people who were also hungry for spiritual enlightenment and knowledge about their past lives. We were obviously all fascinated by the wheel of the soul; the continuous cycle of birth and death that ultimately leads us to lessons learned and missions completed.

My early morning excitement became a state of heightened alertness. I was determined to get as much as possible out of this eagerly awaited seminar. When we all settled in, Dr. Weiss, the facilitator, led us through a series of group and individual experiences, which were aimed at eventually exposing our past lives to the light of our present day reality. One of these exercises was very helpful to me even though it did not give me any insights into my past lives. This exercise had each of us sitting and facing one other person. The lights in the room were dimmed and our eyes were closed. After Dr. Weiss helped us to reach a meditative state, we were told to open our eyes and stare at our partner's face. We were told that this was a spiritual projective technique that allowed our souls to come forward and to possibly give us hints of our previous incarnations.

The outcome of this exercise was not what I expected, but was extremely enlightening nonetheless. My partner in this exercise shared an observation that she considered to be very unusual because she had never experienced anything quite like it before. She told me with excitement in her voice that she had seen a bright light coming out of the right side of my head. Her excitement was immediately transmitted to me when I realized that this observation verified my relatively new awareness that I had had a near death experience at the age of three. Information from the many books on near death experiences that I had read came crashing into my mind. My partner's experience was obviously connected to the fact that near death experiences often activate the right frontal lobe of those who undergo it. This area of the brain is the doorway for psychic and spiritual experiences to come in and its activation makes many near death experiencers more psychic and more open to spiritual experiences and information. Putting this knowledge together with what my partner had just seen made me realize that the light that was emanating from the right side of my head was proof that this side of my brain was working overtime. I understood that what was going on in the right side of my brain was the true cause of my intuitiveness and of the otherworldly experiences that I had been having recently. I shared my partner's observation and my subsequent insight with Dr. Weiss and the other three hundred and fifty people in the seminar. Dr. Weiss explained, "This light, or aura, is an electromagnetic field that surrounds all living things and is also used in healing." He finished by emphasizing that the right frontal lobe of my brain had been activated by my near death experience and applauded me for making this discovery on my own. The remainder of the workshop helped me to sharpen my meditation techniques.

Around the time that I attended this seminar, I ordered and received a past life regression videotape. My desire to explore and to understand my past lives was extremely strong and I was determined to use whatever means possible to accomplish this goal. Our older son, Jay, and his close friend from dental school, were living with us temporarily. One night, the three of us decided to watch the videotape to find out what kind of information we could get about our past lives. Jay was certainly very ready for this experience because during his regression he had a very vivid memory of a lifetime in Holland during the eighteenth century. It turned out to be an extremely emotional experience because he saw himself as a little boy who had died young. He was absolutely sure that I was in that lifetime with him, although he could not tell me what our relationship had been in that incarnation. It was not hard for me to accept the reality of a past lifetime spent with my older son because we had always felt very strongly bonded to each other. All of the books on reincarnation that I had read and all of the seminars that I had attended had prepared me for this eventuality because they had taught me that groups of souls reincarnate together. I understood that the soul who is your mother in this lifetime might have been your son in a previous incarnation and your husband in yet another past lifetime. I knew that this was an important milestone in my spiritual search for the true essence of my sacred self.

A few months after this small group journey back to another lifetime, I tried the past life regression tape again. This time it was a solo voyage and not a group excursion. I wanted to find out what would happen when I tried to regress myself when I was alone. To my delight, almost as soon as the voice on the videotape started to count backwards and suggested that I see myself in a past incarnation, I found myself back in the past lifetime in Holland, which Jay had described so vividly a few months prior to this. The big difference between the two regressions was that I could see what Jay could not. I was his much older sister in this lifetime. As if I was watching a historical movie, I could see myself suffering much guilt and feeling tremendous hopelessness in this lifetime because my sweet little brother had died so young and I had not been able to save him.

The past life relationship that I had shared with Jay explained the simpatico that we have always felt. This made my desire to experience and to explore other incarnations even stronger than before. I was burning to know what subsequent past life regressions would reveal to me. It wasn't too long before another past life regression workshop was advertised in our local newspaper. Thanking the Higher Power for its speedy answer to my ardent request, I immediately signed up for it. The Yellow Brick Road to spiritual understanding was opening up before me and like Dorothy in *The Wizard of Oz*; I was ready to dust off my ruby slippers and to go skipping up the Yellow Brick Road, in the hope of discovering my sacred self.

I drove to the New Age shop where this seminar was being given almost trembling with eager anticipation. Ten other people were attending this workshop. The facilitator was a young man whose enthusiasm for past life regression was swiftly transferred to the group. After listening to a lecture, which described the way in which many of our talents and affinities and our phobias and infirmities travel with us from lifetime to lifetime, the group was helped to reach a meditative state and then led down a path to another lifetime.

Soon after my eyes closed, I saw myself as a young gypsy woman, a dancer who lived and performed in countries, which border on the Mediterranean Sea in the beginning of the eighteenth century. Marvin, who is my husband in my present lifetime, was my father in this Mediterranean incarnation. We traveled from town to town in a gypsy caravan with Marvin driving our horse drawn wagon. Wherever we entertained, Marvin played the guitar while I danced. Dancing was my life and music was his. Our love for these two things came across very strongly in this regression. As I shared my regression with the group, I was struck with the similarity between that long ago lifetime and my present incarnation. Music and dance are still extremely important to Marvin and me in our current lifetime. Marvin has spent a large part of his working years as a professional musician, and dance has always been an important avocation for me. Music, Latin and Gypsy music in particular, has always been a shared source of enjoyment for both of us. I chuckled to myself when I recalled that even the first dance that we shared when we met so many years ago in the Boom Boom Room was a Latin dance, the Pachanga.

As I drove home from this enlightening workshop, I finally understood why we both felt that we knew each other when we first met. My soul had connected to something familiar in Marvin's soul. What we had both felt at our first encounter is called soul recognition and occurs when the immortal parts of our beings recall a past lifetime or lifetimes that we have shared together. This discovery caused a question to form in my mind. Was it possible that Marvin and I had shared more than one past incarnation together? Only time and further investigation would answer this question.

I was beginning to feel like a metaphysical Sherlock Holmes. My spiritual sleuthing had helped me to find out that my soul had shared at least one past lifetime with my husband and at least one more with my older son. These unexpected revelations spurred me on to reading and learning more about reincarnation. My reading taught me that many of the phobias that plague us in our present lifetimes come from experiences that we had in previous lives. This new information motivated me to start probing deeper into the fears that had been troublesome to me in my childhood.

The first thing that came to my mind when I thought of my childhood terrors was an irrational fear of Native Americans, especially braves on the warpath. Throughout most of my youth I suffered from recurrent nightmares in which I was being chased and ultimately killed by frightening looking Native American braves covered with war paint. I can also still remember sitting in the movie theater with my older sister on Saturday afternoons with my jacket over my head whenever the film that we were watching had scenes of brutal warriors attacking wagon trains of pioneers. My first reaction after unearthing this fear and exposing it to the light of my new belief in reincarnation was that I had been one of these pioneers and that I had been killed by a marauding war party.

This speculation proved to be untrue. What happened next proved to me that when someone has the intention to become enlightened that is exactly what happens. For the very first time in my life I had a spontaneous past life regression. One day, with no warning whatsoever, I could see the past life in question as if I was watching a movie on a screen. I saw myself as an older Native American Squaw, alone in her teepee, who was being attacked, raped and killed by a war paint covered brave from another, more hostile, tribe. What triggered this spontaneous past life regression is still a mystery to me. Was it my probing and ultimate acceptance of the fact that I had been killed by a Native American brave in a past lifetime that had encouraged my subconscious mind to release this buried material into my everyday consciousness? Or was it possible that I might have met someone who had played a role in this particular past lifetime that triggered this totally unexpected past life regression. In retrospect, the possibility is strong that this spontaneous past life regression was merely a rehearsal for a very powerful and important regression that occurred in the future.

Very shortly after this spontaneous past life regression, I received a telephone call from my husband's cousin Charlotte, which led to more spiritual discoveries. Charlotte invited me to attend a seminar in a bookstore in Boca Raton that was being given by a well-known local astrologer. Since I had never been exposed to astrology to any degree before, I accepted with enthusiasm. The ongoing revelations, which I was experiencing in my continuous search for spiritual understanding of my soul's sacred journey, made me even more eager for further enlightenment and insights.

After listening to a very interesting lecture, I filled out an astrological questionnaire and paid for a private reading. My birth number turned out to be an eight, which is the total of my two ubiquitous spiritual numbers, two and six. These two numbers also appeared as the first two numbers in a list of the planets that influence me astrologically. The appearance of these three numbers told me that I was in the right place at the right time. Life, which I had once thought functioned in a random and haphazard fashion, was reinforcing what I had recently learned about it; it functioned in a very orderly fashion.

As I listened to the rest of my astrological reading, the orderliness of life was further reinforced. By merely looking at my date and time of birth, the astrologer told me that I had had a home based business, which consisted of selling products that take care of and protect the Earth. For the very first time I realized that it must have been in the stars that I would run a business from my home, which consisted of selling products that would protect the environment. This new discovery was another mind-boggling example of the orderliness of life. It took me a little time to absorb the fact that operating a business, which had occupied so many of my waking hours for fourteen years was predestined by the position of the planets at my exact moment of birth.

The excitement of this new discovery motivated me to further explore what I had just learned. A trip to a bookstore and further reading taught me that our souls actually select the exact time that they will enter the new body, which they have chosen as a vehicle for their next Earthly experience. I also learned that our souls would eventually experience being under every sign of the Zodiac in order to learn all of the lessons that the school of life can teach them. A Virgo in this lifetime, I am sure that I have been or will be a Leo, a Sagittarius, a Cancer and every other sign of the Zodiac at some time or other in my quest for ultimate perfection and total understanding. This enlightening experience also convinced me that, because of its organization, life will always provide for those of us who were interested, the information, signs and symbols necessary for the identification of our soul's sacred mission and reason for being in physical form at this time. All that I had to do was to show my mystical mentors in the non-physical dimension that this was my intention. Then I had to keep my ears, eyes and my sixth sense open and ready to receive.

I recall that someone once told me that I should be careful about what I wish for, because my wish could actually come true. Very shortly after my experience with the astrologer and my realization that God has a great deal to tell us if we are willing to listen, something very unusual happened.

It was a beautiful, sunny Florida day. The sparkling blue sky was almost totally cloudless. I was standing at our community's satellite pool and talking to neighbors who were seated in front of me. During a short pause in our conversation, one of my new friends pointed to a spot in the sky directly above my head and said, "Barbara, don't look now, but there is a small cloud shaped like an arrow that is pointing directly at your head." I immediately turned around and looked up at the sky. My neighbor was right. Right above me, a cloud that looked like a fluffy white arrow painted on a bright blue canvas, was pointing directly at me. Within seconds of observing this strange phenomenon, my original shock gave way to the insight that, since nothing happens by accident, there was a message in this for me. I intuitively knew that God, my spirit guides and my Higher Self were letting me know that I was on the right track and that I had been singled out and given the ability to observe and to understand the signs, symbols and synchronicities with which they communicate with us. Sharing this experience with Marvin opened the doorway for other insights to flood in. These insights brought me the awareness that this task was to be taken very seriously. They also made me understand that I would ultimately have to share what I learned with others. Despite the fact that this was an awesome responsibility, I knew that I would eventually be grateful for the direction that it would give my life. Time and experience have taught me that I can never allow myself to become complacent. There is an important cosmic job to be done. I must never allow myself to forget that I am in training to do it! When I shared these insights with some of my metaphysical friends and mentors, they helped me to understand that sharing what I learned about signs, symbols and synchronicities was part of my soul's sacred mission. My spiritual responsibilities had been spelled out for me and I was determined to accomplish this mission.

The enlightening experience at the pool put me on the alert. All of my senses were heightened in preparation for the discovery of experiences that would propel me further up the Yellow Brick Road of spiritual understanding.

Life had become so exciting, filled with new friends, new insights and new revelations, that I decided to throw myself a little birthday party. I invited some of our new friends to celebrate. I threw myself into a frenzy of food preparation and game planning. The day of the party arrived and everyone on the guest list came to join in the fun. Two of the friends knowing of my interest in psychic development, brought me a book on just this topic. After a really successful and fun filled party and the subsequent clean up, I started to read this new book. Before I finished the first chapter, I knew that this book was the teacher that I needed at this time. This insight brought a smile to my lips because it finally made me aware of the fact that whatever I needed to support the next step in my spiritual development always seemed to come to me in the most convenient and effortless way. I found out much later on that this is always what happens when someone is on the right spiritual path.

Two suggestions that were very important in speeding up my psychic development seemed to jump right off the page and right into my mind. One recommendation was to start a journal in order to record all of my metaphysical, psychic and spiritual impressions and experiences.

This journal would be a place where I would record the dreams, synchronicities, insights, spontaneous past life regressions, after-death communications, and incidents of ESP, that were becoming more and more prevalent in my life.

The second suggestion that I connected to was the recommendation that I start a collection of objects that were symbolic of spirituality. Two of the objects that were recommended were angels and pyramids. The thinking behind this suggestion was that owning these objects would bring spiritual power to the owner.

I found these suggestions to be so exciting and so empowering that I immediately bought a journal and some small pyramids and figures of angels at a local New Age store. I wanted my spirit guides, guardian angels and God to know that I meant business. I was counting on them to remove any roadblocks and obstacles that I might encounter on the remainder of my spiritual journey.

Purchasing my first journal, naming it my Psychic Journal, and beginning to record psychic and spiritual impressions and insights into it, has proven to be one of the most fruitful and significant things that I have ever done. Putting sacred and psychic communications, thoughts, learnings and experiences into writing has virtually opened a floodgate that allowed even more of the same to come through. My Psychic Journal has proven to be such a powerful help to me in my spiritual quest that I have made almost daily entries into it since its inception. Even if something seems relatively insignificant to me at the time of its entry, it very often takes on new importance in light of subsequent entries.

Just about a year after I started to make entries into my Psychic Journal, I had an unusual experience that validated the importance of this practice. One early morning, I was jolted out of a restful sleep at about 4:00 A.M. Since I had previously learned that this was one of the most psychic parts of the day, I lay quietly in my bed, just waiting for something to happen. As I lay there in quiet anticipation, a thought, which I knew was not of my mind, shot through my consciousness. This thought consisted of only two words, "lucid notebook". I took this thought very seriously, even though I did not know exactly where it came from. I speculated that it could have come from my Higher Self, that part of my soul that remained in a loftier dimension or from one of my spirit guides or even from God. This message left me feeling a little confused. I have always thought that the word 'lucid' means clear and understandable. I could not see how this definition applied to my Psychic Journal (which was the only notebook in my life at the time). Despite this confusion, I entered this strange thought into my Psychic Journal and promising myself that I would look up 'lucid' in the dictionary in the morning, I went back to sleep.

As soon as I awakened in the morning I headed straight for the bookshelves in the little room where I keep my books and my angels and which I refer to as my "angel room." One of the several definitions of 'lucid' in our dictionary was the unexpected, "suffused with light." As I reread this definition several times, I realized that it was very appropriate to what I was trying to achieve by keeping a Psychic Journal. This Journal was starting to bring more "light" in the form of spiritual inspiration and enlightenment into my life. The word "light" had very spiritual connotations to me because of part of my training. When I studied the Kabbalah, I learned that the word "light" was synonymous with God. Whoever or whatever put the thought *lucid notebook* into my mind was obviously informing me that I was doing the right thing and that I should continue to do it. As soon as I closed my dictionary, I decided to rename my Psychic Journal and call it my Lucid Notebook. I find it very interesting that ever since I changed the name of this Journal, the number of psychic and spiritual phenomena, which I have experienced, has increased. Changing the word *Psychic* to the word *Lucid* has definitely suffused my journal with extra spiritual light, much to my joy and satisfaction.

Lessons From Chapter III

* Starting a psychic journal can help you to speed up the process of spiritual enlightenment. Give this journal a spiritual name and record every psychic or spiritual experience or insight that you have into it.

* Starting a collection of articles that have spiritual meaning will also speed your way to spiritual enlightenment. You can collect figures of angels or pyramids or crystals or anything else that you feel is spiritual.

* Use these objects to create an altar or a spiritual little room in your home.

* Start a collection of New Age books and tapes. Try to keep all of these sources of spiritual information in your special room or near your altar.

* Meditating often can also help to speed up the process of spiritual enlightenment.

* When we meditate, we relax our bodies and quiet our minds. As we clear away the chatter and the distractions in our heads, it becomes easier to hear communications from our higher selves, our spirit guides and God.

* If you want to be able to pick up the spiritual messages that are always there for us, start to become more aware of your environment. Look for unusual occurrences, like the cloud arrow that was pointing at my head.

* Put these new observations into your psychic journal. Eventually you may see a pattern.

CHAPTER IV

Ruby Slippers on the Yellow Brick Road

*After death communication from loved ones
can heal our lonely hearts.*

Changing the name of my Psychic Journal to my Lucid Notebook actually sharpened my spiritual sensibilities and increased my desire for personal spiritual enlightenment. Since I was beginning to feel that the study of Kabbalah alone was a little too limiting for me, I started to search for someone whose teaching contained the truths of many spiritual beliefs and not just one. I had no idea at the time that I had met such a person already.

A few months after I met Gloria Fleischner and attended her powerful meditation seminar, I received the exciting news that she was going to be teaching Metaphysics and Parapsychology at Palm Beach Community College in nearby Boca Raton. I enrolled and started to eagerly devour everything that Gloria taught. I felt like a piece of parched ground that could not get the water of spiritual knowledge fast enough. This was what I was searching for.

Continuing to attend Gloria's classes, I began to see that there was a side benefit to studying with her. One of these unexpected benefits was meeting new people with a strong interest in what had become my passion, Metaphysics and Parapsychology. One of these people was Ina Werthman, who usually sat behind me in class. We often discussed our interest in what Gloria was teaching during lunchtime and we decided that we would try to pursue these subjects together whenever possible. In time, Ina became one of my companions in my journey along the Yellow Brick Road to my spiritual Oz.

Gloria's classes were particularly enjoyable because she encouraged us to share our psychic and spiritual experiences with each other. Hearing about other people's other-worldly experiences validated my own. After telling the class about the premonitions, which I had had before my father died, and how my friend Sandy's mother had visited me in my kitchen after she had died, I decided to tell them about an after death communication that I had received from my father-in-law. Marvin and I had always spent the High Holy Days of Rosh Hashanah and Yom Kippur with his parents. After Marvin's mother died, his father, a retired pharmaceutical salesman had continued to spend these important family holidays with us. When his father died and the High Holy Days arrived, Marvin was despondent. He desperately missed his father's presence in the synagogue and at the holiday dinner table.

When Yom Kippur, a day of fasting and the holiest day in the Jewish calendar, arrived, Marvin and I went to the synagogue together. But, this Yom Kippur turned out to be important in a different and very powerful way. Marvin's father, when he was alive, had had a penchant for using one word in particular, to express his frequent displeasure. Often feisty as an old man, when he did not agree with someone, he loved to bellow, "Baloney!" While Marvin and I were listening to the rabbi's Yom Kippur sermon, I knew that my husband was brooding about his father's absence. I always enjoyed listening to our rabbi's sermons. This highly educated man was a vegetarian, quite formal and spoke in a theatrical, almost British accent. His sermons were always well written and equally well presented. Never in a billion years would anyone ever expect him to use a word as prosaic as "baloney" in one of his scholarly presentations. That is exactly why I let out a gasp when on the holiest day of the year, he unexpectedly shouted out, "'Baloney!" When the shock of this uncharacteristic event had worn off and I had regained my composure, I leaned over to Marvin and told him that I was absolutely certain that this surprise was actually a communication from his father's spirit. I explained that his father wanted him to know that he was doing fine on the other side and that he was still with him in spirit form. Marvin's depression immediately lifted. He accepted my explanation very gratefully and was in much better spirits for the rest of the day. This mystical experience reinforced my belief in the healing power of after-death communication. There is nothing more comforting than the realization that our departed loved ones are still connected to us.

Attending Gloria's classes provided me with an atmosphere that accelerated my spiritual and psychic evolution. It was not just the acquisition of important metaphysical and spiritual knowledge that speeded my development. Being exposed to the auras and high vibrations of so many people on quests for greater spirituality also proved to be of benefit to me. I reveled in the joy of being able to share my discoveries of all the signs and symbols, which functioned as guides along my spiritual Yellow Brick Road, with these open minded and accepting people.

I told everyone in the class about the number twenty-six and how it functioned as a signpost in my spiritual life. Basking in their acceptance of this discovery, I also shared with this group what I have learned about synchronicities and how these meaningful coincidences have also helped to point me in the right spiritual direction. Everyone, Gloria included, seemed to be fascinated with what I had recently learned; that the Universe is so well organized and in touch with us that it could drop us little hints to guide us on our spiritual way.

An interesting thing happened when I started sharing all of my new spiritual discoveries. This simple attempt to connect to and to help others opened the door for more spiritual discoveries to come in. God and my spirit guides obviously liked the idea that I was sharing with others what they were so lovingly teaching me. It was becoming more and more apparent to me, that one of the major tasks that I was meant to accomplish in my present lifetime, was to be a conduit for the transmission of information about the many spiritual signs and symbols, which were available to guide us.

When the doors between dimensions opened up and the knowledge of more of my personal spiritual signs and symbols started to flood in, I made the discovery that doubles were also one of my most important spiritual symbols. In fact, to my utter surprise, I discovered that the number twenty-six was actually one of these doubles. It dawned on me that the number thirteen, one of the most important numbers in Judaism and in metaphysics and spirituality, was also considered a very lucky number in Marvin's birth family. The acceptance of the power of this number was demonstrated whenever anyone in his family bought a new car. When the car was brought home, all of the relatives would throw thirteen pennies into it for good luck. Attending classes at the Kabbalah Center reinforced my discovery of the significance of thirteen as a part of a guiding spiritual double. During a class in gematria, Kabalistic numerology, I learned that the numerical value for the Hebrew word "ahava", or "love", is thirteen. By using what I call the mathematics of mysticism, I figured out that when two soulmates find each other and join together in love, ahava plus ahava, or thirteen and thirteen, combine to make the number twenty-six, the holiest name of God in Judaism. This was the very first time that I began to think of Marvin and myself as soulmates. This outstanding revelation made tremendous sense to me because something as solid as numbers could be used to steer those of us who were in physical form in the right spiritual direction.

A less complicated expression of the fact that doubles were a prominent spiritual symbol, which helped to guide me on my sacred path, was the prevalence of twins in my birth family. I have twin sisters, twin aunts and twin nieces, who are all alive at this time. My mother added to this prestigious array of double relatives by telling me that her mother had also had twin sisters who had died young.

Entering these new insights about doubles into my Lucid Notebook brought me the astonishing revelation that there were an extraordinary number of other doubles in my life. Interestingly, even the name given to me at birth is a double. In the light of my latest spiritual discoveries, I realized that the name, Barbara, actually consists of two sets of the syllable 'bar' plus an additional 'a.' This discovery led to an equally interesting revelation. I recognized that the nicknames for both my first name and my middle name are doubles. I had always wondered why I was the only one of four female siblings who was given a middle name. My realization of the importance of doubles in my life has finally given me an answer to that question. The middle name, which I was given at birth, was *Roberta*. Since one of the most widely used nicknames for *Barbara* and *Roberta* is *Bobby*, my most unusual nickname is *Bobby Bobby*.

I still find it hard to believe that it took me almost sixty years to figure out the spiritual significance of my birth names. My extensive metaphysical and spiritual reading has taught me that my soul devised doubles as a sacred symbol before it incarnated into my present physical life. It has also led me to understand that nothing happens by accident and that I, therefore, made this eye-opening discovery when I was spiritually ready to receive and interpret it.

My very first awareness of the significance of doubles as an important spiritual symbol in my present lifetime came in a very dramatic and unusual way. Marvin and I had driven from Florida to New York to help our younger son, David, and his then fiancé, Tracy, celebrate their engagement. On the way home to Florida, we decided to visit Ellis Island where we had had our parents' names recorded on the wall of immigrants. We arrived at Ellis Island by ferry and immediately located this historically important outdoor wall. After locating Marvin's parents' names on this wall that was framed by New York City's famous skyline, we proceeded to locate my mother and father's names. As I stood in front of my parent's imprint on American history, I was struck by the realization that the Twin Towers, one of New York's most famous landmarks, were outlined against the sky directly behind their names. This disclosure made me momentarily speechless. It seemed to me that time stood still and waited for me to digest, and to assimilate this striking revelation. I found it hard to believe that all of this trouble would be taken, whether it came from my Higher Self or from God, to help me to identify one of my soul's most important symbols. Time, meditation, and study have taught me that nothing is too large or too difficult for God and our mystical mentors to accomplish in order to help us to find our way back home. I finally turned and walked away from this incredible tableau with the newly acquired knowledge that doubles were a very significant guiding symbol in my personal quest for spiritual understanding. I could hardly wait to get back to our car so that I could enter this magical moment of discovery into my Lucid Notebook.

My new awareness of the importance of doubles as a guiding factor in my spiritual life allowed a torrent of twin symbols to come flooding into my consciousness. For days and nights on end all I could think about was how and where these doubles appeared in my life. One of the most outstanding doubles was the name of the nightclub where Marvin and I met, the *Boom Boom* Room. Then I realized that my double nicknames, *Bobby Bobby*, have double letters in them, as does my married name *Yudell*. The vast majority of the names in our family have double letters in them as well. A sampling of these names are: *Bass, Glasser, Weiss, Isaacs, Shoon, Sussman, Harris, William, Nessa, Jeffrey, Larry, Lillian, Kenny, Charlotte, Manny* and *Maddy*. Even our dog, *Buttons*, has a name with a double letter in it.

This unexpected recognition of how many doubles there were in the names of people in my life was very shortly followed by the startling awareness of how many twin objects and furnishings that I had unconsciously decorated our new home with. As my eyes wandered over our much loved retirement home, I was amused at the number of double candlesticks, bookends, sofas and chairs that abounded in each and every room. Even our address right here in Boynton Beach, a double in itself, and our new phone number, both contained doubles. My Lucid Notebook was beginning to overflow with doubles. I found that this new understanding of how my soul had devised symbols that it could be identified by was very empowering.

My old friend and teacher, Bernie Wagner, had told me about a New Age system called Silva Mind Control that helped people to relax and to use positive imagery to activate their right brains. He explained that it helped people to become more psychic by teaching them to reach and to function in the alpha, or slower brain wave, state of consciousness. He also told me that people who take this course are taught to employ relatively slow brain waves to expand their awareness and their problem solving abilities. Ina and I were eager to take Silva Mind Control training and when Bernie called to tell me that he had located a facilitator in the area, we both immediately enrolled in the class. My experience at Dr. Brian Weiss' past life regression seminar, when a light coming out of the right side of my head was detected, had verified my belief that the right frontal lobe of my brain had been activated by my near death experience. I was anxious to take Silva Mind Control because I knew that further development of the part of my brain that was connected to the otherworldly dimension would most certainly help me on my journey up the Yellow Brick Road to personal spiritual understanding.

When the date for the Silva Mind Control class finally arrived, Ina and I took off for Fort Lauderdale, feeling like two spiritual prospectors, ready to explore and to conquer the unknown. The exercises, that we were involved in during this seminar, truly helped to develop the right side of my brain and proved to me, with no doubt, that we are all connected to each other. To this very day, I still find it mind-boggling that I was able, after many preparatory exercises, to diagnose the illnesses of absent people who I had never met and knew nothing about. This part of the mind control training proved to be a powerful motivator for me. It proved to me that I am, as we all are, very psychic indeed, and that I could use this natural attribute to help me to discover more about my personal spiritual journey and sacred mission. It removed any doubts that I may have had about achieving this goal. Silva Mind Control had succeeded in sharpening my right brain and my ability to function in an alpha brain wave state and was helpful in facilitating the spiritual discoveries, which were yet to come.

Lessons from Chapter IV

* After-death communication is the name for the phenomenon by which spirits in the after life contact living people. There are countless ways that this can occur.

* Communication from the spirit world can come through other living people. My friend, Sandy's, mother, used a light to get my attention. When I realized what this light meant, I carried the message to her daughter.

* My father-in-law's message was delivered to us through our rabbi. In this case he used a word that he knew that we would recognize in order to get his message across.

* We all have symbols by which our souls can be identified.

* When we recognize what these symbols are, they can help us to make personal spiritual discoveries.

* I was fortunate enough to discover that the number twenty-six and doubles are two of my soul's most important spiritual symbols.

CHAPTER V

Meeting the Lion and the Tin Man

*Spirit Guides are sometimes the essence
of people we least expect.*

Before sharing the next event that happened in my quest
for personal spiritual understanding, I have to back-
track to an incident that occurred in 1979 when Marvin and
I took our two young sons to Europe. After we visited
England and the Netherlands, we boarded a train to Paris.
After we got on the train, we discovered that our travel agent
had not reserved the first class seats that we had requested. We were all very tired and did not relish facing a five and
one half-hour trip in uncomfortable second-class seats.
Marvin communicated our distress to the conductor who
suggested that he walk up and down the aisle to try to locate
a private compartment, with room for the four of us. He told
us that if the people in that compartment did not object, we
should settle in and that he would collect the additional
money later on. Marvin looked and quickly came back with
the good news that there was an American woman traveling
with her teen-age daughter who said that they would be very
happy to share their compartment with us.

As soon as we were settled in our seats, I realized with
whom we were traveling. The teen-age girl was a seventeen-
year-old actress by the name of Jodie Foster. I remembered
her from the movie, *"Taxi Driver"* and from *"The Courtship of
Eddy's Father,"* a situation comedy that appeared on television in the late sixties and the early seventies. The five and
one half-hour trip passed very pleasantly. When we reached
Paris, we said our good-byes to Jodie and her mother. We

thanked them for their kindness in sharing their compartment with us and also for the recommendations, which they had made for the rest of our trip.

This little encounter became an anecdote in our family's history. I always thought of this chance meeting with fondness, but I did not think that it was of any particular importance in my journey toward spiritual awareness until July of 1997, eighteen years after its occurrence. At this time, about two weeks after the completion of the course in Silva Mind Control, Marvin and I took off for Chicago for Hadassah's annual national convention. I had founded a chapter of Hadassah, the largest woman's humanitarian organization in the United States, in our new retirement community and was functioning as its first president. This organization has always been very dear to my heart because it saves lives and does intensive medical research in its two hospitals in Israel. It also helps to improve the lives of women and children in the United States. After the convention, Marvin and I were planning to visit his first cousins in Seattle, Washington and intended to finish our trip by driving into the Canadian Rocky Mountains.

As soon as the limousine picked us up to take us to Palm Beach International Airport on the first leg of our trip, the number twenty-six started to pop up all over the place. The limousine driver used the number twenty-six at least three or four times in his conversation alone. Then, when we finally arrived in Chicago, I noted with amusement that our room was on the twenty-sixth floor of the hotel. This seemingly innocuous fact caused my spiritual antennae to stand up and take notice because experience had taught me that a preponderance of the number twenty-six appearing in my life was always a harbinger of some kind of important spiritual event or insight. My anticipation of such an event or insight was greater than usual because the year, 1997, also added up to twenty-six. Happy that I had brought my Lucid Notebook with me, I excitedly entered my observation of these twenty-sixes and my speculation about what this meant into it. I also added that my mind was open and that

I was ready for whatever the flurry of twenty-sixes was going to bring my way.

The spiritual insights and events that I had anticipated did not take long in coming. That evening, after dinner in the hotel, every delegate attending the convention, was taken to the Navy Pier for a celebration honoring the 100th Anniversary of World Zionism. We were celebrating this auspicious event because Hadassah supports the two largest hospitals and medical research facilities in Israel and is, therefore, a Zionist group.

At the Navy Pier, Theodore Bikel narrated an informative show about the life and work of Theodore Herzl, the father of Zionism. As the show progressed I was struck by the fact that Herzl was born about the same time as Sigmund Freud, the father of psychoanalysis, and that they both lived in the same area of Vienna for most of their lives. The meaningful coincidences surrounding these two famous men jumped right out at me. I had recently discovered that Freud was one of my spirit guides. I put this together with the fact that my father and Marvin's mother were both born in Vienna, and that I had felt compelled to start a Zionist organization, which owed a debt of gratitude to the father of Zionism, Theodore Herzl. As I sat in the Navy Pier, listening to Theodore Herzl's story, I had the strange feeling that my spiritual story had something to do with Vienna.

The way in which I found out that Freud was one of my spirit guides is an interesting part of my quest for personal spiritual understanding. When Marvin and I were attending the Kabbalah Center, we took part in a group meditation, which was supposed to help us to find some of our spirit guides. We were informed that we might not connect to a spirit guide immediately, but that we should continue to do this meditation on our own until we achieved our goal. Nothing happened during this group exercise. This did not faze me. I was determined that I would continue this meditation on my own so that I would eventually meet a least one of my sacred helpers. I meditated on a regular basis, but did not discover any spirit guides until Marvin and I took our third trip to Israel in 1995. During this trip, Marvin was driving our rental car around Jerusalem while I sat next to him with my eyes closed. I did this because I thought that it was preferable to meditate than to watch my husband compete with the suicidal drivers that surrounded us. While I was meditating, I asked to be introduced to one of my spirit guides. To my astonishment, as I made this request, a picture of Sigmund Freud floated up into my mind's eye. This revelation seemed so outlandish to me that I decided not to tell Marvin about it. He usually believed everything that I told him, but this was a little bit too far out. Why would such an illustrious spirit want to be my spirit guide? The very next day found us driving around Jerusalem again. My eyes were again closed in meditation. I opened them when I felt the car stopping for a traffic light. When my eyes fell on the street sign of this road that we had never been on before, I had the greatest surprise of the trip. We were on Sigmund Freud Street. What an outstanding way to corroborate something that I found hard to believe. Sigmund Freud was one of my spirit guides.

Now I sat in the Navy Pier in Chicago, Illinois, wondering if Theodore Herzl was also one of my spirit guides. I actually had good reason to think this way. Theodore Herzl was the father of Zionism and I had felt compelled to start a chapter of a Zionistic organization. I even found the builder's advertisement for the retirement community in which we now live in Hadassah magazine. Did Herzl, the founder of Zionism, encourage me from the other side?

As I sat in the Navy Pier, trying to deal with the multitude of soul-searching questions coursing through my mind, a strong inner knowing enveloped me. My Higher Self told me that the spirits of these two eminent Jewish men, Freud and Herzl, were definitely my spirit guides and that they had been serving as such since my birth in 1938. The stage seemed to fade from my perception as I contemplated what had just been revealed to me. I could now understand why I had always had such a deep interest in psychology and psychotherapy and had almost made this my life's work.

Was this why my younger son, David, had decided to become a psychologist? Was all of this connected to the fact that my father and my husband's mother were both born in the same section of Vienna as Freud and Herzl? It was hard to keep up with the influx of questions that this significant insight was producing. As I sat next to Marvin in stunned silence, I could actually envision Freud and Herzl looking down from heaven, trying to encourage a Jewish-American woman, with roots in Vienna, to help the cause of Zionism. I spent the rest of the evening in a confused daze. My impatience to get back to our room to enter my new insights into my Lucid Notebook was overwhelming. It would take another year to finally get the answer, which would tie up all the loose ends that my questions were creating.

At least one of my questions had been answered. I now knew why so many twenty-sixes had popped up since we had left Florida. It was swiftly becoming obvious to me that this trip was really a spiritual voyage of discovery. I even saw the theme of the Hadassah Convention as a synchronicity, which validated that I was on the right track in my quest for personal spiritual understanding. The theme was, "If you will it, it is not a dream." I was startled by the fact that this was actually the theme that I was working on in my life. I was trying to bring my dream of understanding my soul, its journey and its mission, into conscious reality. All the books that I was reading and all of the courses and seminars, which I was attending, were helping me to see the connection between my soul's sacred mission and what I was and would be accomplishing in my present lifetime.

When the Hadassah Convention was over, Marvin and I flew to Seattle, Washington to visit with Marvin's cousins, Reva, Maddy and Jim. After the pleasant visit, we rented a car and took off for southwestern Canada and the Canadian Rocky Mountains. When we reached Banff, a tranquil little ski resort nestled in the snow capped mountains surrounding it, we checked into a hotel on the main street of the town. It was in Banff that I had an experience that also

explained the preponderance of twenty-sixes and synchronicities that we were encountering on this trip. In retrospect, I recognize that this experience was meant to occur
in 1997 because the numbers contained in this year add up
to twenty-six. It has also become quite clear to me that this
experience was connected to the chance meeting that we
had with Jodie Foster in 1979, which also adds up to twenty-six.

After we checked into the hotel, we unpacked and we ate
dinner. Since there was nothing else to do at night in this
quiet little town, we decided to go to the movies. Jodie
Foster's latest movie, *Contact* was playing. The memory of
the experience that we had shared with Jodie Foster and her
mother in Europe in 1979 was nowhere in my conscious
mind when we took our seats and the movie started. But,
obviously, my subconscious mind had an agenda of its own.
The film started and we rapidly became engrossed in what
we had been previously told was a metaphysical story. Jodie
Foster played the part of a sonar astronomer, working for
SETI, whose job it was to listen for sounds of extraterrestrial life in the Universe. When a sound was identified and it
was established that it came from the vicinity of Vega, a star
situated twenty-six light years from Earth, my ears opened
wide and my entire being snapped to attention. The number
twenty-six had put me on the alert. This was the very
moment that my intuition told me that something spiritually important was about to happen.

The sonar astronomer, played by Jodie Foster, was chosen to travel into space in a vehicle, which was built to the
specifications of the aliens whose radio waves she had
picked up. Instead of reaching outer space, Jodie's spaceship started to shake violently and fell apart. Time and
thought have made it clear to me that what happened to the
sonar astronomer when the space vehicle fell apart was very
similar to what happened to Dorothy in *The Wizard of Oz*.
She was blown into a reality that was very different than the
one she had previously known. As the spaceship was being
destroyed, Jodie began to float down onto a terrain that

looked exactly like the surreal beach, which I had recently envisioned in Silva Mind Control when we were asked to imagine a place of ultimate peace and tranquility. Seeing Jodie standing in this serene tableau that was almost an exact duplicate of my imagined heavenly place of sanctuary, caused me to be ever more on the alert for some kind of spiritual message. This was obviously a synchronicity, which was meant to catch my attention. I could almost hear my Higher Self telling me to pay attention to what was going to happen next.

All of my senses were standing up at attention. I waited breathlessly for the other worldly message to come in. As I waited, I could see an amorphous figure slowly drifting down a long stretch of luminous white sand that was framed by a cloudless blue sky and the sparkling azure sea. As this shapeless mass drifted toward the sonar astronomer, played by Jodie Foster, it began to take on a more distinct form. With a gasp, I realized that this amorphous form had become the astronomer's father, who had died when she was quite young. What happened next made it difficult for me to breathe. My intuition was prodding me to recognize that there was a message in this film from my father. This accounted for the appearance in this movie of the number twenty-six and the synchronicity of the heavenly beach scene. As I sat speechless in the movie theater, I struggled to accept the fact that my father's spirit had chosen such a complicated way to send me a message, two exposures to Jodie Foster, both in years that added up to twenty-six. My inner confusion was slightly diminished by the memory of a spiritual truth, which I had read about in books on metaphysics and spirituality. The metaphysical fact that I remembered was that dead parents will try to get through to their living children in any way that they possibly can.

I left the theater with a multitude of questions buzzing through my mind. Was I imagining this or did I really get a message from my father in this film? If this incident was not a product of my imagination and there truly was a message for me in this movie, what exactly was this message? As we walked back to our hotel, I told Marvin what had transpired during this film. I was thankful that he did not accuse me of being totally insane. Then I did something that I have never done before but have done many times since, I silently asked God to send me a sign, possibly in the form of a synchronicity, to validate my belief that there really was a message from my dead father in the movie, *Contact*.

When we returned to our hotel, I put a detailed description of this mystical experience into my Lucid Notebook. Then I tried to get it out of my mind. I didn't want the confusion that was making my head spin to ruin the rest of our vacation. I decided to trust God to send me a sign that what I had just experienced was indeed true. I also decided to trust that, if there were authenticity in what had just transpired, I would ultimately understand the message that it was bringing to me.

As I have subsequently found out, God never takes too long to verify an important truth. In this case the answer came within a very few days. When we left Canada and headed back to Seattle, we decided to drive around the Olympic Peninsula to get a more complete picture of what the Pacific Northwest was really like. We decided that we would locate available restrooms and use them before we entered the Coastal Highway. We didn't have too much luck in this quest, so Marvin suggested that we use the facilities in a nearby hospital. After doing just that, we climbed back into our car to continue our sightseeing. As we pulled out of the hospital's parking lot, I instinctively looked up at the street sign above our heads. I chuckled to myself when I saw that the street that we were on was Schweitzer Way. I laughed because this was certainly the sign of validation, which I was waiting for. My maiden name and, therefore, my father's surname, was Schweitzer. Since the message in the movie was from my father, I could not have hoped for a more appropriate synchronicity. I was overjoyed that I had received proof that my father had sent me a message, through Jodie Foster, in the movie *Contact*. It would take a little longer to understand what the message was.

I was beginning to see that the Higher Power and all of life were working together to leave me little hints to guide me on my spiritual path. I always seemed to intuitively know which things in my environment were clues and which were not. Some of these clues made sense right away and some took a little longer to expose their meaning. Whether I understood a particular clue or not, I always entered it into my Lucid Notebook. Invariably the meaning of the hints that I did not understand became apparent to me at some later date. During our stay in Banff, it occurred to me that there was significance in the fact that I had received a mystical message from my father's spirit in Alberta, known as the Wild Rose Province. I had this thought while we were walking in front of our hotel in Banff. When I looked across the street, my eyes fell on the sign for the Rose and Crown Hotel. The name of this hotel seemed significant to me because I had recently intuited that the rose and the crown were two very important spiritual symbols in my life. I knew that these symbols were pointing at discoveries that I would make sometime in the future. When I returned to our hotel, I recorded these symbols in my Lucid Notebook. This done, I knew that I had to be patient. Eventually my mystical mentors would reveal the meaning of these symbols.

When we returned to Florida, I found a message on my answering machine that ultimately brought a wonderful, spiritual validating tool into my life. The message informed me that there was a local angel shop that was going out of business and was having a huge liquidation sale. As soon as I heard this message, I intuitively knew that there was something on sale in this shop that was of spiritual importance to me. I decided to pay a visit to the angel store. Once there, I was going to allow my intuition to lead me to the article waiting for me. When I entered the shop, I was overwhelmed by the quantity of wonderful sale items. How was I going to find exactly what I needed to further my spiritual development at this particular time? I took a deep breath and decided to leave all conscious judgment at the door. Then I walked through the store and waited for my intuition to nudge me and to let me know what to purchase. Every step that I took became more and more depressing. I couldn't seem to connect to anything. As I walked past the checkout counter, which was the last stop before leaving the shop, I was attracted to a blue box with a picture of an angel on it. This box contained a pack of cards and a corresponding book that was entitled Universe Angel Cards. As soon as I saw this box, my intuition let me know loud and clear that this was what I had driven all the way from Boynton Beach to find. When I told the owner of the store that I wanted to purchase these cards, she shuffled them and asked me to pick one. I was pleasantly surprised when I picked the card that was the duplicate of the picture of the angel on the box. This was proof to me that this was the spiritual article that I was supposed to buy. Time has proven that I was right. These wonderful angel cards have proven time and again to be spiritually validating and guiding. They have helped to clarify and to verify all of the mystical experiences and discoveries, which have come my way since I found them.

It did not take too long for this divination tool, which I was sure had been sent to me by one of my mystical mentors, to prove its worth in assisting me on the Yellow Brick Road toward personal spiritual knowledge. A few weeks after I made this purchase, I walked into our community's clubhouse and showed these cards to our social director, Jennifer. This spiritually sophisticated young woman was always ready to share mystical experiences and insights with me. When I showed her my new purchase, she informed me that she owned these cards too. Jennifer then told me that the card that she picked the most out of the 85 cards in the deck was the Angel Baby in the Lotus card. Since this was the card that I picked most of the time too and since it corresponded to page 26 in the accompanying book, I knew that Jennifer had been sent to me to help me in my spiritual development. I was not wrong.

When I told her that she seemed to be in unusually high spirits and much more enthusiastic than usual, Jennifer shared the origin of her euphoria with me. She told me, "I attended a group Reiki healing in Hollywood last night. This is a Japanese system of spiritual hands on healing. I sat under a huge metal frame pyramid when all of this was going on. When the Reiki practitioners started to work on me, I felt a sharp rise in body temperature." When I questioned this, I was told that this occurred because the energy of the Universe comes in at the crown or top of the practitioner's head and then travels through his body and into his hands. Sitting under a pyramid intensifies this energy. As I listened to Jennifer describe how natural spiritual healing occurs, an unexpected insight popped into my mind. I realized, with total clarity, that all of us are like little pyramids. The energy of the Universe comes into our bodies at the crown chakra at the top of our heads. This inspiring insight, which I was sure came from my Higher Self or a spirit guide, convinced me that the next step in my journey toward a greater knowledge of my soul would be the experience of a group Reiki healing under a pyramid.

I entered the Reiki Center in Hollywood, Florida with the intention of discovering what I would find out about my soul while sitting under a pyramid and exposing myself to intensified Universe energy. A huge pipe metal pyramid covered the room. I was allowed to sit under this pyramid during the group Reiki healing because this was my first experience with this form of hands on healing. After we were seated, we closed our eyes and listened to the Reiki master recite a prayer, which stated that our intent was to cure illness and to achieve world peace. When the prayer was completed, beautiful ephemeral music began to waft through the room. I could feel the hands of a Reiki practitioner directing the intensified Universe energy to all parts of my body. As I slowly drifted into a state of ultimate relaxation, I could actually feel heat coming out of the hands that had been trained to be channels for Universe energy, love and healing.

What happened next brought me closer to the knowledge of what my immortal soul, the Godlike part of me that I so ached to understand, was really like. As the Reiki session continued, I could see the Earth floating in space on the mental screen formed by my closed eyes. This image was so real that I could even see wispy white clouds drifting over our planet's surface. As this beautiful tableau floated in front of me, I could see my arms reaching out and embracing our troubled planet. Huge tears of joy and relief began to roll down my cheeks as waves of love for the Earth and all of its inhabitants began to emanate from deep within me. At that moment, I could feel all judgment suspended. I knew that if I could cure all of the ills of the world with my love, I would certainly do so. I felt like Mother Earth, brimming over with unconditional love for her children.

When I opened my eyes and shared this life altering experience with the rest of the group, I was told that this Reiki share had opened up my heart chakra, a whirling center of spiritual energy located near my heart. This middle chakra, in a series of seven chakras, stretching from the bottom of the human torso to the crown at the top of our heads, is the seat of unconditional love. This Reiki, hands on healing, had opened my heart chakra and had allowed all of the love, which was stored up within my soul, to come pouring out. When I returned home and entered this powerful experience into my Lucid Notebook, I recognized that the long green oval light, surrounded by a golden halo, which I had seen in my kitchen when my friend Sandy's mother died was actually unconditional love emanating from Edith's soul. I now understood that green, the color of growth, healing, and the subconscious mind is also the color of love and the heart chakra. This mystical green light was Edith's way of asking me to love and to help her daughter to cope with her mother's death.

This dramatic expression of unconditional love seemed to me to be connected to the spontaneous episodes of total non-judgmental love, which I had been experiencing more and more frequently over the last few years. These feelings would descend upon me very suddenly and unexpectedly. Recently, as I drove around in my car, a little black child on a bicycle passed me. From out of nowhere, a feeling of intense unconditional love swept over me. These short lived, but always welcome feelings, would usually be directed at minorities, poor and disabled people, those most in need of unconditional love. The most significant effect that these episodes of intense, non-judgmental love have had on me was that they have brought me closer to knowledge of my immortal soul and its godlike nature.

LESSONS FROM CHAPTER V

* We all have invisible bodies, which work in conjunction with our physical bodies. These bodies, which are called the etheric bodies, possess an etheric spinal cord, which is called the sushumna. The sushumna is an exact replica of the spinal cord in the physical body.

* The etheric body possesses force centers, which correspond to the force centers in our physical bodies, which are called glands.

* The invisible force centers of the etheric body are called chakras. Chakra means "wheel of energy" in Sanskrit. There are seven chakras along the sushumna or etheric spinal cord.

* The three lowest chakras or centers of consciousness, the root, the navel, and the solar plexus, form the lower self, or carnal being. Someone who lives in the consciousness of these lower chakras will live a life of lust, greed, selfishness and hate.

* The first chakra is the lowest one. It is called the root chakra and is located at the base of the spine and the groin. Red is the color of this chakra. It relates to our animal nature and to survival.

* The next highest chakra is located just below the navel. It is orange in color and is called the sacral chakra. This chakra relates to reproduction, sexuality and health.

* The chakra that is next highest is called the solar plexus chakra. Its color is yellow and it relates to issues of worthiness and our sense of identity.

＊ The middle chakra is the heart chakra. Its color is pink or green and it is responsible for love and for higher consciousness. The heart chakra is the gateway to the higher, more spiritual chakras.

＊ Above the heart chakra, we find the throat chakra. This chakra is blue and it relates to self-expression, creativity and the search for truth. People who are seeking spiritual enlightenment live in the consciousness of the heart and the throat chakras.

＊ The sixth chakra is located in the middle of the forehead and is known as the third eye chakra. Indigo is its color. It relates to the qualities of intelligence and psychic powers.

＊ The seventh chakra is called the crown chakra. It is located above the head. Its color is violet and it is the link between the individual and the Universe.

CHAPTER VI

Glinda, the Good Witch, Speeds up My Journey on the Yellow Brick Road

Our past lives reveal the lessons we are here to learn in this incarnation.

I continued to attend Gloria Fleischner's Metaphysics and Parapsychology classes on a weekly basis. Gloria was just like the Good Witch, Glinda, whom Dorothy met in *The Wizard of Oz*. Her psychic development classes were very helpful. They were helping me to piece together my soul's spiritual journey through eternity. Her group past life regression sessions helped me to uncover some of the places that my soul had been before it incarnated as Barbara Schweitzer Yudell. I knew that I had to learn where my soul had been in the past before I could understand what it was doing in my present body.

Through participation in one of Gloria's past life regression seminars, I realized that my soul was once in the body of a Roman man. As soon as I reached a deep enough meditative state, I could see myself as a male who was dressed in a toga and in sandals, which were laced all the way up to my knees. When Gloria asked me to tell the class about this lifetime, I responded with, "I think that this lifetime was before the time of Christ. I am a Roman man who was an athlete when he was younger and is now a writer or a scribe." From my present vantage point, I understand that this past life regression was merely a rehearsal for a later, more detailed, trip back to this lifetime that would take place in a one on one setting.

In another past life regression, I went back to a lifetime in Ireland, in the fifteenth or sixteenth century. I saw myself as a strong willed young boy who was barefoot and wore knickers and a long sleeved ruffled white shirt. This picture of myself in another time was set against a backdrop of a roadside inn, which was owned by my parents. Looking more deeply into what was going on in this lifetime brought me the awareness that I was responsible for taking care of the horses and the carriages that were owned by the people staying at the inn. The discovery of a past lifetime in Ireland was not at all surprising to me. It left me with a feeling of completion because it explained why I have always had an affinity for the Irish people and why I have always wanted to visit Ireland.

Exploring my past lives was becoming very exciting. The details of the lives that I was beginning to access were immediately entered into my Lucid Notebook, as soon as I returned home. It was becoming increasingly clear to me that past life regression was a very important tool in my quest for knowledge of my soul's essence. These little glimpses into my Earthly sojourns motivated me to read more and more books on reincarnation. The information that I gleaned from these books and from the many classes and seminars on past lives, which I was attending on a regular basis, increased my fascination with this important spiritual topic. The more I learned about reincarnation, the more I wanted to know about it. I learned that our souls come back to physical life not just to learn spiritual lessons, but also to experience all aspects of being human. Every returning soul must experience being male and female, rich and poor, a member of every race, and even what it is to live under the influence of every sign of the zodiac. I also learned that there are many clues in our present lives, which can help us to determine who and what we were in other incarnations. Some of these clues come in the form of affinities for certain countries and cultures. Very often, how we dress or decorate our homes, or where we like to travel to on our vacations, will point directly at one of our more significant past lives. Even strong phobias and dislikes can be hints of what happened to us in the past, when our souls resided in other bodies. The most fascinating thing that I learned about reincarnation was that the talents that we possess in our present lifetime could give us insight into who we were in a lifetime centuries ago. Not only do talents travel with us from lifetime to lifetime, they actually gain strength with each subsequent incarnation. This probably explains why Mozart was composing great music at such a young age. His musical genius had obviously been traveling with him from lifetime to lifetime for many centuries.

Gloria's next psychic development class took us on a shaman journey. This proved to be very exciting because it helped to shed light on the total picture of my soul's sacred mission and spiritual odyssey through time. After the entire class had stretched out on available sofas, beds and carpeted floor spaces, Gloria, like a medicine man or witch doctor in a Native American tribe, started to chant and to beat on a drum. Before too long we were all in a deep trance. The first part of the journey was to the lower world. In the distance I could hear Gloria telling us, "You will be meeting your power animal on this inward trip." I knew that power animals were an important Native American phenomenon. I had no idea what my power animal would be. Within seconds of being alerted to watch for this power animal, I bumped headfirst into a tall and elegant giraffe. This was quite a surprise. My surprise diminished slightly when I thought of the spelling of the word giraffe. The name of this animal contains a double letter, which fits in with my discovery that doubles are one of my soul's spiritual symbols.

Later discussion helped me to understand that the giraffe is probably the best power animal for me. Like this elegant, long necked animal, I always have my head in the clouds. This condition comes from the fact that I am an idealist, a visionary and a dreamer. I always expect more from people than they can ever realistically live up to. Also, like the giraffe, I try to look down through the metaphorical clouds at the tiny world below me to convince myself that in the total scheme of things, our problems are really very small. Finally, the most obvious similarity between my newfound friend, the giraffe, and myself is that we both have the propensity to stick our necks out. While the giraffe does this to survive physically, I do it to survive emotionally and spiritually. Having my head in the clouds, like the giraffe, and being an idealist, makes me very sensitive to the perpetration of injustice. If I feel that there is a wrong to be righted, I will do anything within my power to correct it. Like Archangel Michael, I am constantly trying to protect and to defend others.

After leaving my newfound power animal, I journeyed into a rainforest. While I admired the lushness of the vegetation and the beauty of the subtropical animals that lived and thrived within this lushness, an insight popped into my mind. I suddenly recognized the truth in the statement that we are all connected and that either all of us will survive together or none of us will survive at all. I saw, with great clarity, that one of the contracts that I had agreed to before I incarnated into my present lifetime was that I would help to care for and to protect the environment. This insight helped me to recognize that it was no accident that I started, built and ran a natural, biodegradable product business from my home for almost fourteen years. It also validated the fact, that even after retiring from this business, I continue to use all of these safe, non-polluting products and am always trying to encourage others to do the same.

In the wink of a shaman's eye, I traveled from the rainforest to a river that was situated at the bottom of a canyon. As I surveyed my surroundings, I could see multitudes of Native Americans standing on the shore. I was floating down this river in a very large canoe with many human traveling companions. All of these fellow travelers were strangers to me. I knew that they represented humanity as a whole. I also realized almost immediately that the Native Americans on the shore, known for their spirituality and their connection to the Earth, were symbolic of the many spirit guides and guardian angels who were helping me to navigate down the river of my soul's sacred odyssey. This part of my shaman's journey reminded me of the twenty-six-word poem, *Grand Canyon*, the allegory for my spiritual journey, which I had written on a cross-country trip with Marvin in 1966. I could now see that this mystical canoe trip was an allegory for a much broader trip, the spiritual odyssey of all humanity. This tableau made it clear to me that either we, as a species, learned to get along and to be kind and considerate to each other, or, the canoe would sink. We could no longer ignore the reality that we are all connected in our journey through this thing called life. One errant passenger in the canoe of life could tip the boat and we would all go down together.

As I continued to survey my surroundings while I floated down the river in the canoe, I could see an eagle circling in the sky. My eyes also fell on a large jade green rock on the shore. I found these two aspects of my shaman journey very interesting, but I did not understand their symbolism until I participated in the post voyage class discussion. Others in the class helped me to understand that the eagle was a symbol of spirituality and the soul unfettered by a human body. This was a position that I often longed to be in. Much later on I recognized that the seagull in my poem, *September Sea,* bore a similar symbolism to the eagle in my shaman journey. Going inside helped me to see that despite the symbolic similarities of these two avian creatures, there were still striking differences in their functions. The seagull in *September Sea* represents my soul flying out of my body to heaven and back during my near death experience in 1941. The eagle represents my soul connecting to other dimensions while it is still entrenched in my human body. The class discussion also helped me to see that the color green of the large jade rock on the shore represents Universal love. Green is the color of the heart chakra, through which we give and receive love. The fact that it was a rock, a Universal symbol of strength and stability helped me to see that this was a representation of the positive benefits that love can produce. This allegorical green rock underlined what I have known for a very long time, that bringing love into the world is a Universal mission. Love truly makes the world go round. Without love everything would die.

After all of us were satisfied that we understood the significance and the spiritual content of everything that we had encountered in our shaman journeys to the lower world, Gloria started to beat her drum again. We took off on a journey to the upper world. Almost immediately, I found myself going straight up in a huge, colorful hot-air balloon. As I rose higher and higher, I could see Archangel Michael flying by with his wonderful sword of protective blue light. I found this particularly exciting because I had just learned, through a series of synchronicities, that Archangel Michael was one of my guardian angels. I even had a framed poster by my bed of a Marc Chagall's painting of this powerful spiritual being. The significance of this symbolic sighting came to me immediately. I recognized that I had vowed before I was born, that like Archangel Michael, I would protect and care for people and that I would also try to teach them to protect and to care for themselves.

After my encounter with my invincible guardian angel, I traveled to a crystal city that glowed with the reflection of the northern lights that framed it. The spiritual feeling that this scene engendered was intensified by the beautiful sound of bells ringing in the background. This entire picture seemed very familiar to me. Was this what I saw when I had my near death experience at age three? Or was this a regression back to a past lifetime on the breathtakingly advanced island continent of Atlantis? As I asked myself these questions, my Higher Self gave me an answer that I did not expect. I was told that this idyllic scene was merely a reminder that my husband, Marvin, and I have had many lifetimes together and that our souls and our sacred mission are intertwined. Perhaps our souls, separated for a short time, met again in an ethereal city such as this one when we both had near death experiences in October 1941. Whether or not our souls had a reunion in heaven before we met again in the physical world was not really important. What was important was that we were soulmates and that we would be together for eternity.

The last thing that I saw on my shaman journey to the

upper world was a big dark spot, which faded into a bright white spot. When the drum stopped beating and I returned from my shaman journey to the upper world, I shared this last experience with Gloria and the rest of the class. I was told that what I had just seen was my future death. My soul had symbolically traveled into the dark tunnel that takes us to the other side. Then, after encountering the white light of heaven, my soul had rejoined my physical body in its everyday reality. This incredible shaman journey had brought me into closer contact with my immortal soul. The feeling of lightness and completion that it left me with still lingers.

The same instinctive desire to rise higher spiritually by doing good deeds that had prompted me to start a chapter of Hadassah, a women's humanitarian organization, also motivated me to be instrumental in starting a spiritual support group called SOUL. SOUL was an acronym for Seekers of Universal Light. Those of us who founded this group saw it as a means of connecting like-minded people to each other and to the kind of mystical experiences, which would help to facilitate our spiritual ascension, our progression to the perfection of God.

Forming a spiritual support group was something that I had wanted to do for a very long time. As I started to get in touch with my own spiritual nature and the awareness that we as human beings were always connected to and guided by evolved beings on the other side, I decided that it was my sacred duty to share my awareness with others. I also felt that by founding a chapter of humanitarian organization such as Hadassah and a spiritual support group such as SOUL, that I was forming more evolved communities for more evolved souls. This was important to me because I knew that these groups were necessary for those of us who were yearning for a kinder and a more spiritual way of life. These more evolved groups were essential because they encouraged the qualities of kindness, love, fairness, and respect for and service to others. These were the virtues, that when fostered, would help all of humanity to ascend. An interesting message appeared in my life at just about the same time that I finally understood what had really motivated me to found more evolved communities for more evolved souls. I was driving in my car on September 26th, a very appropriate day to receive a mystical message, when I found myself behind a mini-van with a very obvious bumper sticker. The slogan on this bumper sticker summed up what I had just intuited to be part of my soul's sacred mission. "Civility for the new millennium," was a very appropriate abbreviation for what I was attempting to do by founding a chapter of Hadassah and the spiritual support group, SOUL.

When I was convinced that my Hadassah chapter and our new SOUL group were strong and would survive, I started to turn my attention to other things. I was beginning to have a very powerful desire to visit Vienna, Austria. A strong gut feeling kept nagging at me and telling me that visiting Vienna would connect me to important spiritual information that would ultimately unlock many of my soul's most significant secrets. This strong inner knowing was based on the discoveries that Sigmund Freud, the father of psychoanalysis, and Theodore Herzl, the father of Zionism, were my spirit guides and that both of them were born at just about the same time, in the same area of Vienna. The fact that Marvin's mother and my father were born in the same area of this Austrian city at later dates, also fanned the flames of my intuitive fires. The synchronicity of these connections to Vienna was pointing me in the direction of a visit to this city on the Danube.

I will forever be thankful that I have a husband who is supportive and who doesn't feel threatened by a highly intuitive wife. Perhaps the fact that we are soulmates is part of the reason for this. When I explained the reasons behind my desire to visit Vienna, he wholeheartedly agreed with my decision. He felt, as I did, that since we were both connected in Israel through his father and my mother, that we probably were also connected in Vienna through my father and his mother.

As usual, my mystical mentors did not disappoint me.

They brought me a synchronicity verifying the veracity of my intuitive desire to visit Vienna even before I asked for one. Since Marvin and I had just started a high-protein, low carbohydrate diet, we decided to pay a visit to our local supermarket to stock up on appropriate foods. As I walked into the store, I was greeted by a huge display of canned Viennese sausage. After my initial astonishment at the rapidity of this corroboration, I started to giggle. I could actually envision my spirit guides having a good giggle too. As I laughed, I thought of how grateful I was for the guidance of my mystical mentors and for the spiritual sense of humor that they entertain me with as they joyfully lead me on my spiritual journey.

What happened next was something that often occurs when people are making good progress along their spiritual paths, I started to experience episodes of lightness. At first, I found these sensations frightening. I would be standing at a dance class or a SOUL meeting and all of a sudden I would feel like a tree swaying in the wind. The metaphysics book that I was reading at the time helped me to understand that mystical experiences, prayer or dance can give the participant an incredible feeling of lightness. This lightness occurred when the soul was being nourished. When I gave it some thought, this made sense to me. I recognized that when the soul is fed what it needs, it moves higher, to more ethereal dimensions. I could also see that when the soul is drifting upward, it makes the physical part of us feel lighter and on the ascent too.

I had always loved to dance. Now I recognized that dancing has always been a form of nourishment for my soul. The act of dancing often made me feel as if I was drifting out of my body, up to the top of the room and then skyward into the floating clouds. The feelings of weightlessness, which have always been produced by dancing, were now being achieved by the other spiritual activities, such as meditation, which I was now taking part in.

My increased involvement in more spiritual pursuits not only produced occasional weightlessness but also speeded up the appearance of synchronicities and spiritual symbols and signs in my life. My Lucid Notebook was filling up at an accelerated speed with mystical observations and insights. Having finally become aware of these little hints and bits of guidance from the holier side of life made me feel more connected to the unseen and less dense dimensions. My experiences had finally convinced me that I was never alone. I knew that I was always connected to love, support and guidance from invisible loving beings. Every day brought me new spiritual adventures and ever increasing expectations. I was developing a perfect trust in my intuition and in the fact that every question that I asked would be answered. All that I had to do was to keep my eyes and my ears open for the guidance that was coming in from the realm of the unseen. It was rapidly becoming apparent to me that my ego was beginning to take a back seat, allowing my Higher Self to climb into the driver's seat. There was no turning back. I was climbing the mountain of spiritual discovery and I was enjoying the increasingly rarified atmosphere.

The spiritual support group that I had founded, SOUL, or Seekers of Universal Light, was proving to be very helpful in connecting me to information about the immortal part of me. One of the first activities that we experienced in this group setting was automatic writing. I had heard and read about this means of connecting to the realm of spirit but had never had the opportunity to be exposed to it. Gloria Fleischner, who had more experience in the use of metaphysical techniques than we did, had graciously agreed to lead us in this activity. She had told our excited group the month before that all we needed in order to be successful in automatic writing was a pad, a pen and an open mind. On the evening selected for automatic writing, we started out by doing a relaxing meditation, which was followed by a recitation of the twenty-third psalm. We then closed our eyes and put our pens over clean sheets of paper. We were told to keep our eyes closed while we allowed our hand to write freely. I was filled with a feeling of dismay as I obeyed these instructions explicitly. I was sure that when I opened my eyes, all that I would see was a page full of kindergarten scribbles.

When our writing time was up and we were told to open our eyes, I was amazed to see the word 'Web' written as clearly as if my eyes had been open during this exercise, right in the middle of the page. The rest of the page was filled with the juvenile scribbles that I had anticipated, except for two more discernible words about an inch below the word 'Web.' These two words were *proud marriage*. After sharing my results with the group, I sat in a quiet state of awe for a considerable time. I had actually connected to the invisible realm of spirit and had received information from an unseen spirit guide. I felt as if a brand new world had opened up to me. I could hardly wait to get home so that I could enter this unexpected communication into my Lucid Notebook.

When I returned home after the SOUL meeting, before I entered the results of my first attempt at automatic writing into my Lucid Notebook, I spent some time trying to figure out what the two messages that I received meant. I tackled the word 'Web' first. The first meaning of the word 'Web' that came to me was the computer definition. The 'Web' in computer lingo stands for the Internet, which is a connection between people the world over. Opening my dictionaries and giving the definitions of this word some thought, I recognized that the word 'Web' is a symbol for all connections. I entered all of this into my Lucid Notebook. I then added that I thought that this was the most appropriate message that I could have received from my first attempt at automatic writing. I reached this conclusion because the theme of connections and contacts, which actually are connections, had been popping up in all of my supernatural experiences for quite a while. I was learning to understand and to identify the signs, symbols and messages that connect those of us who are in physical form to our guides and mentors on the other side. Even more important than this, I had decided to write this book in order to share with others what I was learning on my journey toward spiritual enlightenment.

When completed and distributed to the public, this book would be the strongest connection to others that I would ever achieve. This was probably the exact moment that the title of this book started to formulate in my subconscious mind. My spiritual odyssey was helping me to discover the connections that my soul had to other souls, whether in physical or non-physical form, to God, to my spirit guides and guardian angels, and even to the many past lives that I had led.

The words *proud marriage* were a little harder to understand. I knew that my husband and I were soulmates and had probably spent many lifetimes together on our spiritual treks through eternity. I also knew that I was proud of the positive ways in which we interacted with and helped other people. It even occurred to me that the message *proud marriage* was a corroboration of the veracity of the mystical mathematics equation that I learned about in my study of Kabbalah. I was sure that this equation, 13+13=26 or ahava+ahava=Yud Hay Vov Hay related to my marriage. The word ahava is the Hebrew word for love and is equal to 13 in Kabalistic numerology, while Yud Hay Vov Hay, the tetragramatton or holiest name of God in Judaism, is equal to 26. The prevalence of these numbers in the marriage that Marvin and I share seems to me to be a validation of the importance of the message *proud marriage* that came through in my first attempt at automatic writing. From my present vantage point, I can see that the most significant definition of this message, *proud marriage,* was waiting for me when I got to Vienna.

The many spiritually revealing messages that were finding their way into my life had a profound effect on me. They actually lessened my interest in the ordinary activities that keep most retired people happy. I was traveling faster and faster up the highway of spiritual awareness. I was beginning to feel as if someone had given me a great big how-to book on connecting with my spiritual self. As I thirsted for more and more knowledge this book rapidly became my Bible. Whenever I opened this metaphorical Bible, I always seemed to refer back to the chapter on reincarnation. This occurred because all of my spiritual and metaphysical investigations and experiences had convinced me that I would never really understand my sacred mission on Earth and my soul's spiritual journey until I took the time to delve further into my past incarnations. It was becoming rapidly apparent that one could never really know where they are going until they take the time to find out where they have been. I saw myself as a student, who was ready to learn, so I was not surprised when the teacher that I was waiting for appeared out of the blue. Ina, my SOUL group co-founder, called to tell me about an all day seminar on reincarnation, sponsored by the Association for Research and Enlightenment founded by Edgar Cayce, to be held in our area. Since I was absolutely convinced that this was the area of spirituality that I had to delve into at this particular time, I sent in an enrollment check immediately. I then waited patiently for the day of the seminar to arrive.

At long last, the day of the past-life regression seminar arrived and Ina and I drove to Plantation to attend this greatly anticipated Edgar Cayce event. When we arrived, we entered the hotel conference room to join more than one hundred other people, all of whom were eager to discover who and what they were in their past lives.

Shortly after we took our seats the seminar began. The first session of this conference consisted of a lecture on the meaning of reincarnation. We discussed the way in which reincarnation helps our souls to grow and to evolve. The facilitator stressed how examining our present lives could help us to determine whom we were in a past life and even where we lived during this earlier incarnation. I found this very interesting despite the fact that most of this material was not new to me. Previous exposure to the theory of reincarnation had already convinced me that looking at the talents, affinities, phobias and dislikes of our present lives could disclose much information as to who we were in a past lifetime.

After the morning session was over and we returned from lunch, the seminar leader helped us to reach a deep meditative state. Then she suggested that we go back to a previous lifetime that would help us to understand who and what we were in our present lifetimes. As soon as I reached the appropriate meditative state, I saw myself as a young woman during the nineteenth century. I had long dark carefully coifed hair and was dressed in a manner that suggested that I was of affluent or noble status. As the regression went on, I realized that my husband in this lifetime was a rich and powerful man, which explained my appearance and the charitable activities in which I could see myself involved. When the seminar was over and I returned home, I added this seemingly innocuous past life regression into my Lucid Notebook and then put it out of my mind. In time I would discover how very important this lifetime that I had just accessed was in my soul's overall spiritual development.

My spiritual search continued. Attending classes and reading books on metaphysics and spirituality were proving very helpful in connecting me to pieces of information that helped me to understand my soul and its sacred journey. I was reminded in one of my classes that the color green is synonymous with unconditional love and healing and intuition and the subconscious mind. This reminder hit very close to home. It made me think of Dorothy in *The Wizard of Oz* and how this metaphysical tale related to my own spiritual journey of discovery. When Dorothy, on her personal sacred odyssey, eventually reached the epitome of greenness, the Emerald City, she finally discovered that everything that she had been looking for was inside of her already. This made me recognize, with utmost clarity, that Dorothy was loving and intuitive before she reached the Emerald City. I began to realize that, like Dorothy, I too was becoming more loving and more intuitive and that, also like Dorothy, I needed no external wizard to help in my development. Everything that I needed to know about my soul and its sacred journey were inside myself all along.

These new insights sparked my intuition and led me back to the poetry that I had written on a cross-country trip with

Marvin in the 1960's. When I located these poems and reread them, I began to see one of these little verses in a different light. This poem was about the Rocky Mountains. In the light of my recent discoveries about myself, I now recognized that this poem was really a testimony to the fact that I had been growing more loving and more intuitive for a very long time. These attributes, which were considered to be products of the green heart chakra, came out loud and clear in this poem.

Rocky Mountains

Proud they are, like sinuous steeds,

Their green manes sweeping high,

The pinto peaks, aloof and cool,

In the cloudy corral of the sky.

What I could see now, from a spiritually more knowledgeable vantage point, was that the green mountains were a metaphor for my swiftly growing intuition; my unconscious knowingness and my ever-increasing capacity to feel and to send unconditional love. The green manes sweeping high were now seen as an allegory for my strong desire to reach upward to more lofty dimensions in order to ascend spiritually. I also understood that " the cloudy corral of the sky" was symbolic of my conscious mind or ego, those parts of me that were always trying to obscure my unconscious longing for greater spiritual growth and awareness.

As I reread all of the poems in my cross-country collection, I could see that the one entitled *Welcome* also spoke of my spiritual connection to the color of the heart chakra and of unconditional love and intuition, the color green.

Welcome

Rolled out, extended, a welcome mat of green,

With dipping hills and miles of road,

And swiftly changing scenes.

> A land of beauty, highs and lows,
>
> And towns both large and small,
>
> And all its people beckoning,
>
> Come out and pay a call.

After I reread this poem several times, I sat back and gave it some thought. Before too long, I could see layers of spiritual meaning in a poem that I had written on a cross-country trip in 1966, years before my quest for spiritual knowledge and understanding of my soul ever came into my conscious mind. What I had thought of as an innocuous or even frivolous poem took on the meaning of the masters. On the surface, I could see that this poem was a communication from my Higher Self, which was trying to encourage me to spend more time in that part of me that was connected to the color green, my subconscious mind. As if by magic, the meaning of the "welcome mat of green," spread out before me. It was symbolic of the unconscious and intuitive part of me. I could also see that "all the people beckoning" was a metaphor for my Higher Self, the part of me that was always trying to steer me onto the sacred path of green, a road leading to my personal spiritual evolution and ascension.

Continued rereading of this poem also helped me to understand that it also contained a deeper and more mystical meaning. I saw that the "swiftly changing scenes," the "highs and lows," and the "towns both large and small," were in reality an allegory for all of the past lives that my soul had had through the ages. How amazing! My Higher Self, aware of all of my soul's past incarnations, was trying to communicate this awareness to my conscious mind well before I had even accepted the theory of reincarnation.

The next entry in my Lucid Notebook supported a very important spiritual truth; our souls are all connected, whether they are in heaven or in a suit of flesh on the physical plane. It also underlined the fact that our mystical mentors, on the other side, are always trying to contact us in order to help us along on our spiritual journeys. It was the anniversary of my father's death and Marvin and I were at the bowling alley, participating in our community's weekly bowling league. Our team consisted of four people. Every week we bowled against a competing team, which also consisted of four people. Every team member's initials and scores were recorded on computer monitors, which were located above every lane. After we had finished bowling our first game, the members of both competing teams looked up at these monitors in order to know when we could start bowling our second game. As we did this, eight people witnessed something quite unexpected, something that only I understood. My initials, B.Y., magically changed to my father's initials, F.S. This had never happened before. After everyone involved expressed shock and consternation and wondered why this had happened, we proceeded to bowl our second game. It was obvious to me that my father's spirit, desperate to get through to me, had used the media that was most convenient at the time. I entered this unusual occurrence into my Lucid Notebook with a very perplexing question; what did my father want to tell me? The simple act of putting this question into my Lucid Notebook comforted me. I intuitively knew that in time I would discover the answer to my question.

Questioning what my father was trying to tell me in this unusual communication from the other side was not the only query in my mind. My head was abuzz with countless questions about my soul, where it has been, where it was going and what it was trying to accomplish. My intuition had been repeatedly telling me that I should delve deeper into my soul's past lives in order to understand it better. Since other members of my spiritual support group, SOUL, shared my fascination with reincarnation and past life regression; I decided to ask those who were interested to join me in a video induced past life regression session. The date was scheduled and everyone arrived in an eager frame of mind, ready to explore a past life. I put the video into the VCR and let myself drift into a hypnotic state. Within seconds I was transported back about one hundred years to someplace in Europe. I saw myself as a beautiful young woman with long dark hair who was married to a wealthy and influential older man. When I came out of my deep meditative state, I reported to the rest of the group that this past life regression was identical to the one that I had had at the Association for Research and Enlightenment reincarnation seminar just a few weeks before this. I entered this regression and its similarity to the one that I had had at the Edgar Cayce workshop into my Lucid Notebook when I returned home. I also entered what my intuition was whispering into my ear. It was trying to tell me that the two almost identical regressions had something to do with what my father's spirit was trying to tell me.

My progression along the Yellow Brick Road toward sacred enlightenment and knowledge of my soul was teaching me the importance of unconditional love. I was also learning how much more spiritual and powerful it was to have respect for and to cooperate with others, rather than to compete with them. As soon as I entered my acceptance of these spiritual attributes into my Lucid Notebook, my mystical mentors honored me by sending me a validating synchronicity. Someone in my SOUL group gave me a copy of a beautiful Native American legend, written by who I understand to be an anonymous author, which they had received over the Internet. Like all synchronicities, this spiritual little allegory came to me at just the right time. It expressed the way in which souls that are seeking a connection with God should operate. I feel that by sharing its beauty and spiritual wisdom with others that I am doing the work of my soul:

Colors

Once upon a time the colors of the world started to quarrel: all claimed that they were the best, the most important, the most useful, the favorite.

Green said, "Clearly I am the most important. I am the sign of life and hope. I was chosen for grass, trees, and leaves— without me all animals would die. Look over the countryside and you will see that I am in the majority."

Blue interrupted, "You only think about the earth, but consider the sky and the sea. The sky gives space and peace and serenity. Without my peace, you would all be nothing."

Yellow chuckled, "You are all so serious. I bring laughter, gaiety and warmth into the world. The sun is yellow, the moon is yellow, and the stars are yellow. Every time that you look at a sunflower, the whole world starts to smile. Without me there would be no fun."

Orange started next to blow her trumpet. "I am the color of health and strength. I may be scarce, but I am precious for I serve the needs of human life. I carry the most important vitamins. Think of carrots, pumpkins, oranges, mangoes and pawpaws. I don't hang around all of the time, but when I fill the sky at sunrise and sunset, my beauty is so striking that no one gives a thought of any one of you."

Red could stand it no longer. He shouted out, "I am the ruler of all of you. I am blood—life's blood! I am the color of danger and bravery. I am willing to fight for a cause. I bring fire into the blood. Without me the Earth would be as empty as the moon. I am the color of passion and of love, the red rose, the poinsettia and the poppy."

Purple rose up to its full height. He was very tall and spoke with great pomp. "I am the color of royalty and of power. Kings, chiefs and bishops have always chosen me for I am the sign of authority and wisdom. People do not question me—they listen and obey."

Finally Indigo spoke much more quietly than all the others, but with just as much determination: "Think of me. I am the color of silence. You hardly notice me, but without me you all become superficial. I represent thought and reflection, twilight, and deep water. You need me for balance and contrast, for prayer, and for inner peace."

And so the colors went on boasting, each convinced of his or her own superiority. Their quarreling became louder and louder. Suddenly there was a startling flash of bright lightning—thunder rolled and boomed. Rain started to roll down relentlessly. The colors crouched down in fear, drawing close to one another for comfort.

In the midst of the clamor, rain began to speak, "You fool-ish colors, fighting amongst yourselves, each trying to domi-nate the rest! Don't you know that you were each made for a special purpose, unique and different? Join hands with one another and come to me."

Doing as they were told, the colors united and joined hands. The rain continued: "From now on, when it rains, each of you will stretch across the sky in a great bow of color as a reminder that you can all live in peace. The rainbow is a sign of hope for tomorrow."

And so whenever a good rain washes the world, and a rainbow appears in the sky, let us remember to appreciate one another."

This beautiful and spiritual little story seemed to me to be a direct communication from my soul to my everyday per-sona, or ego. As I entered this charming tale into my Lucid Notebook, it dawned on me that I already knew the spiritu-al truisms contained within it. Memories of a book, which I had written in college for a children's literature class, came flooding into my mind. My book was about warring clocks and the clockmaker who helped them to live in peace rather than about competing colors, with the rain as the peace-maker. The similarities between these two stories helped me to see that my soul has been communicating with my ego for a very long time. I was obviously not ready to connect to and to learn about my soul when I was in college. Thankfully my soul, or Higher Self, continued to prod me and to lead me in the right spiritual direction. Spiritual truisms that I have been aware of on a soul level for a very long time were now coming to the surface of my mind. Since I am convinced that nothing happens by accident, I recognize that they have come to the forefront of my mind at this time because I have to include them in this book.

A Higher Power validated my decision to include the spir-itual little Native American tale about the colors of the rain-bow and the rain in this book the very next day. It did this in the most unusual way. When I awoke the following morning, I looked out of my window and decided that since it was a gloomy rainy day, I might as well sit down at my computer and do some writing. I decided to write the portion of this book that was about the colors of the rainbow and the rain. A short time after I started to add this story to my book the computer went completely crazy. Whole paragraphs jumped from one computer page to another, the font size kept changing and everything that I wrote was being underlined. I gallantly continued to type until my frustration became so great that I had to take a break. After taking a shower and getting dressed, I sat down at my computer again, and tried to resume typing. My frustration continued to grow because the break had not helped. My computer was obviously having a nervous breakdown. Despite my growing frustration, I continued to type. As I typed the word "rain" it finally dawned on me that a message in the form of a synchronicity had just come in from the invisible side of life. I was writing about rain while it was raining and pouring outside. As soon as I recognized what my mystical mentors were trying to tell me I could feel gooseflesh running up and down my arms and my computer started to function normally. After my astonishment had worn off, I realized that this very dramatic synchronicity had been sent to me in order to validate the spiritual principle of love, respect and cooperation that I was trying to share with others.

After the computer went back to its normal operation, the rain stopped, and I sat back and breathed a sigh of relief. My reaction to this striking synchronicity, which had been sent to me from the non-physical side of life, was one of gratitude. I was humble enough to recognize that I could not complete my earthly mission or even write this book without the help of what I affectionately call my mystical mentors. Their guidance and frequent validation of my insights, intuitions and spiritual discoveries have always kept me on the Yellow Brick Road that leads to sacred enlightenment. I now see that this help has been with me since the beginning of time, even when the illusionary separation of physical life has lulled me in to the false belief that I was alone and without assistance.

LESSONS FROM CHAPTER VI

✳ People who have died will try to contact their living relatives in any way that they possibly can. These messages are very often meant to comfort or to guide those who are still alive.

✳ Dead parents and other relatives will often come to living loved ones in dreams.

✳ They may send messages in movies and television shows.

✳ Those on the other side often use computers to send messages to living loved ones.

✳ Dead relatives sometimes use flashing lights to catch the attention of those of us who are still living .

✳ Scents of perfumes and other odors very often let us know that a dead loved one is around and may have a message for us.

✳ Some people report that they have had after-death communication with loved ones

✳ Many people have reported contacts with deceased loved ones during an out-of-body experience. An out-of –body experience occurs when a soul leaves its physical body for a short time. This can happen when a person is asleep or awake and in an alpha, or slower, brain wave state. When a soul leaves a physical body temporarily, it may journey into a spiritual dimension and meet dead relatives.

✳ A number of after-death communications occur just as people are falling asleep or waking up. People are usually in an alpha brain wave state at this time. This slower brain wave state allows spiritual phenomena, such as after-death communications, to come in.

✳ Very often people report hearing a dead relatives voice.

✳ Dead children very often come to living relatives in the form of birds and butterflies.

* They often come to living parents in visions. These visions may occur when someone is awake, in a very relaxed state.

Chapter VII

Meditating Upon My Spiritual Journey

Pay attention to your dreams. They can be the windows and doorways to your soul's lessons in this incarnation.

After I reflected upon what happened to me next, I recognized that I had been sent a message that came to me directly from God. The timing of this mystical message could not have been more perfect, since it contained a form of a rainbow and came to me right after I was given a copy of the Native American legend, *Colors*, which was about the colors of the rainbow.

This definitely otherworldly communication came to me early in the morning while I was still lying in bed in a hypnagogic or semi-hypnotic state. The time of this communication was no surprise to me. These early morning hours brought in similar spiritual communications and insights to the ones that I received upon awakening at 4:00 A.M. This particular communication happened during daylight hours because it involved natural light. The room was still dark because the blackout shades were down. As I lay in this almost total darkness, I could see a brilliant beam of pure white light coming through the space between the two window shades in the corner of the room. This ethereal beam of sparkling light was surrounded by something that I have never seen before, a rainbow halo. As I lay in my bed staring at this wondrous spiritual light, I realized that this celestial circle of colors was refracted from the brilliance of the heavenly white light beam, which it embraced. My reaction to this wondrous and serene beam of light was at first very matter of fact and low key. It wasn't until quite a while later that I finally reached the conclusion that this communication of light was actually a manifestation of God.

The fact that this celestial communication came to me very shortly after I received the Native American legend, *Colors*, made it much easier for me to understand its meaning and significance to my spiritual journey. Both *Colors* and the children's book about clocks that I had written in college, stressed the spiritual truism that we are all connected. They also emphasized the Universal truth that love, respect, and cooperation are more sacred than competition, rivalry and hostility. The overall message that came to me through the synchronicity of these communications was that all of us in human form should try to put our egos on the back burner and let our higher selves, or souls, come through. Native American and Aboriginal people have always seemed to be more aware of this than those of us who have been brought up in more "civilized" societies. While we stress competition and rivalry, they stress community and cooperation with each other, with the land and with the unseen forces.

Each and every time that I received a message from the unseen part of life and added it to the entries in my Lucid Notebook brought me closer to a blissful state of gratitude for my ever-increasing connection to God. It was becoming apparent to me that the more time that I spent meditating the easier it was becoming for me to identify and to understand the spiritual messages that were constantly coming into my consciousness. An example of this occurred on March 10, 1998. Even though I was not feeling well, Marvin and I had gone out for lunch and to buy a birthday gift for one of our friends. As we were driving to our destination, I attempted to forget about how awful I felt by concentrating on the license plates on the cars that surrounded us. Very shortly after I started this activity, Marvin allowed another car to get in front of us. As this car maneuvered into position I saw that its license plate was 426 GDC. As I read these three numbers and three letters, a little light bulb went off in my head and I recognized that there was a message in them for me. The message that I picked up from this license plate was, "For 26, God sees." I felt that this little message in a license plate referred to me because 26 is my omnipresent spiritual number and the vast majority of the communications, which come to me from the other side come in on this number. This message, like all other spiritual communications, added to my growing feeling that we are never alone. Love and protection always surround us from the non-physical dimension.

I was becoming more and more alert and sensitive to the appearance of spiritual messages. Besides coming in on the mystical number 26, they also found their way to me from the other side on the wings of synchronicities. One meaningful coincidence that was sent to me to bring me closer to knowledge of my soul came in the form of books. We had just discussed the spiritual significance of dreams in Gloria Fleischner's Metaphysics and Parapsychology class. I was also reading about dreams in one of my books on synchronicities and spiritual guidance. During the same week that all of this was going on, two people who did not know each other, both gave me the same book about dreams and dream symbols. When I recorded this synchronistic event in my Lucid Notebook, it occurred to me that the message, which came in with this meaningful coincidence, was that I should pay more attention to my dreams. I decided to take this bit of guidance seriously because it brought me the insight that my soul desired to communicate and connect with me through my dreams.

My intuition was right, because the very next night brought me a vivid dream, which was so crystal clear that I had no trouble at all remembering the smallest details contained within it when I awoke in the morning. I was running away from something unpleasant in this dream. As I fled from whatever was disturbing me, I bumped into John Travolta, the actor, who tried to encourage me not to run away. As soon as I opened my eyes the following morning, I knew what this dream was trying to tell me. I realized that I was running away in my dream because I was under a lot of pressure as president of the four hundred-member chapter of the humanitarian women's organization, Hadassah, which I had recently founded in my community. It was apparent to me that in this dream, John Travolta represented Archangel Michael, one of my guardian angels. My subconscious mind probably picked John Travolta to represent Archangel Michael because he had recently starred in *Michael*, a movie about this powerful archangel and his visit to the Earth. In my dream, John Travolta, or Archangel Michael, insisted that I should stand firm despite the pressures that were weighing me down. He let me know that all would be well in the end. Happily, this turned out to be a prophetic dream. I did what my guardian angel told me to do and eventually everything was resolved. The pressures that were weighing me down disappeared. In retrospect, this dream and the outcome that it produced, proved to me beyond any doubt that dreams are just as important as any other form of spiritual guidance, and should be taken very seriously.

What I added to my Lucid Notebook next, even though it seemed innocuous at the time, proved to be of great spiritual significance at a later date. One of the women who was active in the women's humanitarian organization, Hadassah, handed me a catalog from an Israeli costume jewelry company called Dolphin Or. The company had a local showroom. She suggested that we sell this company's jewelry at our monthly meetings in order to raise money for medical research. When I leafed through this catalog I discovered that the main branch of this company was located in Richon le Zion, one of the oldest towns in Israel and the place where my husband's father was born. Something about this seemingly innocent bit of information set off an intuitive alarm within me. Was this a synchronicity sent to me by one of my spirit guides? Was one of my mystical mentors trying to tell me something? I decided that I would consider my introduction to this Israeli company a celestial clue and would follow it. I contacted our chapter's fund raising vice president and set up a time to visit the Dolphin Or showroom in order to discuss displaying their jewelry at a Hadassah meeting.

I accompanied two of the Hadassah women who worked on fund raising to the Dolphin Or showroom in Deerfield Beach, so that we could speak to the owners of this company about developing a working relationship between our two groups. While I was at the showroom, which was filled with beautiful pieces of costume jewelry, I selected and purchased several pieces to take with me on our upcoming trip to Austria and the other Alpine countries. Many of the pieces that I purchased contained Austrian crystal but the significance of taking jewelry made with Austrian crystal to Austria did not dawn on me until much later on.

It became apparent to me that Dolphin Or had come into my life as a navigational road marker along my spiritual Yellow Brick Road when synchronicities involving dolphins began to pop up in my life. The first meaningful coincidence involving dolphins occurred in Gloria Fleischner's Metaphysics and Parapsychology class. We discussed the fact that dolphins are initiates of the animal kingdom, with aspirations of climbing the evolutionary ladder to ultimately be reborn as human beings. That evening I turned on my television to be met by a reference to swimming with dolphins in Florida.

Over the past eight or nine years, I had become aware of other spiritual symbols, such as the rose, the crown and the pyramid, which seemed to constantly pop up in my life. This awareness piqued my curiosity and I did intensive reading about pyramids in particular. My efforts taught me that pyramids have much spiritual power and tremendous significance in mystical fields. They have been used for the initiation of masters and to draw down and intensify spiritual energy.

When I finally recognized the spiritual importance of these unusual structures, I decided to increase the size of my pyramid collection. I bought stained glass pyramids, crystal pyramids, plastic pyramids and ceramic pyramids.

As my collection grew, Higher Powers validated its importance. Right after I bought a lovely rose quartz pyramid at a showroom in a neighboring town and was walking toward my car, a large red truck with a twenty-six on it turned the corner. The appearance of one of my most powerful spiritual symbols helped me to understand that purchasing a rose quartz pyramid was a very empowering thing to do. I instinctively knew that this empowerment came from the capacity of this popular crystal to enhance spiritual attunement to the energy of love.

Starting a collection of pyramids proved to be a very fortuitous thing to do because it helped to stimulate my intuitive powers. I connected to some very important extrasensory information during one of Gloria's weekly Metaphysics classes. The insights that I received while attending this class were exceptionally powerful because, as I later found out, they were a rehearsal for an important spontaneous past life regression that I was going to have in the immediate future. On the day that I am writing about, I wore a bright purple outfit to class and was besieged with compliments from my fellow classmates. These compliments seemed to work as a catalyst for my intuitive powers because as soon as I took my seat and opened my notebook, I had an intuitive flash. This flash seemed to connect three facts that seemed completely unrelated. The first bit of unrelated information was that purple, a color that I love and look very well in, is a color that symbolizes royalty. I immediately connected this interesting insight to the fact that Marvin and I live on Crown Drive. The third link in this intuitive chain was the metaphysical symbol for the crown chakra, a thousand petaled white and purple lotus blossom. I felt a very strong connection to this spiritual symbol for the crown chakra, the wheel of sacred energy in our etheric body that is closest to God. I feel this connection because I usually pick the lotus card, which is explained on page twenty-six, when I use my Universal Angel Cards, a divinational tool for intuitive guidance. This intuitive flash seemed to point to something to do with royalty. I scribbled this unexpected insight into my class notebook and later transcribed it into my Lucid Notebook when I returned home. The simple act of putting such a complicated insight onto paper made it more concrete. Now all that I had to do was to be patient and to wait for my mystical mentors to explain how these surprising insights related to my soul's spiritual journey.

Many things were happening that strengthened my awareness that I was indeed ascending spiritually. The most significant of these things was that the importance of forgiveness and unconditional love was beginning to take root deep inside of me. I was beginning to understand that when a critical mass of the inhabitants of our planet wanted to live in peace and to espouse unconditional love and forgiveness, we would finally achieve a more peaceful world. This understanding was one of the motivating factors for the trip to Austria and Germany that Marvin and I were scheduled to take. I had finally decided that there were things that I had to do if I wanted to accelerate my spiritual ascension, the process of getting closer to God. One of the things that I had to do was to set aside my anger and hatred for the countries that were involved in the atrocities of World War II. Then I had to visit these countries and to practice the unconditional love and forgiveness that I knew was so important for my spiritual evolution and ascension.

As soon as I made this conscious decision to act in a spiritual and loving way and to forgive the almost unforgivable, my mystical mentors proceeded to validate my new determination. The day that followed the entry in my Lucid Notebook about my resolution to live the principle of unconditional love and forgiveness was April 26th. The day dawned bright and sunny like most days in southern Florida usually do and was filled with validating twenty-sixes and synchronicities. One of my former clients and friends, whose name is also Barbara, even called me from New York to tell me how many twenty-sixes were also appearing in her life. That evening I entered all of the validations of my insights concerning unconditional love and forgiveness and the verification that our upcoming trip to Austria and Germany was the right spiritual thing to do into my Lucid Notebook. I also added my delight in the fact that my invisible helpers were telling me that I was on the right path.

My mystical mentors and my Higher Self continued to drop little hints that I was moving in the right spiritual direction. I soon found out that these little clues were harbingers of what was soon to come. Marvin and I visited our public library to find books and videotapes on the Alpine countries, that we would be visiting soon. We found a video-tape on Switzerland and viewed it as soon as we returned home. Watching this little film about Switzerland convinced me that it somehow figured in my spiritual story. Two facts about this tiny Alpine country were responsible for this intuition. The first bit of information that verified my feeling that Switzerland is of significance to the story of my soul is that it consists of twenty-six cantons or states. The second insight that intensified my belief in the sacred importance that this little European country holds for me was that my maiden name, Schweitzer, means Swiss in German. As these insights flooded into my conscious mind and I entered them into my Lucid Notebook, I thanked God and all of my mystical mentors for the fact that I was ready to receive these heavenly hints and for their graciousness in sending them to me.

In retrospect, what happened next, was the harbinger of the eventual discovery of a tremendously important part of my soul's spiritual mission on this planet. On a brilliant Sunday in early May, Marvin and I joined thousands of other residents of Palm Beach County, for a celebration of Israel's 50th birthday at the Jewish Community Center in Boca Raton. As soon as we arrived and I entered the Center's main building, my intuition led me to an exhibition in the Art Gallery. As I walked around the exhibit I discovered that the Israel-Egyptian peace treaty was signed on March 26, 1979. Using the mathematics of mysticism brought me the unexpected synchronicity of the fact that not only was the treaty signed on the 26th of the month, but that the four numerals in the year 1979 also add up to twenty-six. This discovery was so striking that I decided to do a little further research when I got home. Finding out that "shalom," the Hebrew word for peace, also adds up to twenty-six in gematria or Kabalistic numerology only served to intensify my intuitive feeling that somehow my soul was connected to the signing of this momentous peace treaty. This exhibit of postal envelope art, which was called the Messengers of Peace, was bringing me the intuitive understanding that my soul was also a messenger of peace. It had obviously come to Earth at the end of one millennium and the beginning of another, in order to foster the precept that living a life of peace and unconditional love and forgiveness was what we needed in order to accelerate the spiritual evolution and ascension of all the residents of our planet.

The proliferation of pyramids in these artistic expressions of one of the most momentous peace treaties in history also helped to reinforce my feeling that there was a connection between this event and my soul's sacred mission. Now I knew why I had felt the need to start and to build a collection of pyramids. I felt that my new collection of pyramids was connected in some synchronistic way to the plethora of pyramids in this Messengers of Peace Exhibit. My mystical mentors were using every means possible in their attempt to bring me closer to knowledge of my immortal soul

The date of departure for our trip to Austria, Germany and the other Alpine countries was fast approaching. The last SOUL group meeting before Marvin and I took off on this odyssey was in my home. I will never forget this meeting because it brought me a synchronicity, which I later realized was a forerunner of a striking discovery about my soul that came to me in Europe. One of the founding members of SOUL brought a new woman to this meeting. Arlene walked into my house for the first time wearing a beautiful hand painted denim jacket. The scene on this jacket contained a brilliant yellow sun above turquoise hills and colorful trees and flowers. When we told her how much we admired this jacket, she told us, "I haven't worn this jacket in five years and I have no idea why I wore it tonight." As soon as Arlene shared this with us, the only male member of our group arrived, carrying copies of the twenty-third psalm, which he had volunteered to make up for us. When he proceeded to distribute the copies of this prayer, my mouth dropped open in shock. The graphic that he had selected for the cover of these little pamphlets was identical to the picture that was painted on Arlene's denim jacket. I immediately called the group's attention to this impressive synchronicity and told them, "There is a message some-where in this meaningful coincidence. Unfortunately, we will have to be patient and wait until the message is revealed to us." It would take a few more weeks for the true significance of this synchronicity to come to light.

An impressive synchronicity, which I took as a definite validation of one of the more spiritual reasons for our trip to the Alps, occurred the day before we left on this trip. I had just arrived home from Gloria's weekly Metaphysics and Parapsychology class, during which we discussed the important precepts of unconditional love and forgiveness. I had taken some time to share with the class that my desire to practice these two healing spiritual principles of forgive-ness and unconditional love was part of the reason that Marvin and I were taking a trip to Germany and Austria. As soon as I started to eat lunch, the doorbell rang. It was UPS delivering a parcel. When I opened the box, which the UPS driver had left near my front door, I found a beautiful Waterford crystal angel that was made in Germany that Marvin had ordered for me several weeks before. Since, spir-itually speaking, nothing happens by accident, I recognized that this meaningful coincidence was actually a wonderful and touching affirmation of my desire to visit Austria and Germany in order to forgive and to practice unconditional love. My mystical mentors had given me the best bon voyage gift that I will ever receive.

On May 29, 1998, Marvin and I took off from Miami International Airport, on a Lufthansa plane headed for Frankfort, Germany. I sat in my seat marveling over the fact that I was really going to the countries that had killed my father's mother and older sister and other relatives during World War II. I had even had to stop telling other Jews where I was going. So many of them felt that I was being disloyal by visiting and giving my money to the countries that had done so much harm to the Jewish people. As I quietly sat and thought about this trip, I realized that it had been quite a spiritual leap for me to make the decision to go to Austria and Germany. This trip was necessary for my spiritual evolution. If I had learned anything in my spiritual reading and studies it was that hatred only leads to more hatred. The only hope that the people on our planet had for survival was in the hands of those of us who knew that hatred was destructive to our future. I knew that the world would be a much better place if more of us practiced giving unconditional love on a daily basis. This understanding was one of the reasons that we had decided to take this trip. I knew that it was imperative that I send unconditional love to everyone when I arrived in Austria and in Germany. Maybe it would make a difference. I knew that by doing this I would prevent myself from feeling the anger toward the Germans and the Austrians that had pulled me down for so long. Since I knew that I was going to be sending unconditional love in Germany and Austria, I decided to prepare myself for this by silently sending love to people on the plane.

When we finally landed in Frankfort and started our tour, I realized that the spiritual preparation that I had done on the plane had worked. I had no negative feelings whatsoever about being in Germany. As I continued to spread silent unconditional love to everyone that I passed, I could feel a lifetime load of anger and hatred begin to lift off of my shoulders. I could almost see these negative emotions evaporating into the air. It felt wonderful to allow these heavy feelings to float upward and to disintegrate. My new recognition that harboring ill feelings can only weigh us down and keep us from ascending spiritually made me feel much lighter. As this feeling of lightness steadily increased, I knew that I was getting more in touch with my Higher Self and closer to my spirit guides and to God.

I boarded the tour bus the following morning filled with hopeful anticipation. We were headed for Switzerland and arrived in Lucerne in just a few hours. Our tour guide, a charming English lady, Mary, reminded me of her namesake Mary Poppins. The very first thing that Mary took us to see in Lucerne was a huge wall sculpture of a dying lion. She explained that this wounded lion was a memorial for the twenty-six members of the elite Swiss Guard who had been killed on this spot while trying to protect Marie Antoinette and King Louis the 16th during the French Revolution. Surveying the wall and listening to Mary triggered a very strong intuitive feeling in me. I knew that there was a message for me in the story that this memorial was telling us. The fact that there was a twenty-six in this story made the intuitive alarm bell ring even louder. I had no idea of what my Higher Self or my mystical mentors were trying to tell me, but I made a mental note to include all of this in my daily entry into my Lucid Notebook anyway. Experience had taught me that all intuitive messages that came into my consciousness would eventually be deciphered.

As we headed to the Palace Hotel, where we were going to spend the night, I became more and more excited. Twenty-six, the sacred road marker that I could count on to help me to navigate up my spiritual Yellow Brick Road, seemed to be everywhere. It even appeared in the number of our hotel room. These little celestial clues, which were being sprinkled in my path, put me on the alert. Something important was going to happen, but I had no idea when.

As the trip progressed, my excitement continued to build. The beautiful weather and the gorgeous panorama of the Alps fueled the intuitive fires that were glowing inside of me. When I awoke on June 2nd, or 6/2, I prepared myself for what I knew was going to be an eventful day. This day was no different than any other day that had a combination of 2 and 6 in their date. Insights seemed to pop into my conscious mind all day long. One of the most significant insights was that I had reincarnated into my present lifetime as a Jew in order to give myself the opportunity to practice the ultimate in unconditional love. I had decided to visit and to forgive the people of the nations responsible for perpetrating the most horrific crime in recorded history. I had decided to do this so that I could prove that by overcoming hatred and vengeful thoughts and by demonstrating unconditional love, I could somehow help the entire world and myself to ascend spiritually. I knew that if more and more of us could accomplish this, the world would be a better place.

Little heavenly hints of important spiritual things to come sprang up throughout our tour of the magnificent little country of Switzerland. Twenty-sixes seemed to be everywhere. The four numbers on my ticket for the cable car and cog railroad, which took us up to the top of one of the Alpine mountains, added up to twenty-six. Then, to my surprise, when we reached the top of the mountain, there stood a large openwork pyramid. This unexpected pyramid beckoned to me to stand under it so that I could absorb the invigorating Universal energy, which it was drawing down. When I think back to this exciting time, I recognize that my mystical mentors were doing whatever they could in order to prepare me for the spiritual discoveries, which I intuitively knew were coming.

The next day found us on our tour bus headed for Chamonix, a lovely little ski resort nestled in the beautiful French Alps. As I relaxed in the bus and enjoyed the scenery as it sped by, I had an unexpected spontaneous past life regression. I saw myself quite clearly as a woman in a white, close fitting bonnet, which was tied snugly under my chin. A severe, long sleeved, full-length black outfit covered the rest of my body. On top of this black dress were two pieces of stiff white fabric, crossed over my chest. As I tried to understand what this picture meant, my Higher Self brought me the immediate awareness that I had spent a previous lifetime as a nun in this Alpine region of France. Keeping the connection to my Higher Self open brought me the further information that I had lived in a remote convent in this beautiful Alpine region of France around 1523. When

I added these four numbers up later on, I was not surprised to discover that they added up to 11, a double and another hint that special spiritual things were going to happen. The most significant detail that I could perceive about this lifetime was that I had taken a vow of silence when I entered this convent and had upheld this vow for my entire life. Having this spontaneous past life regression verified an inner knowing that I had had for a long time; I had spent a previous lifetime as a nun. My only reaction to the discovery of this past lifetime was a feeling of pity for the fact that I had spent an entire lifetime in total silence. This regression also brought me an understanding of why I talk so much in my present lifetime. I decided that the next time that I am told that I talk too much, I will merely state that I am making up for the lifetime of total silence, which I spent as a French nun in the sixteenth century!

Seeing the amusing way in which this past lifetime was connected to my present incarnation, prepared me for the equally humorous verifying synchronicity, which awaited me in the next hotel that we were scheduled to stay in. After arriving at the Mirabeau Hotel, and going to our assigned rooms, I picked up a colorful brochure that was displayed on one of the dressers and immediately let out an extremely loud belly laugh. Marvin looked at me and asked, "What's so funny?" When I finally caught my breath, I answered, "The hotel that we are staying in is part of a chain called the Silence Hotels. I find this hysterical, because I just had a spontaneous past life regression on the bus, which took me back to a lifetime as a French nun who took a vow of silence and didn't say a word for her entire career." As I told my husband why my funny bone had been tickled, I could actually visualize my spirit guides, in another dimension, trying to suppress the giggles that were bubbling up within them. My entry into my Lucid Notebook that evening included my delight at having mystical mentors who actually have a sense of humor.

On June 8th we finally arrived in Vienna, which I considered the highlight of our trip because I intuitively knew that something spiritually important was going to occur here. The vast number of twenty-sixes that popped up all day long convinced me that my intuition was indeed right. Other signs and symbols, which I knew were meant to prepare me for whatever was going to happen, also started to appear. As we were driving toward our hotel, I spied a license plate that seemed to hold a message for me, ME5597. I instinctively knew that the ME part of this license plate stood for my husband, because they are the initials for his two given names, Marvin Emanuel. The second part of this car license, 5597, added up to twenty-six, which I was sure referred to me. The message that came through to me was that my husband, Marvin, was going to be involved in whatever was going to happen in Vienna.

The other message, which came on another license plate wasn't as clear-cut, but spoke to my Higher Self nonetheless. What I saw on this license plate was BR 19 PM. The closest that I could get to a message in this license plate was, Barbara Roberta met Marvin on the 19th of the month. This made sense to me because Marvin and I met on April 19th. The only meaning that I could get for the P was that I knew Marvin in a past life. When later events occurred, I learned the true meaning of the letter P.

After we settled into our hotel and had dinner, our tour guide took us to a Mozart and Strauss concert in what looked like the music room in a royal palace. Champagne was served while we seated ourselves on delicate gold leafed French chairs. Soon after this, six beautiful young musicians, dressed in costumes from Mozart's time, came in with their string instruments. After the musicians had settled down and tuned up, out came two opera singers and two ballet dancers, who were also dressed in period costumes. Then the beautiful soulful music started and I closed my eyes in order to enjoy it more deeply.

As soon as I closed my eyes, I saw myself back in the Vienna of the 1800's. I was a beautiful, slim young woman with long dark hair, who was regally attired. I was wearing an exquisite ball gown, which was worn over many crinolines. I was dancing around the elegant ballroom of what must have been my home. It was evident to me that I was a married woman and the affluence of my surroundings convinced me that my husband in this lifetime was rich and powerful.

When the music momentarily stopped and I opened my eyes, I immediately knew that I had just had a spontaneous past life regression that had been brought on by the ambience created by the concert that we were attending. As I sat in my little French chair and waited for the music to resume, I slowly became aware that this past life regression was an extension of the two regressions that I had recently experienced back in the United States. I could clearly see that the two similar regressions that I had had with my SOUL group and at the Edgar Cayce Association of Research and Enlightenment seminar, were actually rehearsals for this, much more intense regression. The beautiful chandeliers, mirrored walls, elegant carpets and little gilded French chairs had most certainly been a great part of the catalyst for this extremely vivid past life regression. This experience left me feeling very shaky, but I decided not to tell Marvin about it yet. It was too new and had to be mulled over and digested.

I awoke the following day filled with excitement and positive anticipation. Would I find out more about this unexpected past life regression and what connected me to Vienna on this sparkling Austrian day? After breakfast, our entire tour group was taken by bus to the Schonbrunn Palace, the summer residence of the Habsburg dynasty, the royal family that ruled the Austro-Hungarian Empire. We entered this magnificent home and after meeting our local Viennese tour guide, started a tour of the Schonbrunn Palace. As we followed our guide from room to room, the number twenty-six kept popping up everywhere. It didn't take me too long to recognize that this little string of twenty-sixes was leading me to an important metaphysical discovery. Perhaps this was the day when I would find out the importance of Vienna in my soul's spiritual journey.

As we continued to follow our tour guide through this royal residence, I began to feel more and more at home. The longer that we remained in the palace, the more that it reminded me of the spontaneous past life regression that had taken me by surprise at the concert the night before. Memories of the two similar regressions that I had had in Florida before we left on this trip also kept popping into my mind. Something shocking happened next. A totally unexpected question came into my conscious mind. Was it possible that I had been Elisabeth Habsburg, Empress of Austria and wife of Franz Josef, in my very last past lifetime? This question popped into my mind from out of nowhere and sent my thought processes reeling.

We ended our tour by walking into the palace's gift shop. The question that had stopped me in my tracks just a few minutes before entering this shop kept echoing in my mind. Empress Elisabeth, or Sisi, as she was affectionately called, was assassinated in 1898, in Geneva, Switzerland, making 1998 the 100th anniversary of this popular monarch's death. All of Austria, including the gift shop of the Schonbrunn Palace, was covered with pictures of Sisi, in commemoration of her assassination 100 years before. Her face appeared on boxes of candy, tins of coffee, coffee cups and souvenirs of all kinds. I browsed through the huge display of souvenirs hoping to find some kind of validation of the surprising insight that I was having such trouble accepting. My browsing stopped when I came to a display of Barbie dolls that were designed to depict Empress Elisabeth in one of her most regal ball gowns. Since my name in this lifetime is Barbara and since Barbie is actually a shortened form of my name, I recognized that this was one of the corroborations of the discovery of my past lifetime as Empress Elisabeth that I was looking for. Something told me to pick up a box containing one of these dolls in order to locate the product's serial number. As I did just that my intuition let me know what I was going to find out before my five physical senses received the information. Just as I expected, the serial numbers on the box that contained the Barbie doll added up to

twenty-six. My intuition let me know that this was a communication from my mystical mentors, a communication
that was meant to make me a little more comfortable with
the discovery that I had spent a past lifetime as Empress
Elisabeth Habsburg.

These little heavenly hints that corroborated the validity
of my startling past life regression started a flood of questions that came tumbling into my conscious mind. Was the
reason that I had felt so compelled to visit Vienna in 1998
related to the fact that all of Austria was celebrating the
100th anniversary of Sisi's assassination in 1898? Was this
one of the reasons that my father's spirit had been coming
back to me over the past few years? Was this why Freud and
Herzl, who lived and worked in Vienna during the time that
Empress Elisabeth was alive, were my spirit guides? All of
these questions and more were reeling around in my brain
as we left the gift shop and the Schonbrunn Palace. I had
numerous entries for my Lucid Notebook on our return to
the hotel.

We had signed up for the daylong tour to Budapest,
Hungary, scheduled for the next day. We awoke with eager
anticipation of our one-day visit to another country. After
eating breakfast, we piled onto our tour bus and took off for
Hungary. I had put my insights about my past lifetime as
Franz Josef's wife on the back burner and had no expectations of any metaphysical happenings in Hungary.

When we reached Budapest, we met with our local
Hungarian tour guide and began a walking tour of this
beautiful city. The route that our walking tour took, which
culminated at Saint Mathias Church, was strewn with twenty-sixes. Something unexpected was going to happen. When
we entered the church and I looked around, I was impressed
by its beauty. Besides its smaller stature, the only other
thing that differentiated this cathedral from the many other
European churches and cathedrals that Marvin and I had
visited in the past, was that this cathedral had five organ
balconies instead of the usual one or two. While we were all
appreciating the majestic beauty of this edifice, our tour

guide informed us that this was the church where Emperor Franz Joseph and Empress Elisabeth had been coronated King and Queen of Hungary.

I have had feelings of déjà vu at different times through out my life, but none of these glimpses into past lives had ever been as dramatic, or as all encompassing as the one that I experienced in Saint Mathias Cathedral. This feeling was so strong that I found it difficult to breathe. I was incredibly relieved when we left the church and I could take a deep breath of fresh air. As I filled my lungs and mulled over what had just happened, I was filled with the awareness that I had been in this cathedral before, albeit not in my present lifetime.

As we walked toward the river and the next part of our tour, I closed my eyes and silently asked my mystical mentors and my Higher Self if it was true that I was Empress Elisabeth of Austria in a past life? As soon as this question was posed, a scene of myself as Empress Elisabeth walking down the aisle in Saint Mathias Church, floated across the mental screen of my closed eyes. Was this knowledge that had most certainly been released from my subconscious mind the real reason that I had felt compelled to come to Austria in 1998, and why I had chosen a tour that would allow us to spend a day in Budapest?

When we started the second part of our tour on a boat that floated down a river, which separated Buda from Pest, the tour guide told us that Sisi was even more revered in Hungary than she was in Austria because she was as beautiful as a fairy tale princess and was not Austrian by birth. She was born in Germany, into the Wittlesbach family, German royalty who were related to the Habsburgs, the royal family of Austria. Since the Hungarian people were being ruled by the house of Habsburg and felt that they were being denied autonomy, they liked the fact that Emperor Franz Joseph's wife, Elisabeth, was not Austrian. The last bit of information about Sisi that our tour guide shared with us was that the love that the Hungarians had for Sisi was mutual, and that Sisi found herself playing the role of intermediary between Franz Joseph and the Hungarian people.

On the bus ride back to Vienna, our tour guide, Mary, filled in much missing information about the elusive Empress Elisabeth. I eagerly absorbed what she was saying. We were told that a twenty-six year old Italian anarchist named Luigi Lucheni assassinated Sisi on September 10, 1898 in Geneva, Switzerland by striking her in the chest with a sharpened file while she was leaving her hotel with her companion. She was traveling, as was often the case, without her husband, Franz Joseph. As Mary spoke, I used the mathematics of mysticism and figured out that the numbers in the year 1898, added up to twenty-six. I was astonished by the incidence of two twenty-sixes in the story that Mary was telling us about Sisi's assassination. After giving this some thought, I decided that the synchronicity of twenty-sixes was actually additional proof that I had been Empress Elisabeth in a past lifetime.

I spent the rest of the bus ride back to Vienna in total silence, with my eyes closed. All of the information that I had received about Empress Elisabeth was whirling around in my mind. I was desperately trying to make sense of it. If it was true that I had lived a lifetime as Empress Elisabeth of Austria at the end of the nineteenth century, this in itself would answer some spiritual questions that had been plaguing me. It would explain why two illustrious men of Viennese birth, Sigmund Freud and Theodore Herzl, would become my spirit guides after their deaths. The obvious explanation for this was that they were born and lived in Vienna at the time that Sisi reigned as Empress of Austria. Why shouldn't they, both Jews themselves, guide this adored monarch who was now a Jewish-American woman? Things were beginning to make more and more sense to me. Despite this, I knew that I could not tell Marvin about my astonishing discovery until my mystical mentors sent me some more concrete proof that all of this was true. This decision made me close my eyes again and ask my heavenly helpers for a sign, a symbol or a synchronicity that would prove that my memories of a past lifetime as Empress of the

Austro-Hungarian Empire were valid. Satisfied that my heart felt request for verification had been made, all that I could do now was to wait for a response.

The next morning, after I had recorded the startling occurrences of the day before into my Lucid Notebook, we went downstairs to have breakfast before boarding our tour bus and resuming our tour of Austria. While waiting for our bus to arrive, one of the other members of our tour group handed me a magazine called "Vien", which means Vienna in German. As I glanced through this pictorial magazine, which was written in both German and English, my attention was drawn to a two page illustrated article on Empress Elisabeth and the 100th anniversary of her assassination in 1898. This article highlighted the exquisite collection of jewelry owned by this beautiful and popular Empress. It also included photographs of some of her favorite pieces. As I admired these replicas my mouth dropped open in shock. A pair of Sisi's favorite earrings and matching ring were an almost exact duplicate of a costume jewelry pendant and matching earrings, which I had purchased at Dolphin Or and taken on the trip with me. As the shock of this discovery wore off, I recognized that this was the synchronicity, which I had asked for the day before; the meaningful coincidence, which validated the authenticity of my past lifetime as Empress Elisabeth. When we returned to our room to freshen up before we took off on the rest of our tour, I showed Marvin the picture in the magazine and the almost identical jewelry, which I had with me. I then explained that this was the meaningful coincidence that I had asked for and that proved the veracity of my past lifetime as Empress Elisabeth. He told me, " Yes, I believe you, but don't tell anyone else about this discovery until you check it out even further."

The next verifying synchronicity came when we left Austria and traveled back into Germany. Our next stop was Munich, where we were supposed to stay at the Sol Hotel, part of a Spanish chain. I gasped when the bus stopped at the front door because the hotel's logo was remarkably similar to the twenty-third psalm graphic, which had been brought to our SOUL group, and the painting on the denim jacket that another one of our members had worn to the same meeting. As I sat in the bus, staring at the hotel's logo, my Higher Self informed me that the meaningful coincidence that occurred at our SOUL group meeting before we left Florida, was meant to prepare me for the spiritual discoveries that I was going to make in Austria and Hungary.

When this wonderful, spiritually revealing trip was completed, we returned home to the United States. After I had finished unpacking, I decided to reread the entries, which I had made into my Lucid Notebook during our trip. A little intuitive itch was telling me that there were spiritual understandings in my journal that I would connect to when I reread what I had recently written. This rereading was very gratifying because it connected me to the awareness that the number fifty is also an important symbol in my spiritual scenario. The first thing that led me to this understanding was my realization that Israel, which figures prominently in my spiritual story, was established fifty years after Sisi's assassination. By identifying this fact, I encouraged other examples of the significance of the number fifty in my life to come to the surface. This spiritually significant number appeared when I founded a chapter of Hadassah, the largest women's humanitarian organization in our country, in our community. This chapter turned out to be the 50th chapter founded in Palm Beach County, Florida and was honored as such. This memory brought the memory of another significant fifty to the forefront of my mind. At about the same time that I founded the Hadassah chapter, my husband and I joined the Civilian Observer Patrol, or COP, a volunteer group, which helps to protect our community. Interestingly, the identification number of this group is 50. My continued studies of Metaphysics and Parapsychology later verified my intuitive discovery of the importance of the number fifty as a spiritual symbol.

As soon as I settled back into my regular routine as a retiree in an active adult community in Boynton Beach, Florida, I called my teacher and mentor, Gloria Fleischner.

When Gloria answered the phone, I excitedly told her, "Gloria, you won't believe what happened on our trip. I had a spontaneous past life regression back to a lifetime as Empress Elisabeth of Austria. I was a Habsburg and Emperor Franz Joseph's wife. After this happened, I asked my spirit guides to please send me a corroboration that this regression was true. They did this in a very unusual way. I was given a magazine that had a picture of the same earrings and pendant that I had with me on the trip." Gloria accepted this story without expressing any shock. After discussing the significance of this discovery we decided that the very next step in putting together the pieces of my spiritual puzzle should be some formal past life regression sessions. We both felt that a structured trip back to my past lifetime as Empress Elisabeth of Austria, while in a hypnotic state, would certainly shed light on my soul's sacred mission and the direction that it is taking in my present lifetime. Gloria suggested that I do some research in the interim. I agreed to this and then scheduled an appointment for a formal individual past life regression session with Gloria.

Since 1998 was the 100th anniversary of Empress Elisabeth's assassination, the Internet furnished me with some very worthwhile information about Sisi's lifetime. This was combined with some biographies of her less than happy life that were not easy to come by. The interesting biographical information that I put together from these sources started out with me being born in this previous lifetime as Empress Elisabeth of Austria on Christmas Eve of 1837 in Munich, Bavaria, Germany. My parents were Duke Maximilian and Maria Ludowika, daughter of the Bavarian King. I grew up at Possenhoffen Castle far from the pomp and ceremony of the royal court. I developed like my sisters and brothers into an unconventional, freedom loving and extremely sensitive person.

In the summer of 1853, at the scenic Salzkammergut town of Bad Ischl, I met Emperor Franz Joseph of Austria. Franz Joseph's mother, Archduchess Sophie, was my mother's sister and my aunt, making him my first cousin. He was supposed to marry my older sister, Helene, but defied his mother's marriage plans and fell in love with me. I was only fifteen at the time of our meeting and had accompanied my sister, Helene, and my mother on this trip to Bad Ischl to meet the Emperor rather accidentally. Our royal engagement was celebrated only one day after our meeting.

As Sisi, I became the sensation of Austria and on April 24, 1854 I married Franz Joseph in the Vienna Augustine Church. The festivities lasted for more than a week. All of the pomp and ceremony made me feel like a fish out of water and I spent much of my time crying rather than celebrating.

In 1855, I gave birth to my first child; a daughter who was named Sophie after my aunt and mother-in-law. The following year, I gave birth to another girl, who we named Gisela. The long awaited Crown Prince, Rudolph, arrived in 1858. I had done my duty as a wife and as Empress of Austria by producing an heir to follow in the footsteps of his father, Emperor Franz Joseph of Austria.

I found out that as Empress Elisabeth I was considered a fairy tale princess, but unfortunately my private life was far from a fairy tale. Since I was young and freedom loving, the strict life in the royal palace made me feel trapped and unhappy. My mother-in-law and aunt, Sophie, was less than kind to me. This was one of the reasons that I spent much of the early years of my marriage in isolation and illness. The strict court etiquette appalled me and caused me to immerse myself in rigorous exercise and horseback riding. Later on in my marriage, I tried to escape by spending a lot of time in Madeira and Corfu, while the public was told that I was very ill and had gone for a rest cure. To make matters even worse, my mother-in-law took my children away from me with the excuse that I was too immature to be responsible for their upbringing. This accomplished; my mother-in-law and the royal court raised them.

Many of my marital problems were created because my husband, Franz Joseph, even though he professed his love for me, had little time to spend with me. He ruled over an empire of 50 million people, leaving me very lonely. Despite these marital problems, our fourth child, Marie Valerie, who

I considered a gift to the Hungarian people, was born in 1868, ten months after Franz Joseph and I were coronated as King and Queen of Hungary. I also learned that this coronation came about because I energetically promoted it.

Further research taught me that Hungary was part of the Austro-Hungarian Empire that was ruled by Franz Joseph, and wanted desperately to gain equal footing with Austria and that I, as Sisi, used the power that I earned as Franz Joseph's wife to help the Hungarians to accomplish this. Through this experience, I attained a position of respect and affection in Hungary, which has lasted until the present day. My mother-in-law and her royal cohorts were very much angered by the fact that I loved the Hungarian people. I learned how to speak Hungarian and spent more time in Budapest than in Vienna.

As I continued to do my research on my past life as Sisi, I was happy to discover that my beauty was not my only attribute. Besides being an accomplished equestrienne, I wrote poetry and studied languages.

Unfortunately, there was also much tragedy in my lifetime as Sisi. I lost my daughter, Sophie, in 1857, and my favorite cousin, King Ludwig II of Bavaria, in a tragic manner. Then revolutionaries shot my brother-in-law, Emperor Maximillian of Mexico. My worst tragedy, one that I was never able to get over, was the suicide of my son, Rudolph, in 1889. If these tragedies were not enough, a 26-year-old anarchist, Luigi Lucheni, assassinated me in 1898. After my son committed suicide, I became obsessed with the thought of death. I had already displayed a curiosity concerning spiritualism, but after this tragedy at Mayerling, I became more serious about it. It seems that I wanted desperately to communicate with Rudolph's spirit, and finally find out why he killed himself. The God that I began to believe in was the "great Jehovah," which was divergent from the religious beliefs of my upbringing, Catholicism.

This last morsel of information about myself in my lifetime as Empress Elisabeth of Austria was the most fascinating of all. It made me wonder if this might be the reason that I incarnated as a Jew in my present lifetime. If anything, it certainly explains my interest in Metaphysics and Spirituality. I am swiftly becoming what I could not be in my lifetime as Sisi, a believer and not a belonger.

Other similarities between Sisi and myself jumped up at me from the pages that I was reading too. Sisi was known as a poet, and I have always found that poetry writing comes very easily to me. Also, I am as freedom loving and as individualistic in my present lifetime as I was when I lived my life as Empress Elisabeth of Austria. I dislike regimentation, ostentation and phoniness in any form. My research has taught me that I am truly Sisi's child.

It was several weeks until the date that I had scheduled for an appointment with Gloria Fleischner for a formal past life regression session back to my lifetime as Empress Elisabeth. In the interim, I was finding out more about one of the most important symbols in my spiritual life, doubles. These twin symbols had started to pop up in my life again, possibly as a validation of my interest in an important past lifetime. As I thought this, it occurred to me that the nickname in my Empress Elisabeth life, Sisi, was also a double.

What happened next proved to me that my heavenly helpers do not like to waste time. Since I had to wait a while before my scheduled appointment with Gloria, I decided to accept when my friend, Ina, called to invite me to come to her home for a session on altered states. After everyone had settled in and introductions were made, the leader of the group assisted us as we fell into a deep meditative state. To my delight, I had a past life regression back to my lifetime as Sisi. I saw myself as an eight-year old girl running through a beautiful green field in Bavaria, Germany. The trees and the flowers were in full bloom and the scene was filled with happy children, who were running, playing tag and dancing to the spirited music that filled the air. There were also many adults, horses and dogs included in what seemed to be some kind of a celebration. When I came out of my trance and answered the questions posed to me by the group, I was pleased to realize that my father in my present lifetime had been a close relative in my lifetime as Sisi. I also recognized that my present husband, Marvin, had also been my husband in my Empress Elisabeth incarnation.

Shortly after this informative past life regression I decided that an idea, which had been germinating in my mind for a very long time, was going to take root and that I was going to write this book. As soon as I made this decision, Marvin handed me an envelope of pictures of our Alpine trip, which he had just picked up. As I admired pictures of Schonbrunn Palace, St. Mathias Cathedral and the beautiful Alps, the phone rang. It was our local bookstore calling to inform me that the book that I had ordered, which had some information about Empress Elisabeth had just arrived. This little synchronicity brought a smile to my lips because I knew that it had been sent to me by my mystical mentors as a validation of my decision to write a book, in which I would share what I was learning about my soul and its journey, with others. I went to bed that night with visions of the book that I knew that I was going to start writing very soon dancing in my head. This must have jumpstarted the intuitive process in my subconscious mind, because I awoke at about 4:00 A.M. the following morning, with insights about my past lifetime as Sisi flooding into my mind.

As I valiantly tried to get all of these insights into my Lucid Notebook before they sped away, I was astonished to discover how many clues appeared in my present lifetime that led back to my past incarnation as Empress Elisabeth. The first and possibly the most striking hint of my royal past life is our present address; we live on Crown Drive. I could now see that my subconscious mind was probably responsible for this selection. The very next clue leading back to my lifetime as an Empress was that the house model that I chose to have built is the Castleton and that the other models that we could choose from were the Royal Court, the Majestic Manor and the Tiara. Even the area of the adult community where our house is situated is called Regency Cove.

The heavenly hints connecting my present lifetime to my

past lifetime as Sisi continued to inundate my consciousness. My research had informed me that as Sisi, I got married at sixteen and became an Empress, or Queen.
Amazingly, this connected to the fact that when I was sixteen in my present lifetime, my family moved from the
Bronx, New York to Queens, New York. Then at seventeen, I
entered Queens College, where I received my Bachelor's
degree and my Master's Degree. After teaching for a few
years, I met my future husband, Marvin at the
Fontainebleau Hotel in Miami Beach, Florida. The
Fontainebleau Hotel is named after a royal palace in France.
I found these revelations quite astonishing, because what
had previously been merely innocuous pieces of personal
information had just been transformed into startling connections between two of my lives.

As I mulled over the mass of clues, which bridged the gap
between my present lifetime and my incarnation as
Empress Elisabeth, I realized that the most significant hint
in my lifetime as Barbara Yudell that I had really been Sisi,
is my maiden name, Schweitzer. Schweitzer means Swiss in
German, a double-pronged clue to my past lifetime as Sisi.
The first part of the clue links the German origin of my
maiden name, Schweitzer, to my place of birth in my lifetime
as Empress Elisabeth, Germany. The second part of this
same clue, Swiss, links the meaning of my maiden name,
Schweitzer, to the country where I was assassinated in my
lifetime as Sisi, Switzerland. Another clue in a name that
links my lifetime as Barbara Schweitzer Yudell to my lifetime
as Elisabeth Habsburg was my husband's middle name at
birth. When my husband was born he was named Emanuel
Joseph. It was changed to Marvin Emanuel later on. Since I
recognized that Marvin was my husband in my Sisi lifetime
too, I have determined that he carried his middle name from
his past lifetime as Franz Joseph into his present lifetime as
a linking clue between these two lives.

I had done the research on Empress Elisabeth's life as
Gloria had asked me to do. Now I waited patiently for the
day of my formal past life regression session to arrive. When

the day finally did arrive I awoke in the morning filled with excitement and anticipation. Seconds before I picked up my handbag and my sunglasses in preparation for the trip to Gloria's house, the doorbell rang. The mailman had dropped off a package containing puzzle books, which I had ordered several weeks before. When I opened the package, I was pleasantly surprised to find that puzzle book 26 was the one that was on the top of the pile. I intuitively knew that this was a message of validation from my mystical mentors. They were validating my decision to be hypnotized so that I could access my past incarnation as Empress Elisabeth of Austria. The humor in this exceptionally well-timed confirmation did not escape me. My spirit guides had used a puzzle book to validate my decision to go inward in order to solve personal spiritual puzzles.

I arrived at Gloria's house on time for my appointment, feeling nervous and filled with doubt. Questions flooded my mind. Would I be successful at going back to my past lifetime as Empress Elisabeth of Austria? If I did go back, how much of this life would I be able to access? But, despite my many apprehensions and doubts, I was ready and willing to be put into a hypnotic trance in an attempt to relive part of my past lifetime as the beautiful Empress of a kingdom of fifty million people.

After I settled into a comfortable recliner in Gloria Fleischner's office, I closed my eyes and listened as she led me through a series of breathing exercises. When I reached a state of deep relaxation, Gloria proceeded to use visualization, in order to balance my chakras, the invisible wheels of spiritual energy or the organs of my soul. She first asked me to visualize the color red washing through my root chakra, the chakra responsible for our animal nature and survival, at the base of my spine and my groin. I then went on to visualize the color orange, washing through my sacral chakra, the invisible wheel of energy located just below our belly buttons, which is responsible for sexuality, reproduction and health. Going still higher, I visualized the color yellow washing through my solar plexus chakra, which is responsible for our sense of identity and issues of worthiness. When we finished with the chakras of our lower self or carnal nature, she asked me to go up to the middle chakra, which is green and is called the heart chakra. After I visualized the color green washing through the chakra that is responsible for higher consciousness and love, I went up to the throat chakra. I visualized the color blue washing through this chakra, which is responsible for creativity and self-expression and the search for truth. After this, Gloria asked me to go up to the third eye chakra in the middle of my forehead, and to visualize the color indigo washing through this invisible wheel of spiritual energy, which is responsible for the qualities of psychic powers and intelligence. The last of the seven chakras, which Gloria asked me to visualize, was the crown chakra at the top of my head. She asked me to see the color violet washing through this chakra, which contacts us to the Universe and all of its spirituality. After this essential balancing of my spiritual energy centers was completed, Gloria led me across the other dimensional Rainbow Bridge that connects us all from one lifetime to another.

When I got to the other side of the Rainbow Bridge, I could hear Gloria telling me to look down at my feet and to describe what I saw. I immediately followed her directions and found myself on a dirt road in what I instinctively knew was Austria. Behind me I could see a rustic, rough-hewn wood-hunting lodge. When I looked up I could see that I was a beautiful and slender young woman of about twenty or twenty-five, who was holding a riding crop, a leather stick that was used to prod horses, in her right hand. I was dressed in a velvet-collared riding outfit and dark riding boots. My skirt was hiked up at the side for ease in sidesaddle horseback riding and there was a military style hat on my head. My thick and beautiful dark hair had a velvet ribbon in it, which tied it up at the back of my head, under my hat. Under my coat, I could see a ruffled white blouse, which was fastened at the neck by a large, jeweled brooch. On my wrist was a simple gold bangle bracelet and the only ring on my fingers had a large, dark red stone, which I thought might be a carnelian.

The hunting lodge behind me was constructed of a coarse, dark wood that seemed to me to be flattened logs. This lodge with its many colorful shutters had no name or numbers on it. As I looked around, I could see that there were other men and women with me. The women were dressed in clothes that were quite similar to mine and the men were wearing short pants, or knickers, knee socks and feathered hats.

My horse was a magnificent fawn colored animal with a lighter colored flowing mane. As this horse waited patiently for the hunt to begin, I put on leather riding gloves that were almost the same color as this powerful animal. It was obvious that this horse was mine because it nuzzled me as I stood near it. Its reaction to me made me feel that we had bonded during many previous hours of horseback riding.

It was a beautiful day in early fall. The air was crisp and the sun was shining brilliantly through the trees. There were many medium sized dogs barking excitedly in anticipation of the upcoming hunt.

The many servants present helped all of us on to our horses. When I had mounted my beautiful, long legged and thick maned horse, we took off after the frantically barking dogs.

Following behind us were two servants on horses, laden with drinks and refreshments. The excitement of the hunt made my face flush with color and the strands of my hairs that were sticking out from under my hat blew in the wind. The air around me bristled with electricity as I enjoyed the exhilaration and the feeling of power that riding on this splendid animal gave me.

I watched as the dogs lost the scent of the animal that we were chasing. After a less than successful hunt, we all returned to the hunting lodge, dismounted and entered this rustic building. While my guests were served refreshments, I excused myself and went to another room to remove my hat and to comb my hair and repair my makeup. The inordinate amount of time and energy that I devoted to this task made me aware of the fact that I was certainly very vain in this lifetime. A bit of sadness crept into this vivid past life regression when I realized that even though I enjoyed the company of this group in my lifetime as Sisi, I was heartbreakingly aware that these people needed my power and my status more than they needed my friendship.

At this point in my regression, I could hear Gloria suggesting that I move forward by five or ten years to a future time in my lifetime as Elisabeth of Austria. The scene shifted immediately. As I looked around these new surroundings, I saw myself looking about ten years older than I had at the hunting lodge. I was about thirty or thirty-five. I was in a palatial home in what was probably Vienna. It was obvious to me that whatever happiness I had felt at the hunting lodge, ten years prior to this, was completely gone. My clothes were much more formal than they had been in the first part of my regression and my hair was combed into a much more mature and regal hairdo. As I took in the physical part of this scene, I also picked up what was going on emotionally. I was trying to figure out how I was going to avoid fulfilling an important but deathly boring royal duty. I was supposed to greet and entertain dreadfully stuffy officials and their wives. My companion was trying to help me to accomplish what needed to get done with the least amount of pain possible. After a while, and because I trusted my companion, I started to nod my head in acceptance of the advice that she was giving me.

The conversation between me, as Empress Elisabeth of Austria, and my trusted companion, revealed that my husband, Franz Joseph, expected me to meet and to welcome some foreign dignitaries and to be witty and charming. I did not want to do this because I despised the phoniness, the protocol and the pomp and ceremony of the royal court. I desperately missed my large, carefree and loving birth family, who despite the fact that they too were royalty, lived in an unconventional and freedom loving way. I felt like a delicate little bird that had lost its freedom and had been placed in a gilded cage of a prison, with no avenue of escape. My husband (and cousin) was very correct and stodgy; he always did what was right and expected this of me, too. There was a constant look of disappointment on his face because I was rebellious and refused to do things that were the correct things to do. All I wanted out of life was to be left alone and to get out of the stifling environment I found myself in, in order to get to a place like Corfu or Madeira, where I could bask in the sunshine.

Gloria interrupted this depressing scenario. I heard her voice, as if through a dense fog, telling me to move another five or ten years into the future, to a later point in the past life regression that I was so engrossed in. Again the requested change was instantaneous. I immediately saw myself at about age forty or forty-five, in another big house, probably another palace in a country other than Austria. My first reaction to this scene was that the mood was definitely happier than it had been in the last part of my regression in the palace in Vienna. The happiness, which I felt at this time, came from the fact that some of my relatives from Bavaria had come to visit me. I had the feeling that they had come to visit in order to celebrate a holiday with my family and me. I was smiling because it was wonderful to hear what was going on in the place where I was born and where I spent so many happy years growing up, surrounded by my large and loving family. As I saw myself totally enjoying being around these joyful and relaxed members of my family, an insight flashed through my mind. I saw with clarity, that my mother-in-law in my present lifetime was my mother in my incarnation as Sisi. This explained the closeness that we always felt for one another from the first time that we met until the day that my mother-in-law died.

As I continued to relive this particular part of my past life as Empress Elisabeth of Austria, I began to understand that the restrictive and critical atmosphere of the royal court of which I was a part was slowly destroying my health. I was very thin and very pale and I had a deep, racking cough, which made my throat and my chest hurt. When the coughing was at its worst, my ever-present companion brought me a cup of tea with honey and brandy in it. This soothing medicinal brew could only do so much because my constant feelings of not fitting in had taken a heavy toll on my emotional and physical health.

Gloria, whose voice seemed to be coming from a far away place, interrupted my complete absorption in this telling scene from my lifetime as Sisi. As I brought my attention back to this voice, I could hear Gloria asking me what message I was receiving from this trip back to my incarnation as Empress Elisabeth of Austria. The message, which immediately flashed into my mind, was that it was extremely important to be happy. Also that being happy comes from doing what you want to do, not only what you are told that you have to do. I continued to share with Gloria that I had learned that joy is as important for our well being as the food that we eat, the water that we drink, and the air that we breathe. As I continued to talk, I knew that my Higher Self was speaking to Gloria and telling her that I had also learned that being kinder, less critical, and more accepting of others differences, was as important to our health as joy.

After my Higher Self had finished sharing the lessons that I had learned in this lifetime as Empress Elisabeth, Gloria asked me to push ahead in time about five or ten years in this past incarnation. Before Gloria had finished her verbal instructions, I saw myself as a very depressed and ill Elisabeth. It was very sad to see myself as a very weak, very thin Sisi, completely dressed in black. The pain and the heaviness in my throat and my chest were worse than they had been in the past and my depression, which was exacerbated by my son Rudolph's suicide, was almost impossible to bear. It was evident that I was in one of my palaces and that my husband was in another part of this regal building. My ever-loyal companion gave me some medicine to lift my mood and to relieve the pain, but it did not help. All that I wanted to do was to get out of the gloom of the palace and to go someplace where the sun would be shining.

The scene shifted for no apparent reason, and I found

myself being helped into a horse drawn carriage by my companion and my driver. Together we rode in this closed coach and finally got to a place where the sun was brilliantly shining. We entered another residence, where my companions encouraged me to eat, gave me my medicine, and distracted me with games, music and walks in the sunshine. Nothing that they attempted to do seemed to lift the veil of sadness that was pulling me down. As I watched this scene, from the perspective of another lifetime, I realized that much of this depression stemmed from the heavy load of guilt about my son's suicide that I carried around with me. I had not been a very good mother. It pained me that I was not around enough. I tortured myself with the thought that I was off traveling somewhere when my son needed me.

As Gloria's voice started to interrupt me again, I could feel a dense dark cloud descending upon me. When she asked me to go to the end of my lifetime as Sisi, I could feel a horrible fear gripping at my throat. I told her, "Gloria that is something that I absolutely cannot do. I cannot experience the trauma of my assassination again." My terror at the mere thought of reliving my brutal murder at the hands of a deranged anarchist was the final proof that I needed to convince the rational part of me that I actually did live this lifetime as Elisabeth of Austria. Panic such as this was something that I could never have made up.

When I returned to the present, Gloria and I discussed what I had just experienced in the fascinating past life regression that she had initiated. I told her that this inner journey back to my previous lifetime as Empress Elisabeth had left me with a final message, which was really a summary of the previous messages that I had shared with her when I was in trance. The final message was that I, in my lifetime as Sisi, wanted to be a channel of love and light wherever I went. I accomplished this to some degree when I was in Hungary, a country where I was accepted and where I could live with more freedom and without the strict etiquette and pretensions of the Viennese royal court. The happier atmosphere that I lived in whenever I was in the royal palace in Budapest made it easier for me to be the channel of love and light that I so desperately wanted to be. This blessing, which was given to me by the Hungarian people, was what motivated me, as Empress Elisabeth, to help them achieve autonomy with Austria.

After I left Gloria's house, I spent some time thinking about how my past incarnation as Empress Elisabeth Habsburg of Austria has affected me in my present lifetime. I came to the conclusion that what has carried over from my lifetime, as Sisi to my present life is a love for freedom and travel and a total distaste for phony and pretentious people. My strong desire for individuality and my positive attitude and fun loving nature also seem to be outgrowths of this past lifetime among the royalty of the Austro-Hungarian Empire. The most important carry over from my lifetime, as Sisi to my present lifetime is my desire to be a channel for love and light. My introspective evaluation of how my past lifetime as Empress Elisabeth has influenced my present life brought me the gratifying knowledge that I am stronger in this lifetime than I was when I lived as Sisi. With the strength of will, which I am sure is due in some part to what I underwent in my lifetime as Sisi, I have managed to overcome obstacles and ill health, which I carried with me from that past incarnation into the present. My introspection also brought me the understanding that the things that I like most about myself, such as my caring and positive attitude, my sharp sense of humor, fun loving nature and enthusiasm for life are my twentieth and twenty-first century way of being a channel for love and light. My experiences in my Austro-Hungarian lifetime and in this one as well, have also taught me that it is much easier to bring love and light into the world if you first bring love, light and joy into your own life. As I thought about the connection between my incarnation as Sisi and my present lifetime as Barbara, a terrible irony struck me. The irony lies in the fact that someone so revered by Germans and Austrians in the nineteenth century incarnated in the twentieth century as a member of a religious group that these countries wanted to annihilate. The

final outcome of my soul-searching was the clear understanding that what truly connects us to our past incarnations are the lessons that each lifetime teaches us. If an
astral artist could paint a picture of a soul's spiritual journey from incarnation to incarnation, what would be revealed
is a chain of lessons learned.

One of the most important insights that came out of my
past life regression back to a lifetime in the court of the
Habsburgs was that Marvin was my husband in that lifetime too. This awareness clarified something that I could
never really comprehend. I now understood why Marvin and
I felt that we knew each other when we first met. Our souls
recognized each other because we had spent at least one
lifetime together. I am glad that we have been given another
chance at creating a successful and happy marriage.
Though my husband has carried some of the traits that
were troublesome to me in our Habsburg life into our present life, we have managed to overcome our differences and
to create the marriage that I wanted so badly when I lived as
Sisi.

My exploration of my past lifetime in the royal court of
Vienna spurred me on to continued reading on the topic of
reincarnation and corroborated my insight that our past
lives are like a spiritual chain of lessons learned. I also saw
more clearly than before that this reincarnational chain of
lessons is strung together by the craftsmanship of karma, or
in laymen's terms, "what goes around, comes around." My
introspection also made it crystal clear to me that a belief in
reincarnation and karma is important if we want to improve
the ethics within our society. If everyone believed that their
deeds would have consequences in more than one lifetime,
I am sure that it would affect their morality for the better
and would lead to kinder and more principled behavior.

The torrents of connections between my past lifetime as
Empress Elisabeth and my present lifetime kept pounding
away in my mind. My past life regression back to a lifetime
as Sisi and the research that I had done about this past
incarnation, have made me aware of the fact that one of the

things that I loved the most in my Empress Elisabeth life was the sunshine. This discovery creates a direct link between my Sisi lifetime and my present life, because sunshine is also one of my favorite things. This love for the sun, a love that has spanned at least two lifetimes, is probably responsible for the fact that I was born into this lifetime with an olive complexion that makes it very easy for me to obtain a tan. This love for Sol is definitely responsible for my husband's early retirement to Florida and our status as year round residents of the Sunshine State. I have finally achieved in this lifetime what I desperately longed for in my royal past life, freedom to live my life in the light.

A striking synchronicity that most certainly reinforces the truth of this insight came in the form of a movie. While I was rewriting this book a movie called *Sunshine* was making the rounds of the local theaters. This film was about a Jewish family whose name translated to *Sunshine* who lived in Hungary. *Sunshine* traces their history through the nineteenth and the twentieth centuries. In one scene in this film, a member of this family, an official of the Hungarian government, walks into Franz Joseph's office for an important meeting. There on the walls of the Emperor of the Austro-Hungarian Empire's office were several portraits of his wife, and my past incarnation, Empress Elisabeth of Austria.

Pinpointing the sun as a fundamental connection that linked my Empress Elisabeth lifetime to my present lifetime, reminded me of the many other little meaningful coincidences concerning the sun that had evidenced in my life prior to and during our trip to the Alps. One clue in the form of the sun, which was meant to connect me to my past incarnation as Sisi, showed up in the graphic on the cover of the 23rd Psalm, which was distributed at the very last SOUL group meeting before Marvin and I took off on our trip to the Alps. The importance of this clue was magnified by the fact that the appearance of this same sunny scene on a new member's jacket turned it into a synchronicity. The impact of this sunny link between lives was further magnified by the brilliant sun logo on the Sol Hotel that we stayed at when we were in Munich, Germany, where I was born in my lifetime as Sisi. The appearance of all these heavenly hints about the sun and how they connect my Sisi life to my present lifetime have brought me the insight that the sun is also a symbol for the spiritual light of God. I have longed for this light as Sisi and I long for it now as Barbara. This insight has made it possible for me to look at these two life-times and to finally recognize that Sisi and Barbara are one. Writing this book also helped me to understand how much I actually accomplished in my lifetime as Sisi. I overcame almost insurmountable obstacles and managed to be a channel for love and light that improved the lives of millions of people.

LESSONS FROM CHAPTER VII

* The Swiss Psychiatrist, Dr. Carl Jung coined the word "synchronicity" for the phenomenon of meaningful coin-cidence.

* A synchronicity is a principle of connectedness. It is a coincidence in time of two or more events, which are not related to each other by cause and effect.

* Synchronicities are meaningful coincidences, which are sent to us from the invisible spiritual dimension, in order to guide and direct us.

* You can sensitize yourself to synchronistic occurrences.

* Hold a question in your mind. With this question in mind take a random walk, explore a library or bookstore, or browse through a magazine or newspaper. See if words, subjects or things jump out at you, which seem mean-ingfully related to your question or to other things that have happened that day.

* Start a synchronicity journal and record all of the thoughts and observations that you had while doing the suggested exercises.

* Before too long you will be noticing the meaningful coin-cidences that are constantly being sent to us from the

invisible side of life in order to guide us.

* When you have a spiritual insight and you need corroboration of its veracity, ask your spirit guides and the Higher Power for a synchronicity. Be patient. It will come.

* You can use the déjà vu in your life as a clue to past lives.

Ask yourself these questions:

* Have you ever had the experience of going to a new place and having the feeling that you have been there before?

* Have you ever met someone for the first time and had the feeling that you have met him or her before?

* Have you ever felt an unexplainable dislike or like for a person that you have met for the very first time?

* Do you have an affinity for a particular historic era or a particular country's culture?

* Do you have talents and skills in things that you have not been trained to do?

* Do you have unexplainable nightmares or recurrent dreams?

* Do you have unexplainable irrational fears?

* Keep a reincarnation journal and put the answers to the above questions into it. Before too long the memory of a past life may come to you in a dream or in your waking life.

CHAPTER VIII

The Illuminated Yellow Brick Road

More souls are coming to Earth to help make our planet as peaceful and as loving as heaven.

I have always felt that the world would be a better and a more spiritual place if people could find contentment in simpler things; things like love, positive relationships, fun and helping others, rather than the accumulation of material things, money and power. When I delved into my past lives, I was pleasantly surprised to find that this basic outlook on life, which can be summed up by the admonition, "be careful what you wish for," for sometimes the more that we have, the more complicated our lives become, has spanned many of my lifetimes. It seems to be a true connector from one lifetime to another.

As I browsed through my Lucid Notebook and began to see and understand the connections between my lifetime as Empress Elisabeth of Austria and my present lifetime, many more insights about my soul's spiritual mission and my sacred journey through eternity came tumbling down from my Higher Self. Doing research on Sisi had helped me to see that she was very kind and cared about people from every station of life. Besides helping the Hungarian people to gain autonomy with Austria, she was involved with many charities and was loved by all because of her warmth and charm when dealing with the down trodden. This information about Sisi seemed to me to be a synopsis of my soul's mission in my past lifetime as Empress Elisabeth. Even though my life in this past incarnation was tragic, by helping the Hungarians and those in need, I managed to bring light, love and peace down to our physical world. All of this coincided with what I was learning by reading my metaphysical and spiritual books and by taking classes in these subjects. My spiritual studies had taught me that the dimensions of heaven and Earth were becoming closer and, therefore, more similar to each other. I had also learned that more souls are coming to Earth to help make our planet as peaceful and as loving as heaven. By reviewing the total panorama of my lifetime as Sisi and also my present lifetime, I have come to the conclusion that I am one of these souls. Mulling over this insight helped me to see the truth in it. I have spent a good part of this lifetime trying to encourage others to be kinder and nicer to each other.

I named this special group of souls, of which I had just intuited that I was a part of, the Emissaries of Light. This title seemed appropriate to me because it was the name of a worldwide prayer for peace that came in over the Internet on Holocaust Memorial Day, which I and many of my more spiritual friends, said together. I found out later on that the *Emissaries of Light* is a book written by peace activist, James Twyman. The fact that this Emissaries of Light prayer was said worldwide on Holocaust Memorial Day brought me another powerful intuition. I saw, with extremely clear spiritual vision that I as a Jew and as an Emissary of Light, came to Earth at the very beginning of the Holocaust as a channel for love and light in a world that was desperately in need of just that. I am also quite certain that many more members of this highly evolved and peace-loving group, which I call the Emissaries of Light, also came back into the flesh at the same time that my soul did. We volunteered to come down into a world gone mad in order to bring light and love onto a planet that was in dire need of it.

The Emissary of Light intuition was so strong that I did not ask for verification of it from my mystical mentors. What happened next demonstrates the strength of the support that our spirit guides and God give us when we are on the right path. When I looked up at the digital clock on my desk as I was writing this, I was astonished that it was 6:26 P.M. Again the Universe used the spiritual number twenty-six to verify the validity of my intuitive feelings and insights. It is hard to express how grateful I am to God and my spirit guides for their support and for the rapid and powerful way that they give me validation that I am on the right spiritual path.

Something wonderfully mystical happened the next day that I am absolutely sure was connected to my intuitive feelings about being a member of a group of evolved souls, which I call the Emissaries of Light. I was on the stage of our clubhouse theater rehearsing for an upcoming tap dance recital. Our teacher, Josette, a kind and spiritual woman, was demonstrating a new dance routine in front of the class. As I watched her dancing, a wondrous thing happened. She began to glow with an angelic light that was so beautiful that it almost brought me to tears. As I stood in total silence, marveling at this awe-inspiring scene, I saw our teacher as the wonderful spiritual being that she is under the dense coat of flesh that we all must wear to survive in the physical dimension. I knew that this experience had been sent to me as an important message from another dimension. The message that came in loud and clear was that when our souls enter the physical dimension we are all given these coats of flesh in order to make us forget who we really are. I was being reminded that we are really magnificent spiritual beings having a human experience and not just human beings having a spiritual experience. As I continued to watch the incredible light emanating from Josette, a feeling of unconditional love and bliss began to fill my heart and soul. I instinctively knew that God had painted this sacred picture for me. This was our creator's way of helping me to understand that if all of us on Earth today would substitute love for hate and forgiveness for revenge, everyone of us could become an Emissary of Light and the gap between heaven and Earth would be narrowed.

When I awoke the following morning, the wonderful ethereal experience that I had had during tap dance rehearsal the day before was still with me. As I lay in bed in a semi-meditative state before rising and starting my day, I made a life altering decision. I had seen the magnificent spiritual being inside of Josette's dense coat of flesh. The message that I received from this paranormal experience was that I should take the time to see beneath a person's physical façade in order to see the magnificent spiritual being that they really are. Then I took this one step further by resolving to try to see the soul in people like my next-door neighbors, who were negative and gave me a hard time. I couldn't fool myself into believing that this would be an easy task to accomplish, but I knew that it was essential for my spiritual ascension that I at least try. I was beginning to understand that this vision of light had been sent to me because I needed to be reminded that part of my soul's mission was to encourage others to look beneath the surface for the immortal part of those that they knew. If this occurred it would speed up the process of bringing our planet Earth closer to the ethereal dimension of heaven. I could now see quite clearly that I, as an Emissary of Light, had to reach out and to teach others to see the divinity in themselves and others. This would be the first step toward making a paradise on Earth.

I entered all of this intuitively obtained knowledge about my membership in a group of spiritual people who were involved in a movement toward peace on our planet, into my Lucid Notebook and waited for additional information to come in. I asked and within days, I received. Things happen fast when you are on the right path. I turned on my television and within seconds found a show about Walk-ins on the Science Fiction Channel. The subject of Walk-ins, who are advanced souls from the non-physical dimension who return to Earth and enter the bodies of living people by previous agreement to help them in some way, has always interested me. I gasped when the narrator of the show said that Anwar Sadat, the assassinated ex-president of Egypt, swore that a walk-in spirit came into his body and was responsible for getting him to sign the Israeli-Egyptian

Peace Treaty on March 26, 1979. My intuition wasted no time in telling me that this was the information that I had asked my invisible spiritual helpers for. The two twenty-sixes, one the day of the month and the other from the addition of the four numbers in 1979 jumped out at me. They reinforced my inner knowledge that the Israeli-Egyptian Peace Treaty had something to do with the Emissaries of Light and, therefore something to do with me. I would find out in due time how accurate my intuition about the Emissaries of Light and my membership in this group really were.

I had made an appointment with Gloria for another past life regression and was wondering if this was the correct path to take. As usual, all that I had to do was to pose a question and keep my eyes open and almost immediately the answer appeared. This time it came in the form of a license plate. The message in SAR777, which would probably mean nothing to 99.99% of people, jumped out at me as soon as the car with this license plate on it passed by. The first part of this license, SAR, was the main part of the answer to my question of whether or not I should continue with past life regressions. I intuitively knew that SAR meant souls are reincarnating. The second part of the message was a little harder to decipher. My reading and studies had taught me that seven is the number of spiritual initiation. I had also learned that three is also a very spiritual number. It is the number of the trinity and of manifestation of thought and moving forward. When I put the entire intuitively deciphered message that I got together, the answer that I received was that learning about reincarnation is a very spiritual thing to do because souls learn their most important lessons when they are in the flesh. When I returned home I thanked my guides in the invisible realm and entered this message into my Lucid Notebook. I then called Gloria and made an appointment for another past life regression session.

This past life regression would not be as structured as the first one. Gloria and I had decided that my Higher Self would direct me to the incarnation that I needed to know about at this specific time in my present lifetime. As I settled into Gloria's recliner and closed my eyes, I was filled with anticipation, apprehension and excitement. I had absolutely no idea what my Higher Self had in store for me.

After the usual relaxation exercise, Gloria guided me across the Rainbow Bridge, the spiritual connection between the physical dimension and the invisible realm of the spirit. After I had crossed the bridge, I followed Gloria's suggestion to look down at my feet to see what I was wearing on them. I told her, "I am wearing open sandals, which have laces that go all the way up to my knees. Above these sandals is a white flowing toga that is belted with a heavy golden cord." Before I even described what I looked like, my intuition informed me that I was seeing myself in a lifetime as a man who lived during the height of the Roman Empire, over 2,000 years ago. Then I continued to describe my appearance. "I have long hair and a beard and I am about forty-five years-old. My sandals are also gold and I am wearing a large signet ring, which I use to seal important documents, on one of my fingers." I finished the description by telling Gloria that my entire demeanor was one of official authority.

I was walking down a dusty, dirty road towards an expansive field. This field was covered with beautiful gold leafed chariots containing armored charioteers, pulled by magnificent horses. There was an electric excitement in the air as the chariots prepared to start the day's races. I told Gloria, "There is a group of richly dressed and obviously congenial people standing and sitting at tables laden with food and drink at the side of the field. These people seem to be having a very good time. They are eating, laughing and drinking from golden goblets." As I shared all of this with Gloria, I noticed that the Coliseum was in the distance.

As I approached this field, I recognized that it was the Circus Maximus. As soon as these influential people, who I was supposed to welcome, saw me, the air was filled with greetings. These hearty greetings reinforced what I had already picked up; I am a powerful and well-respected man. What happened next was completely unexpected. I seemed to be able to tap in to the thoughts that I was having in this past incarnation. As I looked upon the extravagance and luxurious demeanor of the waiting group and the heavily laden buffet table, I found myself thinking of how inequitable this scene was. While these people were lavishly consuming the best food, I knew that a short distance away were families who barely had enough to eat.

At this point, Gloria's voice came drifting in. I was so absorbed in my past lifetime that I could barely hear her voice instructing me to move forward 15 years or more to a later part of my past lifetime in Ancient Rome. As if by magic the scene changed. I told Gloria, "I see myself in a stooped older body, at home with my wife, who is much younger than I am. I sense a strong feeling of gloom. I am telling my wife that I am being forced to retire from my prestigious official position. I am being put out to pasture because someone's much younger relative has been given my job. It is very difficult for me to accept the fact that I am not indispensable. My loving and loyal wife is having a very hard time consoling me."

The scene changed without any further instruction from Gloria. I could sense an increase in my depression. My obsessive brooding about my vocational rejection has turned me into a bitter semi-recluse. I told Gloria what else was depressing me. "I seem to be very upset that our once elegant society is going downhill. Since my once successful career as a government official was during a highpoint of Roman society, I am very sensitive to its decline. The only joy that I have in my life is the therapeutic catharsis that I get from the biographical writing that I have started. My memoirs are filled with deep dissatisfaction. The people around me are becoming even more selfish, self-indulgent and greedy than they had been before. It is very painful for me to see these people becoming more and more unkind and materialistic.

The deep depression that my past life immersed me in

was pierced by Gloria's voice instructing me to move forward in this lifetime to the time of my death. The very next picture that appeared on my mental screen was of my persona in this past lifetime as a very old and weak man lying listlessly on my deathbed. My ever-loyal wife is spooning warm soup into my mouth. She is trying to convince me that even though my writing was in vain and the majority of my countrymen are calling me a crazy old man, that I have still led a useful and productive life. It is apparent to me that my death from natural causes is imminent and I am greatly saddened to be leaving my loyal wife alone after my death.

Gloria's voice asking me what the final message from this past lifetime was interrupted the gloomy scene that I was reliving. A message came to me immediately. I told Gloria, "This past lifetime has taught me that creature comforts and material possessions would never give anyone any satisfaction. The love that my devoted wife has given me has made me see that in the final analysis the most important values in life are love, sharing and respect for each other. The most important part of my message is that I tried to encourage people around me to be more caring and loving but they did not listen. My wife keeps telling me that I cannot blame myself for this. At least I tried. She is letting me know that the real failure lies in not trying. She is trying to get me to stop torturing myself with the obsessive thought that my life was a failure."

When I finally came out of my hypnotic state, Gloria and I discussed the influence of this past life on my present lifetime as Barbara. Reliving a lifetime as a disillusioned public official in Ancient Rome had really struck close to home. I told Gloria, "This lifetime has made me see that thousands of years and, I am sure, numerous additional incarnations, have not changed my fundamental nature. I am still an idealist who always tries to encourage people to behave in a more spiritual and a kinder way." I added, "My desire to write a book that might encourage others to look inward in order to find their sacred nature has been carried over from my incarnation in Ancient Rome to my present lifetime."

Gloria and I then discussed our shared feeling that this prior incarnation directly affected my lifetime as Empress Elisabeth of Austria. This discussion brought us both to the determination that, although I only wrote poetry in my lifetime as Sisi, I was definitely more concerned with spirituality and kindness than most of the others in the royal court of Vienna whose pretensions and criticisms I was always trying to escape. The main difference between my lifetime as Empress Elisabeth of Austria and my life as a male official in Ancient Rome is that as Sisi I had a major success that lived on after I died. I helped the Hungarian people to gain autonomy with Austria.

Gloria and I both agreed that this trip back to visit my past lifetime in ancient Rome had been very productive and had added much insight into my soul's progression through time. As we spoke about what had just transpired, I instantaneously recognized that my loyal and loving wife in this incarnation was, not surprisingly, my husband in my lifetime as Sisi and my loyal and loving husband in my present lifetime. This welcomed insight helped to reinforce my earlier feeling that Marvin and I are soulmates and that our love is truly eternal.

This past life regression had another important effect on me. It triggered insights about how my lifetime as Empress Elisabeth of Austria has influenced my present twentieth and twenty-first century lifetime. I saw with great clarity, that the desperate longing for greater freedom and individuality, which plagued me in my Empress Elisabeth of Austria lifetime, and which was never really satisfied, has had a direct influence on the way that I am living my life in my present incarnation. These two lifetimes are different in many ways. In my lifetime as Sisi, I got married at sixteen and in my present lifetime I waited until I was almost twenty-six. In my lifetime as Barbara, I had received my master's degree, taught school, been in therapy, shared an apartment with some friends; traveled and paid my own bills before I even met my future husband. As Sisi, I had my first child at seventeen and as Barbara, I waited until I was twenty-eight. Who and what I am in my present lifetime, and how

I achieved the ability to live a life that was ahead of its time, was now exposed to me in great clarity.

As connections between my lifetimes started to come into sharper focus, a quote from Albert Einstein, which I had just seen on television and read about in one of my books, came to mind. "The greatest mystery in the world is its comprehensibility." This quote translated into my new understanding that when one starts to put the puzzle pieces of their life together they see that everything is connected and makes sense. Life had developed an incredible brand-newness and excitement due to my recognition of the astounding connection between my different incarnations.

The very next day brought me another intuitive message from my Higher Self or from my heavenly helpers. This message came in, as it often does, on a license plate. As Marvin and I were out driving, doing some routine errands, my eyes wandered from license plate to license plate. One of these license plates virtually jumped out and screamed, "Read me." Doing as I was told, I read WEB26B. I instantly knew that there were messages for me in this license plate. The letters WEB, because they form another name for the Internet, which connects everyone in the world, spoke to me of communication and of the interconnectedness of all things. I knew that a very effective way to communicate with others is through books. My Higher Self also let me know that there was a message of "congratulations" in this license plate. I had just started to write the book you are now reading, *Discovering Soul Connections*. This otherworldly encouragement was important to me because my soul was wrestling with my ego. My ego, with its perennial big mouth, kept whispering, *"You can't do it,"* in my ear. On the other hand, my Higher Self kept repeating, *"You must share what you have learned with everyone who is interested."* This left me where I usually find myself, right in the middle, desperately trying to keep up the faith and to continue to write this book. This miraculous message in a license plate gave me the courage and the confidence that I needed at just this time to keep me on the right track.

The word, *web*, actually also held a very pragmatic message for me. Marvin and I were talking about buying a computer to help me with the writing of this book. Since it is common knowledge that the Internet, a miracle of modern science and electrical engineering and the epitome of connection, is called the Web, I knew that this message was also a corroboration of our decision to buy a computer.

Since I had made the commitment to continue to explore other past lives in order to gather information for this book, I thought that it would be fun to give the other members of my SOUL group the same experience. After everyone in attendance that night had greeted one another and we had had a short business meeting, I popped a past life regression tape into the VCR and closed my eyes. I had an immediate regression. I saw myself as a Native American woman with bare feet, who lived several hundred years ago and who was wearing a painted deerskin dress. I was tanning the deer hides, which would be used for making teepees, clothing and canoes and decided that this was my job. Painting symbols and pictures on the tanned deerskin was also one of my responsibilities. When I went forward in this lifetime, I recognized that I had a tall handsome husband with long black hair, who hunted for the deer whose skin I ultimately tanned. My regression back to this lifetime came as no surprise to me because I had suspected for a very long time that I had been a Native American in a former incarnation. When the videotape stopped, so did my regression. But, as I later found out, this was just the first installment of a future, more formal and detailed regression back to this same lifetime.

The following Monday, five days after I had relived part of my past lifetime as a Native American woman, I went to Gloria Fleischner's house for another formal past life regression session because I wanted more information about what and where my soul had been in past incarnations. I wasn't sure whether the Native American life that I had experienced during our SOUL group's meeting the week before was a preview of this formal regression or not. With this confusion in my mind, I settled down on Gloria's recliner and closed my eyes. I followed Gloria's voice as she verbally relaxed my body and led me across the Rainbow Bridge into my past. As soon as I got to the other side of the bridge, I saw myself as a barefoot Native American maiden in my teens. I was walking back to my village with a basket of berries that I had just gathered in the woods. As I stepped back and looked at myself, I could see that I was wearing a fawn colored dress that was made of deerskin. This dress had a *V* neckline, was heavily fringed at the hemline and was covered with blue pictures that I had painted with the dye that I made from these berries. On my left ankle was a string of many colored beads that were made from stones and pebbles, which I had painted myself and had strung on strips of tanned deerskin. There was a similar bracelet on my left wrist. As I surveyed my appearance, I took note that my most outstanding feature was my long, straight, shiny black hair that cascaded down my back.

The scene changed and I found myself in my village, in front of the teepee, that I shared with my mother and my father. I was putting the wild berries into a kettle of boiling water that was sitting over the open flame of an outdoor fire. After a little while, I started to stir the berries with a long stick so that they would cook down and release the blue dye that I needed to paint the tanned deerskin.

I could see myself talking to some of the men in the village. While our animated conversation was going on they were showing me the deer that they had just brought back from the hunt. After the men helped me to remove the skins from the deer, I hung these skins on a rope, which I had strung up between two trees. There they remained until the sun and the air had dried them. When this was accomplished, I used the blue dye from the berries to paint them. The pictures that I painted were beautiful. The designs, that were inspired by nature, depicted the sun, the moon, the stars, and the animals, birds, trees and flowers that I loved so much.

When I finished decorating the tanned deerskin and the

paint was finally dry, I stood back and admired my work. I was satisfied that my finished product met my high standards of workmanship and I was ready to barter with the other members of the tribe for the other necessities of life that were needed to sustain our existence. In exchange for these beautifully decorated skins, I received the food and the tools needed to run our household. At this instant I recognized that I was an unmarried only child and that my parents were aging and in need of help. My father had a disability and could no longer hunt. He spent his days gathering roots, berries and seeds and did some fishing in the nearby lake. My mother cooked, tended to the teepee, and made beautiful clothing out of the tanned and decorated deerskin, which I gave to her.

In the distance, I could hear Gloria asking me what my name was in this incarnation. My immediate answer was Blue Rose, for the beautiful blue designs that I painted on the tanned deerskin.

Gloria's questions continued, as she began to explore my love interests. I shared with her that the brave that I am betrothed to is Tall Hunter, the tallest brave in the village. I could see him standing near my teepee, bare-chested, with a bow and arrow slung across his shoulders. He had long, straight black hair and was wearing a short deerskin wrap around skirt and deerskin moccasins.

In answer to the questions, which Gloria was asking me, I said that we were a North American tribe, living in a relatively mild, but certainly not desert like, part of our country. Our village was located on a sparkling blue lake that was surrounded by tall, majestic trees. Because of the ample rainfall, there were many small vegetable gardens in the village. My mother kept a small garden by our teepee, which supplied us and some of our neighbors with vegetables for our cookpots.

The village we called home, consisted of a circle of deerskin teepees around a communal area where a large fire burned most of the time. Just looking at this communal area made me happy, because I knew that it was used for celebrations, shared meals, ceremonies, ritual dancing and story telling. At this point, I saw myself teaching the women of the tribe to dance. These women danced with me at specific times of the month. When we danced there was a full moon and we were expressing our tribe's gratitude for nature's blessings. In my spare time, I helped to make the tom-toms and other musical instruments from the deerskin that I had tanned.

I continued to tell Gloria, "Our tribe was very peaceful and content with our existence. The life that I led in this little self-contained village was idyllic." It was difficult for me to put the wonderful feeling of belonging and being at home that I was feeling as I relived my lifetime as Blue Rose, the Native American woman, into words.

As I drifted deeper into the daily routines in this little paradise by a lake, I saw that many women of the tribe, including myself, had learned how to heal themselves and others by using things found in nature's bounty. Together we gathered the roots and herbs, which centuries of experimentation had taught us would get rid of troublesome physical symptoms.

As I was sharing this information with Gloria, the scene changed and I could see that my beloved little village was bustling with excitement. A very important seasonal ceremony that occurred four times a year was coming up. I saw myself working frantically to get the deerskin that is needed for the extra tom-toms and canoes, which were going to be made for this ceremony, ready.

Gloria's voice intruded on my enjoyment of this past lifetime of peace and harmony. She was asking me to move ahead by about ten or fifteen years in this lifetime. I immediately moved forward in time to find myself married to Tall Brave Hunter and living in the teepee, which my parents had given us. One of our children, a little boy, has died; but I am very fertile and we have several living children. My responsibilities have increased, since I am now responsible for teaching our female children. Tall Brave Hunter is responsible for teaching our male children.

The last fifteen years have made quite a difference in our little village; it is now much more complex. The newer teepees are much larger and more heavily decorated than the older ones. Even our ceremonial dances have become more complicated and intricate.

This relatively short span of years has made me an elder. I am devoting much more time to teaching the younger women ceremonial and religious dances. My female children have taken over most of the deerskin tanning. Things are getting too big and complex for me. I was much happier in the simple world of my childhood when things were more connected to Mother Earth. The younger people of the tribe think that I am old-fashioned because I do not appreciate the tribe's ever increasing progress.

One of the most troublesome changes in our tribal life stems from our young people's curiosity about what lies on the other side of our lake and the mountains in the distance. Their restlessness frightens many of the other tribal elders and me. We spend a great deal of our time trying to convince our restless youth to be content in our idyllic little village because danger lurks behind the hills and the lake. Our younger tribe members do not listen. They want to venture into the unknown. This terrifies me.

At this point, Gloria's voice interrupted my regression and ended the fear and apprehension that I was feeling. When she asked me for a message from Blue Rose's life, I gave her an immediate reply. "The message from this lifetime was that we should all be happy with what we have. Curiosity can be a dangerous thing. Not every place is as peaceful and comfortable as what we have in the here and now." As I shared this message with Gloria, an intuitive thought popped into my mind. I realized that I had been highly intuitive in this past lifetime and that the younger people in my tribe did not trust my intuition. My warnings about the danger of being too curious went unheeded. In the end my intuition was right. This taught me an important lesson, which carried over to my present lifetime. I learned how crucial it is to trust my intuitive feelings.

After I shared this message with Gloria, I could hear her voice asking me to move ahead in this lifetime by another fifteen years. When I followed Gloria's suggestion, I saw that Tall Brave Hunter was dead. He died because he ventured too far from our village on a hunting trip and fell off his horse because the terrain was too rough. I see that I am a much older looking widow. All of my children are married, so that I now live alone in my teepee. Much younger people have assumed the tasks, which were once mine. This has allowed me the time to become an oracle. I predict the future for those who are willing to listen to me. The tribe treats me with respect and has renamed me, Wise Blue Rose.

Even though many members of the tribe have ventured beyond the lake and the distant hills, I refuse to go. My husband's death after straying too far from home has left me even more afraid of the unknown than I was before. I stay very close to home. I love passing on information to our grandchildren and the other little ones in the village. Teaching children to use our tribal symbols in a rudimentary form of writing is one of my favorite things to do.

The fear that I was feeling, while reliving my lifetime as Wise Blue Rose, stopped momentarily as I turned my attention to Gloria's voice asking me to go forward to the time of my death in this incarnation. I had no trouble following her instructions. When the scene shifted, I found myself, as a very old woman, alone in my teepee. There is the smell of smoke in the air and I can hear screams coming from outside of the teepee. Through a haze of fear, I realize that an enemy tribe has attacked and is destroying the village around me. Before I can even think of escaping, one of the attackers enters my teepee and rapes and kills me. As I witnessed this highly traumatic scene, I immediately knew that my intense fear caused me to have an out of body experience even before I was killed. This is why my fear ended as soon as my attacker entered my teepee. Gloria's voice, asking me to come out of my hypnotic state, brought me back to present reality. I gradually left my life as Wise Blue Rose behind and shifted my attention back to Gloria's office and the recliner that I was sitting on. As soon as I was fully out of the deep meditative state that I had been in for the past hour, Gloria and I discussed the lifetime as Blue Rose that I had just revisited, what this incarnation had taught me and how it related to my present life. My first impression was that the synchronicity of my first two initials in my present lifetime, BR for Barbara Roberta, being the same as my initials in this past lifetime, BR for Blue Rose, pointed to the fact that this was a very important lifetime.

Discovering these little synchronistic clues, which connected my lifetime as Blue Rose to my present incarnation, helped me to see the similarities between these two lifetimes. Blue Rose's strong intuition has carried over to my present lifetime. So has her desire for a simpler and less materialistic and competitive lifestyle. I could even see how my Native American incarnation affected my lifetime as Empress Elisabeth of Austria, which came after it. The most important thing that carried over from my incarnation, as Blue Rose to my lifetime as Sisi and my present lifetime is the knowledge of what is really important in life.

Like Blue Rose, and actually like Sisi too, I am always true to my higher values and I am never afraid to communicate what I think is right. Sometimes people have called this integrity. Money and power have never been that important to me. Like Blue Rose and Empress Elisabeth, I am happy when I live by the values of my soul, values like love, joy, friendship, and helping others.

Reliving parts of my life as Blue Rose, not only opened my eyes to the similarities between that life and my present life, it also made me aware of the clues to that past life, which were sprinkled into my present life. The first of these clues starts with the fact that as Blue Rose, I lived in a teepee, which is very much like a pyramid. The second part of this clue is that Paramus, where I spent almost twenty-four years of my present lifetime, is almost identical to the word peremus, which is an ancient Egyptian word that means to go straight up and is thought to be the derivation of the word pyramid. In other, more understandable words, living in Paramus was like living in a pyramid or a teepee. The fact that Paramus is a Native American word makes the connection between these lifetimes even stronger.

Living in either a pyramid or a teepee increases the resident's spirituality because both of these structures point straight up and bring in the spiritual energy of the Light. Interestingly, all of these insights and discoveries connect to the advice that came to me from my Higher Self or my heavenly helpers when I could not sell our house in Paramus. The mystical message that came to me was that in order to sell my house I must resume my spiritual reading and to read about pyramids. When I learned that we are all channels for Universal energy, we finally sold our house. The importance of bringing down spiritual light and sharing it with others was validated very powerfully by the synchronicity of our selling our house to a couple whose last name was a synonym for 'light'.

Having discovered that I lived in a teepee in my past incarnation as Blue Rose, and then finding out that a teepee is actually a pyramid, led to a renewed attempt to find out more about the spiritual significance of pyramids. I took all of the books about pyramids in my "angel" room, where I keep my angel collection, down off the bookshelves and then borrowed another one from Gloria Fleischner. My reading uncovered some amazing synchronicities that convinced me that I was on the right spiritual path.

The first tidbit of information that I gleaned from my reading was that Dr. Ray Brown discovered a submerged pyramid with a large crystal at the top while diving in the Bermuda Triangle in 1968. This newly uncovered information became a meaningful coincidence when it was combined with the fact that one of our closest friends in our new community is a man with the name of Roy Brown. This synchronicity became even more significant when it was combined with the additional fact that our address in one of the places that we lived in the northeast was 26 Brown Circle. This synchronicity opened my mind to the possibility that my soul, in one or more of its incarnation, was somehow connected to the Bermuda Triangle and the great sunken pyramid of Atlantis.

While I was researching information on pyramids, another connection between this submerged pyramid in the Bermuda Triangle and an important symbol in my present lifetime came to light. The number twenty-six, one of the most important spiritual symbols in my present incarnation, is the number of the parallel on which Marvin and I live in Palm Beach County, Florida and is also the number of the latitude on which Dr. Brown discovered the great sunken pyramid of Atlantis.

I was pleasantly surprised when later discussion in our Metaphysics and Parapsychology classes verified my understanding of the spiritual meaning behind these synchronicities. My intuition told me that since the Bermuda Triangle is over what many of us believe is the lost continent of Atlantis, that I have had a past lifetime in this ancient civilization. This interesting insight spurred me on to do even more reading on this lost continent and its remnants near the island of Bimini. This reading captured my imagination and convinced me that my soul, along with many other kindred souls who had lived lifetimes in Atlantis, have come to this area of Florida, in order to rectify the harm that was done when we misused our powers in this ancient civilization.

After I added these telling insights into my Lucid Notebook, the time virtually flew. Before I knew it, it was time for another scheduled past life regression session with Gloria Fleischner. When I arrived at Gloria's home and settled into her very comfortable recliner, I started to listen to her very melodious voice and slipped very rapidly into an altered state of consciousness. As soon as I followed Gloria's directions and crossed over the Rainbow Bridge into another lifetime, I did as I always do and I looked down at my feet. What I saw was a pair of rough leather sandals on feet that were standing on a dusty, country road. When Gloria asked me to take a look at the rest of my body, I saw that I was a young man who was wearing a coarse, burlap like tan robe, which was tied around my waist by a rough looking rope.

My hair was long and straggly and I had a beard. I gasped at my appearance because I looked very much like Jesus Christ. This shock was immediately dispelled when I recognized that I was a shepherd in what is now known as Israel, at the time that Jesus walked the Earth. In my hand, I saw a long pole that must have functioned as a staff, which I used to guide the many sheep that surrounded me. One of these sheep, obviously the leader of the herd had a crude bell around its neck and helped me to keep the other sheep together.

My existence in this lifetime was very peaceful and solitary. I lived alone in a very simple one-room house, where I spent a lot of time writing a book on parchment paper. My writing was done on a crude wooden table in the middle of the sparsely furnished room. Many of my nights were spent out of doors, looking at the starry sky and staying in touch with the Universe. When I was out of doors, I sometimes played a lute or a small flute. I was a vegetarian and made my living by selling the wool and the milk, which I got from my sheep.

My simple and solitary lifestyle allowed me to live very close to and in harmony with nature; therefore, I was always in touch with animals, trees, plants and the sky. Since I was an unmarried only child and my parents were dead, the creatures of the Universe were my family.

Gloria's voice asking me to go forward by about fifteen years in this lifetime impinged upon my blissful feeling of being one with the Universe. When I followed Gloria's suggestion and moved forward by fifteen years, I saw myself looking older and poorer and still tending my sheep. There was dismay in my heart because the last few years had brought tremendous changes that were now threatening my lifestyle. The once small village, which laid at the foot of the hill that was my home, was expanding and creeping up toward my simple house. The idea of moving my sheep and my few meager belongings further up the hill, away from town, came into my mind. I immediately rejected this thought because the land further up the hill was not good for grazing. At this point I made the life altering decision to sell my sheep and to become a teacher, a traveling preacher and a writer. There was a strong feeling within me that it was time to share with others what I came into life knowing and also what I learned during this lifetime. It had become very important to me to teach people to live simpler and more natural lives. I also wanted to show them that they were more connected to the invisible spiritual dimension than they thought.

As I continued to relive my past lifetime as a humble shepherd, I began to see that this was probably one of my most important and most spiritual incarnations. The time period, which I was reliving, was the same time that Jesus walked that part of the Earth that is now known as the Holy Land. I find it quite interesting that in this lifetime I was tuned in to many of the same things that Jesus was teaching. It was quite hard for me to give up my sheep, but I knew that I must follow a higher calling and do more spiritual work. This work consisted of listening to messages from a Higher Power and my spirit guides and of making prophecies and, all the while, going from town to town on my donkey, to share what I had learned with those who would listen to me.

At this point, I followed the suggestion that Gloria was giving me to go forward in this lifetime by about five or more years. I immediately had a vision of myself as a holy man, riding from town to town on my donkey. I listened with rapt attention as I heard myself preaching to those who would take the time to listen to me, about a better, simpler, and holier way of life. Among the few meager possessions that I had taken with me on this holy mission, was the book that I was still writing. In every town that I went to, there were a few kind people who offered food and shelter to an itinerant preacher who had come to share spiritual truths with them.

The truths that I shared with people, who I met on my spiritual odyssey, were about our immortal souls and eternal life. I told people where their souls resided between lives and why they kept coming back into physical bodies. People heard me telling them to love themselves and others and that what they did on this Earth in their present lifetimes, would determine what would happen to them in the future. I also told the few people who were ready to hear what I had come to tell them, that people are essentially good, and that the more good that they seek in others, the more good would come to them. People who listened to me also received hope that suffering is not forever; that they would find peace when they died.

As if the spirituality that I was reliving in this past lifetime was not awe-inspiring enough, my wonder increased when I discovered that I was also a natural healer in this incarnation. I could see quite clearly that the Universal energy that I was a channel for could make others feel better. Wherever I went, healing took place.

The spiritual intensity of this past lifetime had a very profound effect on me. At 3:30 A.M. the following morning, my eyes snapped open, with the clear recognition that I was reliving this past lifetime as a holy preacher to some degree in my present lifetime. Like this holy man, I have given up a worldly career in order to pursue more sacred activities, such as taking courses in Metaphysics and Spirituality. I was also writing a book and was beginning to lecture on, and teach the same subjects. It was becoming increasingly clear to me that I was following the same spiritual mission that I was following almost two thousand years ago.

As I lay in my bed, at the most spiritual time of the day, I stretched my mind outward and upward, enabling me to see a very important connection between my past life as a holy man, preacher and my lifetime as Empress Elisabeth of Austria. Living in the pretentious, political and often unkind environment of the royal court of Vienna was extremely painful for me in my past lifetime as Sisi. I was extremely frustrated because I yearned for a simpler, more private and certainly more spiritual existence. Also, in my lifetime as a reluctant Empress, I spent a good deal of time traveling throughout Europe, far from the phony shallowness of Viennese royalty. I also stretched out a helping hand to the people of Hungary and helped to heal them by obtaining autonomy with Austria for them.

The peace and solitude of the early morning hours also helped me to see how my lifetime as Blue Rose was also profoundly affected by my earlier incarnation as a solitary holy man during the time of Jesus. One of the most important shared values of these two lifetimes was the desire to live a kind and simple life, in harmony with nature. Also, as both Blue Rose and the solitary holy man, I was a natural healer and helped others to feel better by being a channel for healing Universal energy.

My early morning reverie also brought me the memory of a dream that I had had a few days before my past life regression back to my solitary holy man lifetime. In this dream, I was a religious lady in the Israel of today, who wore a hat, and worked with other religious people on a kibbutz or collective farm. The most lucid part of this dream was my purchase of a green sweater. As I began to analyze this dream, my first understanding was that green is the color of the heart chakra and, therefore, of love and kindness. At first I thought that this dream was merely a preview of my past life regression back to my lifetime as a holy man and preacher in the Holy Land of Christ's time. Then I realized that this dream had a much broader significance than this. With an honesty that can come to us only in the wee hours of the morning, I understood that this dream was an allegory for the way I have tried and will continue to try to live all of my lives.

During the next few days, I began to see the little hints and clues that pointed to my past lifetime as a holy man preacher that had been sprinkled into my present lifetime. The first little hint tickled my funny bone. In my lifetime as a solitary holy man, I started as a shepherd and spent most of my time wandering across the Holy Land with my little lambs. In my present lifetime, Marvin and I belong to a bowling league and are on a team consisting of four people, which we call the lambs because the first initials of our four names are L, A, M, B. Another, more serious hint that connects me to my past incarnation in the ancient land, which is now Israel, is that Marvin and I both have very deep roots and thousands of relatives in the Holy Land.

LESSONS FROM CHAPTER VIII

✳ Dreams can help us to better understand our souls and their missions.

✳ When we go to sleep at night our souls leave our bodies and can obtain information from other dimensions.

✳ We may also receive information from our Higher Selves when we dream.

✳ We may dream about past lives or get information about our soul's mission through time.

✳ Recurrent dreams or nightmares are very often just our Higher Self's or our spirit guides' way of connecting us to information about our souls and where they have been in the past.

✳ Pay attention to your dreams and nightmares.

✳ It is very important that you record your dreams in a dream journal or in a general psychic journal.

✳ When you reread your journal, you may discover a spiritual pattern.

✳ Purchasing a book on the spiritual symbology in dreams will help you to glean information about your soul from your dreams.

✳ Dreams may even give you information about your soul's mission.

✳ Pay attention to who you are in dreams and what jobs you are doing.

✳ Dead relatives may also use the medium of dreams to contact you in some way.

* Your spirit guides often use the medium of dreams to help you with your everyday physical life.

* Keep a dream journal and a pen or pencil by your bed.

* If a dream wakes you up, record its contents into your journal immediately.

* Before you fall asleep, tell yourself that you will recall your dreams.

* Try to wake up naturally without an alarm clock. Spend some time recalling your dreams before you get out of bed.

* Review the records of your dreams very often.

CHAPTER IX

Closer to Oz

*Our invisible helpers will always do their jobs,
whether they are asked to or not.*

My middle of the night and early morning connections to my Higher Self were beginning to serve as catalysts for new understandings about how my father's spirit was helping me to understand my spiritual story. I was even beginning to get a clearer picture of what he was trying to tell me when he came to me in the movie, *Contact*, with Jodie Foster. The word *contact* was the most important clue to the solving of the mystery of what my father wanted to communicate to me through the vehicle of this movie. After checking in my dictionary and my thesaurus, I discovered that there were two synonyms for the word *"contact"* that pertained to what I was beginning to perceive as part of my soul's mission and me. These synonyms were *"connection"* and *"communication."* What was most astonishing was that I had given this book the title, *Discovering Soul Connections*, well before I had these new insights about my father's message in the movie, *Contact*. Discovering these two synonyms for the word *"contact"* helped me to see that my father had sent me two messages in Jodie Foster's movie. The first message was that there is a connection between everything in the Universe and that this connection was the reason that my father could communicate with me from the invisible dimension of the spirit. The next message was that I am a communicator and that I have the obligation to use what I have learned about picking up communication from the non-physical dimension in order to teach others to do the same thing. I would find out later on that there was a third, equally important, message in this spiritually revealing movie.

Having these wonderful insights helped me to understand my soul's mission on the Earth, and erased most of the doubts about writing this book, which constantly plagued me. I could now see, with great clarity that my father's spirit had come through to me in the movie, *Contact*, which was originally a book, in order to motivate me to use the vehicle of writing in order to communicate my spiritual learning's to others. When I finally understood this, I could see why the four past lives, which I had accessed with Gloria Fleischner's help, were all incarnations in which I had done some kind of writing. My Higher Self was clearly trying to tell me that communicating what I have learned spiritually in the form of a book, was something that I was obligated to do. My much later discovery of the fact that the channeled title of this book, *Discovering Soul Connections*, contained twenty-six letters was further proof that I was spiritually obligated to write this book.

I was also astute enough to know that my obligation as a communicator of what I had learned about spiritual guidance should not stop at writing. One of my greatest skills was my ability to communicate verbally and I knew that I should, whenever possible, teach others what I had learned myself. This recognition was my motivation for attending a monthly meeting of IANDS, the International Association for Near Death Experiences, with my metaphysical friends. It was a great pleasure to share some of my mystical experiences, including my near death experience, with those who attended this meeting. I knew that people who attended meetings such as these wanted answers about the process of dying and the after-life. I felt that I could help them in some way by sharing what I have learned about these two compelling topics.

After the meeting, our small group dropped in at a local restaurant for something to eat and a chance to chat about what we had learned at the IANDS meeting. Our metaphysical discussion led to our agreement as to why so many of us had followed our spiritual urgings and had come down to this area of Florida at 26 degrees longitude and 80 degrees latitude, right off the Bermuda Triangle. We pooled what we had all learned from different metaphysical and spiritual sources. We then decided that those of us who had felt compelled to move down here had had previous lives on the now sunken continent of Atlantis and had come down to this area to be closer to the sunken pyramid of this once great civilization. Our studies had taught us that when we had lived our lives on the continent that now lay at the bottom of the Bermuda Triangle we had misused our powers and had abused the energies of our powerful crystals. We had all chosen the dawning of the Age of Aquarius to come back to Earth, and to this part of Florida, to rectify the tragic mistakes that we had made on Atlantis and to do it right this time.

When I returned home that night, I felt compelled to take one of my books on Atlantis off of a shelf in my *"angel room."* Reading this book triggered insights that verified my inner knowing that I had spent at least one lifetime on the lost continent of Atlantis. An interesting clue of validation that this insight was correct, was that we now lived about five or ten minutes from the southern Florida town of Atlantis.

Another experience that I now believe was meant to corroborate my new insight about my connection to the pyramids of Atlantis, floated up into my mind at this time. This experience occurred during a trip that Marvin and I took to Egypt many years ago. During this trip, Marvin and I had a photograph taken of the two of us standing in front of the Great Pyramids of Giza. In retrospect, I now see why I selected this picture out of the thousands of family photographs in our possession, to hang in a composite of photographs on our kitchen wall in our house in Paramus. I now understand that I probably selected this photograph because of a subconscious memory of my lifetime around the pyramids of Atlantis. This entire insight made me realize what a wonderful and powerful thing our subconscious mind is.

My insights and my spontaneous past life regressions continued. Keeping my Lucid Notebook and writing this book were all the impetus that I needed to keep the unfolding of my spiritual story going in high gear. One day while I was floating in our community's pool, I closed my eyes and saw myself as a young woman with long dark hair. I was wearing a sarong and had flowers in my hair and encircling one of my ankles. My skin was as brown as a berry and I wore no shoes. As I floated with my eyes closed, I recognized that I had connected to a lifetime that I had lived about three or four hundred years ago, amid the waterfalls and the palm trees of an island in the Pacific Ocean. This regression was so very real that I had difficulty pulling myself back to my present lifetime. As soon as I finally did return to present reality, I remembered a recurrent dream that I had had as a child about a lifetime such as this. I took this as proof that I had just accessed a very important past lifetime.

As I recorded this spontaneous past life regression into my Lucid Notebook, I recognized that what had just happened was probably a rehearsal for a more comprehensive trip back to a past lifetime in the South Pacific yet to come. This strong intuitive feeling came from the fact that Marvin and I were due to take off on a trip to Hawaii soon after this. This unusual occurrence did not shock me because this was not the first time that my Higher Self had given me a preview of a past life regression to come. Only time would tell if my intuition was right.

Before we took off on our Hawaiian odyssey, we accompanied our community's Men's Club on an intracoastal voyage on the Jungle Queen, a popular south Florida boat trip. An important spiritual message came through to me while Marvin and I were waiting to board the boat. This message was not easy to discern. I thank my years of study and my desire to see these messages: no matter how esoteric they might be, for my success in picking up this communication. While we were waiting on the pier, I noticed that the "RA" of the nearby Radisson Hotel's neon sign was blinking off and on. The other letters of the hotel's name were glowing an even red color. As I watched these two flashing letters, I remembered that Ra was an important sun god in Ancient Egypt. This memory triggered an instantaneous recognition of the fact that there was a message for me in these two flashing letters. The reference to Egypt was an important part of the message, because this ancient land was famous for its pyramids. It was also one of the countries that many Atlanteans fled to just before their continent made its final descent into the Atlantic Ocean. This message caused a multitude of questions to go whirling through my head. Was it possible that my Higher Self, or my mystical mentors, were trying to tell me that I had had an incarnation as some kind of a spiritual person in the ancient civilization of Egypt? I thought that it might be possible that in my past lifetime in Atlantis, I might have escaped before this once great continent went down into the sea, and had then found my way to Egypt. When we were finally allowed to cross the gangplank and to board the boat, I tucked these probing questions into the back of my conscious mind to be retrieved as soon as I returned home.

What happened next was probably one of the most unusual and unexpected validations of an important insight that I have ever encountered. As soon as we had settled into our assigned seats on the lower deck of this boat, a large group of Tibetan Buddhist monks, with shaved heads and long maroon gowns, boarded the Jungle Queen. As I marveled over this strange occurrence, I recognized that there were several messages in it for me. The first communication that I intuited was a validation of my insight that I had survived the sinking of Atlantis thousands of years ago and had then traveled to Egypt. I knew that there was also a corroboration of my intuitive feeling that I was some kind of important spiritual person in my past lifetime in Egypt, in this message. The last and probably the most obvious message, was that I had once lived a lifetime as a Tibetan Buddhist monk, possibly one who had been close to the Dalai Lama.

About a week after my striking experiences on the Jungle Queen, Marvin and I hosted a party in honor of my 60th birthday. My friend and spiritual mentor, Gloria Fleischner, gave me a beautiful, double helix clear crystal quartz as a present. She told me that it would help with my spiritual growth and development. After cleansing and activating this gift and making it truly mine, I started to read books that would teach me how this clear quartz crystal could help me in my sacred evolution.

While I was satisfying my curiosity about crystals in general, I connected to the much-needed knowledge of how the lost continent of Atlantis had destroyed itself. I learned that the Atlanteans constructed pyramids of stone and crystal that served as magnetic antennae, which drew down energy fields that nourished our planet. Much of this energy was stored inside these pyramids and threw our Earth out of balance, because the energy was stronger above the surface than it was below it. Then the unfortunate happened. These pyramids became so saturated with the accumulated Universal energy that was brought in by the crystals that they exploded, and Atlantis disappeared under the Atlantic Ocean. These sunken pyramids of Atlantis are now under the water in what is called the Bermuda Triangle. The energy vibrations of these pyramids are still active and explain the eerie phenomena of this triangular stretch of ocean around the island of Bimini.

The most important effect that my accumulation of all of this fascinating knowledge about crystals produced was a verification of my intuition that I had had a previous incarnation on the great continent of Atlantis. My intuition went one step further by convincing me that I had either lived or worked around pyramids during this lifetime.

Shortly after I had these revealing insights, my Higher Self, as it usually does, orchestrated an experience that would further validate what I had just learned about my soul and its spiritual journey. At four o'clock in the morning of the following day, I was awakened from a deep sleep by a very strange dream. In this dream, a series of letters and numbers ran through my head. These numbers and letters were OPEC6226. As I entered this dream into my Lucid

Notebook, its meaning became very clear to me. I recognized first that OPEC is the acronym for the oil-producing cartel of the Middle East. This understanding made me picture an oil well in my mind. The clear image made me gasp. This oil well looked very much like a pyramid. Now that I understood that my dream was about pyramids, I went forward in my analysis. Not only were the numbers 2 and 6 my very own spiritually guiding numbers, but I went on to see that 6226 added up to 16 or 1+6= 7. When I remembered that 7 was the number of spiritual initiation, I immediately knew that this was a past life regression dream sent to me to corroborate my insight about a past lifetime around the pyramids in Atlantis. My final intuitive analysis of this dream was that I was one of the fortunate Atlanteans who had escaped the destruction of this lost continent. My Higher Self let me know that I was lucky enough to leave Atlantis by a boat that took me to Egypt, where I helped to build the pyramids, which were used for spiritual initiation. The last thing that I added to my Lucid Notebook, before I went back to sleep, was that I was thankful that I was remembering and paying more attention to my dreams.

When one is involved in uncovering personal spiritual information, time passes rapidly. One month after my 60th birthday party, Marvin and I took off on a jet plane destined for Hawaii, with a stopover in Atlanta, Georgia. When we landed in Atlanta and we walked off the plane and into the airport, I took note of the fact that we were at gate A26. As soon as I saw this, I told Marvin, "That 26 is not an accident. I've got to keep my eyes open, because something spiritually significant is going to happen on this trip." When we boarded the plane that was going to take us to Hawaii, I became aware of another little harbinger of sacred discoveries to come in Hawaii. The heavenly hint that was waiting for me on the second leg of our journey came in the form of doubles, another one of my spiritual symbols. Directly in the row in front of us sat a pair of identical twins in their 70's, who were exactly alike, from clothing to hairstyles, to jewelry. These two ladies were truly the epitome of doubles. As I observed these mirror images and then put them together with the twenty-six that we had encountered at the Atlanta Airport, I was totally convinced that there were important spiritual discoveries waiting for me in Hawaii. This deduction caused my excitement to mount higher and higher, the closer that we got to the island of Oahu.

We finally arrived in Hawaii, checked in at our hotel in Oahu and met our tour guide. Our very first tour was to Pearl Harbor. During this tour, little messages that added to my excitement kept popping up, to let me know that I was in the right place at the right time. The most powerful of these little celestial clues that validated that I was going to make spiritual discoveries in this tropical paradise came in the form of twenty-sixes.

At Pearl Harbor, the launch that took us out to the Arizona Memorial had a big 26 on it. The next 26 came in the documentary film that told the story of that fateful day in 1941 when Pearl Harbor was attacked by the Japanese Air Force. The power of these messages in the form of twenty-sixes intensified when we left the memorial and walked into the parking lot in order to board our tour bus. There were so many twenty-sixes scattered around the parking lot and on license plates that I couldn't deny my intuition that a message was coming in.

One more heavenly hint that helped me in my spiritual sleuthing came in on a double. When we attended a traditional Hawaiian luau, I went into the gift shop to browse and stopped at a rack of fabric name badges, which had both an English name and the Hawaiian equivalent on it. Palapala, the only double on this rack, was the Hawaiian equivalent of Barbara. I was impressed with the fact that my mystical mentors never rested when they had a job to do. In this case their job was to keep me on the straight and narrow path of spiritual self-discovery.

At this point, another number, which I immediately recognized had spiritual significance, started to spring up. I noted with fascination and awe that wherever we went, the number seven, the number of spiritual initiation sprang up.

The first seven made its appearance when we got tickets for a highly recommended musical show called. "The Society of Seven." After this, sevens started to pop up in every puzzle that I opened to at random. When we finally arrived on the island of Maui and noted that our hotel room was number 707, I intuitively knew that the sacred discovery that I was going to a make in Hawaii was going to be made on this little island paradise in the Pacific Ocean.

When I looked at our itinerary for our stay in Hawaii, the reason for the proliferation of the number seven finally came clear to me. The first trip on our itinerary was a tour of the Heavenly Road to Hana, on the other side of the island, during which we were going to visit the Seven Sacred Pools. As soon as I saw the name of this tourist attraction, I knew deep within the recesses of my being that the important revelation that I was anticipating awaited me at this famous waterfall.

Marvin and I got on the mini-bus that was going to take us to the Seven Sacred Pools with great anticipation. We had heard that this was one of the most beautiful tours of the Hawaiian Islands. When we stopped at the Seven Sacred Pools, I could barely control my excitement. We hiked from the van up to a spot where the entire panorama of these sacred pools lay beneath us. I stood speechless, overwhelmed with wonder, as my eyes drank in the beauty of the little waterfalls that cascaded down the lush green hills toward the sea, stopping to fill the many sparkling pools on the way. While Marvin snapped pictures of this idyllic place, I stood mesmerized by the memory of a lifetime here that occurred in the 1500's. I saw myself as a beautiful Hawaiian woman in a sort of a sarong, with my long, dark hair tumbling down my back. As I continued my spontaneous past life regression, I realized that there were many other women and several little children in the pool with me. This scene was enthralling. We were all laughing and singing as we playfully washed our clothes and ourselves. I was impressed by the frolicsome spirit that made what could have been tedious chores a celebration. While I stood looking at the

sacred pool and the peaceful and happy scene that was filling my mind's eye, I recognized that this discovery was the
reason for my spontaneous past life regression back to a
lifetime as a woman in the South Pacific, which I had had
just before we left on our trip. It also became apparent to me
that this was why I had encountered so many little heavenly hints of guidance during the first few days of our
Hawaiian adventure.

Despite the fact that this spontaneous past life was
remarkably lucid and real, there was still a tiny bit of doubt
in my mind. Was this regression real or was it just wishful
thinking? In order to banish the unwelcome doubt that was
my constant companion; I did what I always do. I silently
asked my mystical mentors for a corroboration of the validity of this spontaneous past life regression, in the form of a
synchronicity, a sign or a symbol. As usual my invisible
helpers did not waste any time in bringing me the confirmation that I asked for. In fact, as usually happens, there
was more than one confirmation. The first verification of the
validity of my spiritual experience came in the form of a synchronicity. As we stood around sharing our delight in what
we had just seen, our tour guide asked us, "Would anyone
like an icy cold bottle of spring water?" After she handed
each of us a greatly appreciated bottle of water, the conversation switched to other places in the world that we had visited. I told the compatible group that Marvin and I had
recently taken a trip to the Alps, which we had greatly
enjoyed. As I shared this with the group of fellow travelers,
something told me to look at the label on the cold bottle of
spring water in my hand. I smiled to myself when I saw that
the name of the company that bottled this water was Crystal
Geyser and that this company was located in the Alps. I
silently thanked my invisible helpers for their prompt confirmation of the validity of the idyllic spontaneous past life
regression, which I had just experienced.

As usually happens when I ask for confirmation of some
spiritual information that has come in and which I doubt,
the corroborations kept on coming. The next confirmation
came in on a double and occurred on the very next stop on

our Maui Island tour. A short while after we boarded the van to resume our day trip, we stopped at the cemetery where Charles Lindbergh's grave was located. When the tour guide told us that the name of the cemetery was Pala Pala, I knew that this double, which means Barbara in English, was another confirmation of my past incarnation at the Seven Sacred Pools of Maui.

The following day found us on a full day circle tour of the big island of Hawaii. When the tour guide told us that we would be driving 260 miles before this tour was over, my conscious mind snapped to immediate attention. As all of my physical senses went on alert, my intuition kicked in too, by telling me to count the number of people in the mini-bus that was taking us on our tour of the biggest island in the Hawaiian chain. A quick count brought me the information, which my Higher Self probably had already, that there were 26 people, including the driver on the bus. When I received this synchronistic information, I might have looked calm on the outside, but inside I was yelling, "Wow." Knowing that two twenty-sixes appearing almost simultaneously was no accident, I could feel the excitement and the anticipation filling every recess of my being as we took off for what I knew was going to be a very revealing tour.

As we drove through eerie fields of solidified black lava, I could feel the spiritual vibes that this unusual island gave off. These vibes became even stronger when we arrived at the Place of Refuge National Park. I listened with rapt attention, as our tour guide told us that this was a place of unconditional love, where Ancient Hawaiians fled to be forgiven for breaking the strict Kapu or Taboo laws of the islands. This area of black solidified lava and symbolic art was haunting in its sacred beauty. I could almost feel the Mana, or spiritual power, in my blood as I walked over the black sand stretches of this ancient refuge. Deep within the recesses of my subconscious mind lurked a faint feeling of guilt, which only proved to intensify my inner knowing that this place played a significant role in my past incarnation in Hawaii. I jotted my reactions down in a notepad that I had with me, promising myself that I would enter them into my Lucid Notebook as soon as we returned to the hotel.

The following day, I found out that there had been a landslide during the night and that the roads that circled this largest of the Hawaiian Islands had been shut down. Now I was sure that my reaction at the Place of Refuge National Park was not a figment of my imagination. I thanked my mystical mentors for holding this landslide off until we had completed our tour of the island. Only time and additional experience would show me why I felt such a strong connection and feeling of guilt at this spiritual Hawaiian park.

I awakened on the smaller island of Kauai the next morning, with visions of the many sevens that were recently occurring in my life, dancing in my mind. Experience had taught me that when I came out of sleep with these intuitive little hints about my soul's journey pouring into my consciousness, it did no good to stop the flood. It was always beneficial to go with the flow. The first thing that popped into my mind was that when I used numerology to add up the numbers in our address in Florida, I got a seven. This insight was followed by the memory of what had occurred in Gloria Fleischner's Metaphysics and Parapsychology Seven classes. We did considerable work in numerology in these recently finished classes and all of my important life numbers, such as all of my names came up as sevens. We had even left Florida on our trip to the Hawaiian Islands on October 7th. This information was followed by the recognition that my first name, Barbara, and my middle name, Roberta, both have seven letters in them. Even my Social Security number contains two sevens. Two more sevens were added to this supernatural collection the very next day, when I found out that Captain Cook discovered the Hawaiian Islands in 1778. As I entered this plethora of sevens into my Lucid Notebook, it occurred to me that having so many sevens in my life supported my strong intuition that my past lifetime in Hawaii was a very important one. This very spiritual number took on another, incredibly significant meaning, within the next two years.

After I made my entry into my Lucid Notebook, I opened one of my puzzle books and turned to a page at random. The puzzle on this page was about license plates. As I began to solve this puzzle, the digits of one of these plates almost jumped off the page at me. The six digits, 4Y7RAB, would probably mean nothing to the vast majority of people, but when I intuitively unlocked their spiritual meaning, I received a corroboration that my early morning insights about the number seven were true. The message that I deciphered from this celestial code was that seven's could unlock part of Barbara Yudell's reincarnation story. Connecting to and deciphering this slightly esoteric message from my mystical mentors gave me great joy. I knew that I had come a long way in my development as a spiritual detective and I was enjoying every minute of it.

On our last day in Kauai, we deposited ourselves on lounge chairs by the hotel pool, which overlooked the Pacific Ocean. I spent most of this absolutely gorgeous day in silent reverie, drinking in as much as I could of the beauty and spirituality of my surroundings. The haunting spirituality, which I had felt in the Place of Refuge National Park in Hawaii, must have seeped directly into my soul because as I sat and looked out at the water, I had a spontaneous past life regression, which was as real as my present lifetime. I saw myself as a man, who was dressed in a white toga-like outfit, on the ancient continent of Atlantis. As soon as I recognized where I was in this past life, I instantaneously knew that my job in this past incarnation was to maintain the crystals in the great pyramids that were sprinkled throughout the vast island. It was obvious that I was a member of the hierarchy of this ancient civilization, who had previous knowledge of the final destruction of Atlantis. As soon as this intuitive knowledge flooded into my consciousness, I saw a picture of myself at a later date in this lifetime, boarding a boat that would carry a chosen few of us to safety. I could actually see this large vessel sailing off into the horizon, as the once great Atlantis sank into the Atlantic Ocean. As the ship continued its voyage across the Atlantic, toward our new home, I was even aware of the intense feeling of relief that I had had at the time, so many thousands of years ago. Realizing that we were safe, we continued our voyage away from a life in which we had abused the energies of crystals and misused scientific technology. This past lifetime was so very real that I did not have to ask my invisible helpers for verification.

An unexpected confirmation of the validity of my spiritual experiences on Maui and Kauai occurred on our first homeward bound flight from Oahu to Los Angeles. The movie that was shown on this flight was *Six Days, Seven Nights,* with Harrison Ford and Anne Heche. There were actually two synchronicities in the showing of this film. The first meaningful coincidence was that there was a seven in the title of this movie, which validated my spontaneous past life regression at the Seven Sacred Pools in Maui. The second synchronicity was that, while we were on tour in Kauai, we were actually shown the spot where this movie was filmed.

The most outstanding synchronicity of validation also happened on this flight from Oahu to Los Angeles. After we saw the movie, I took out my Lucid Notebook and started to enter the absolutely clear and real spontaneous past life regression back to a lifetime in ancient Atlantis, which I had had on the island of Kauai. I also entered the subsequent synchronicities of verification that had followed this experience. While I was doing this, Marvin was sitting quietly beside me reading the airline's magazine. Before I had even finished entering a description of my regression back to Atlantis into my Lucid Notebook, Marvin leaned over and showed me an article about the Atlantis Hotel on Paradise Island in the Bahamas. It dawned on me later on that this was a double synchronicity. The second part of this meaningful coincidence lies in the fact that the Atlantis Hotel, and Paradise Island which we have visited, are located in the Bermuda Triangle, under which a large part of Atlantis is buried. Also interesting is the fact that this aptly named hotel is not far from the spot where Dr. Ray Brown found and removed a powerful crystal from an underwater pyramid, a legacy of the great sunken continent.

I arrived home with a cold and with my head buzzing with the discoveries that I had made about my soul's travels from lifetime to lifetime. The panorama of my sacred journey was coming more and more into focus. Messages that validated my spiritual discoveries kept coming in, asked for or not. Even opening a can of soup brought me a message. The first line of the code on the top of the can read, SEP 00 09038 and the second line read, CX 14AB 1642. This code was amazingly like a mini-autobiography of my present lifetime, or Barbara Yudell was born on September 14, 1938. Even the double zeroes fit in with the newly discovered fact that doubles are one of the ways in which my Higher Self and my mystical mentors communicate with me.

After I unpacked and checked my telephone answer machine and accumulated mail, I decided to do a healing meditation in an attempt to get rid of my cold as swiftly as possible. While I was in a meditative state, I received some interesting insights. I recognized that before we left on our trip to Hawaii, I had done some things unconsciously that would prepare me for the spontaneous past life regression back to a lifetime among the crystals and the pyramids of ancient Atlantis, which I had had on the island of Kauai. For reasons that I didn't discover until we got to Hawaii, I had made the decision to expand my small collection of pyramids by looking for and purchasing others made out of crystal. In retrospect, I understand that my need to obtain these unusual pyramids stemmed from the first stirrings of subconscious memories of an important lifetime in ancient Atlantis.

Life in sunny Florida went on and so did the spiritual events that ultimately wound up as entries into my Lucid Notebook. Something very unusual happened two weeks after our return from Hawaii that was not only supernatural but, as I later realized, actually brought me a very important spiritual message. It was my late father's birthday. Marvin and I were doing some errands and some shopping.

One of our stops was at an automotive store. Marvin went in to this store to check the price of tires, leaving me in the car, with the windows open and the engine off. While I was sitting and waiting for Marvin's return, the strangest thing happened, the windshield wipers started to go on and off by themselves. As I stared at this impossibility, it occurred to me that, since it was my father's birthday, that somehow my father's spirit had accomplished this supernatural feat. After telling Marvin about this strange phenomenon and mulling it over in my mind, I decided that my father had used this paranormal occurrence to send me the message that just as windshield wipers give a driver a clearer visual field, it was apparent that my spiritual perspective was becoming clearer too.

The knowledge that my father's spirit was helping me in my spiritual quest for understanding of my soul's sacred journey was greatly strengthened by this event. It also reinforced my decision to publish this book in 2001, on the 26th anniversary of my father's death and just a few months after my 62nd birthday. This seemed appropriate because it paid homage, not only to my father, but also to the sanctity of the number 26 in my life. As soon as I made this decision, a message from the invisible realm that corroborated my thinking and reinforced its appropriateness came to me in the form of a license plate. I saw the message, WRD 62M, as a clear cosmic confirmation. Obviously the WRD stood for word or writing, the 62 for my age and the M for the new millennium, when all of this was going to happen. This wonderful message of validation brought with it a spectacular feeling of connection to all that is good and worthwhile in the Universe, and a feeling of gratitude for the honor of being part of it.

LESSONS FROM CHAPTER IX

✳ A very reliable way to learn about your soul and its mission on our planet is through the study of reincarnation.

✳ Déjà vus are glimpses backward in time to one of our soul's past incarnations. By entering these déjà vus into a psychic journal and then rereading them you might see a pattern emerging.

✳ Memories of past lives very often come to us in dreams, especially recurrent dreams. Entering these dreams into a psychic journal may help us to determine where our soul has been in past incarnations.

✳ Our phobias are extremely important clues to past incarnations. Traumas from past lives stick to our etheric bodies and are carried with us from lifetime to lifetime.

✳ Your affinities can also point directly to past incarnations. Many people even decorate their homes in the style of their favorite incarnation. If you are partial to a southwestern theme in dress or in home decorating, you might have been a Native American in a past lifetime.

✳ There are several ways in which you can actually access past lifetimes. Watch the newspaper for large seminars on past life regression. Check with your local metaphysical store to see if they offer past life regression workshops. Try to find a certified hypnotist who does individual past life regression sessions.

✳ Accessing past lifetimes can also help us to understand how karma functions in our lives. Karma can be explained by the old saying, "what goes around comes around." It is the soul's schoolroom and a means of compensation and purification. Someone who is a wife abuser in one lifetime may very likely be an abused wife in his next incarnation.

CHAPTER X

Understanding My Mission on the Yellow Brick Road

Life will always provide for those of us who are interested, the information, signs and symbols for the identification of our soul's sacred mission.

I was finding what I was learning in my Metaphysics and Parapsychology classes very helpful in clarifying my understanding of my soul's mission in this lifetime. Learning about our planet leaving the Piscean Age and entering the Age of Aquarius helped me to see my part in this transition. We learned that the Piscean Age, which is symbolized by the fish, was an age of the emotions and that the upcoming Age of Aquarius, symbolized by the water bearer, is an age that is more mental and sharing. The image of this water bearer sharing the water in his jug with others struck very close to home. I was beginning to feel very much like a water bearer whose jug was filled with spiritual insights and understandings. My jug was getting heavier and heavier. I intuitively knew that what was in this vessel, had to be shared with humanity. It was becoming increasingly apparent to me that I really belonged in this age of the intellect and of sharing. I entered this insight into my Lucid Notebook and went on with my life.

An event that happened the following day convinced me that not only was my intuition about an important part of my soul's mission at this time in our planet's history correct, but that this insight was much more significant than I myself realized. I got out of bed very early in the morning to sign up for a tennis court. When I looked up at the early morning sky, I saw a canvas of blue velvet, which contained one small puff of a cloud that looked exactly like a fish that was beginning to lose its shape. As I stared at this unusual painting on nature's blue canvas, I recognized that there was a message for me in this. I intuitively knew that the message was that, yes, the Piscean Age was ending and that the Age of Aquarius was beginning and that I had an important job to do in this new age. Why else was I writing this book, if not to share my spiritual insights, discoveries and understandings with others? My Higher Self and all of my mystical mentors had been pushing me toward the initiation and the completion of this task for a very long time. I silently vowed to take the job of sharing my spiritual discoveries with others much more seriously.

I was beginning to understand that my soul had come into the flesh at the end of the Piscean Age and the very beginning of the Age of Aquarius to share the knowledge that we can all be the Light, with all of those who would listen. My experiences and my intuition were letting me know that there was divinity in all of us, and that we must all become aware of this divinity in order to connect to our Higher Selves and to the Light of God.

Finally understanding a very significant part of my spiritual mission made me even more serious than ever about exposing myself to spiritual experiences and about gathering sacred knowledge. I was beginning to see myself as a link, connecting God's wisdom, to other souls who had chosen to be in the flesh at this time. It was exciting to consider myself one of the initiates who are receiving in order to share with others, at this crucial point in our planet's history, the dawning of the Age of Aquarius. This incredible spiritual insight helped me to understand why I felt better around people who had already connected to the awareness that we are going into a time of higher spiritual vibrations and that, since we are all connected, we must share with and help each other.

The many supernatural experiences that I was being exposed to fostered a need to go to a New Age shop to buy some crystals that would possibly help me to write this book. As soon as I entered the store, I realized the real reason that I was there. In front of me was a display of a book entitled, *The Emissaries of Light*, by James Twyman This title spoke to my soul. It reminded me of how I felt when I was standing in front of the art exhibit in the Jewish Community Center of Boca Raton, which commemorated the signing of the Israeli-Egyptian Peace Treaty on March 26, 1979. At that time, as I stood and stared at the exhibit of postal art that was called the Messengers of Peace, I connected to the intuitive knowledge that my soul was also a Messenger of Peace. This powerful intuition motivated me to buy and to read this book. It was about a group of spiritual people who operated as peacemakers by meditating and sending out Divine Light to the war torn area in which they functioned and to the rest of the world. The book explained that a critical mass of people have been influenced by this Divine Light and are actively seeking peace by trying to bring Heaven and Earth closer together.

Finding and reading this book reinforced my intuition that I too was an Emissary of Light, or a Messenger of Peace. Deep within my heart I knew that my soul was somehow involved in bringing peace to our planet. The theme of cooperation and peace, which was illustrated so beautifully in the Native American tale about the colors of the rainbow, seemed to be emanating from my soul and into my daily life. Was this what the beautiful white beam of light surrounded by a rainbow halo, which came into my darkened bedroom, was trying to tell me? I entered all of this into my Lucid Notebook. I knew that I would find out in due time if my intuition was true.

Information about my soul, its mission on this planet and its journey through time was coming in at a slow but steady pace. This information was entering my consciousness through intuitions, synchronicities and mystical messages of all kinds. It was also coming in through my dreams. There was one dream in particular that seemed to be loaded with past life content. In this dream I was back in our old house in Paramus, New Jersey. The walls and the floors of the house were decorated in dark colors and I could see that I was wearing a tuxedo dress.

When I awoke and thought about this dream, I intuitively knew that it was important and had to be entered into my Lucid Notebook. As soon as I read the last entry that I had made into my journal, I knew that it was connected to the dream that I had just experienced. This entry explained that 10,500 years ago, when the pyramids of Giza in Egypt were probably built, the Orion Constellation and the Milky Way, in the night sky, were the same relative size and the same relative position as these pyramids and the Nile River. This was an outstanding example of the Universal Law, "As above, so below." Using my dream analysis skills helped me to figure out that our old house in Paramus was symbolic of a pyramid. The first thing that connected our house in Paramus to a pyramid was the term peremus, an ancient Egyptian term meaning to go straight up and the possible derivation of the word pyramid. I recognized that the dark colors on the walls and on the floors in our former home were indicative of the fact that I had been inside a pyramid in a past lifetime, possibly as an initiate. Finally, the tuxedo, or formal clothing that I was wearing, probably pointed to the possibility that I had had a high-ranking job in Egypt, possibly around the pyramids of Giza. After my dream analysis was completed, I recognized that this vivid night-time vision was actually a past life regression back to a very influential lifetime in ancient Egypt. Before too much time elapsed I was presented with metaphysical proof that this intuition was correct.

The year 1998, which had been a year of great spiritual discovery, was drawing to a close. Before the year was over, some very important personal spiritual information came in on Christmas day. When I awakened in the morning, an interesting dream was still in my mind.

This dream took place in Germany, where a seminar on underground Judaism was being advertised. The advertisement was in the form of a poster, which had all the colors of the spectrum coming out of it. These colored rays were dazzling and reminded me of a rainbow or the seven spiritual energy centers, or chakras, of our bodies. My immediate interpretation of this dream was that the fact that I was

Jewish in my present lifetime is much more important to my soul's mission and my spiritual journey than I had ever realized. Being a Jew, who has gone to Germany and to Austria and has forgiven the people of these two countries for the perpetration of the Holocaust, has been a very important part of my spiritual journey and has led to a very big leap in the evolution and the ascension of my soul. My dream analysis went even further, to the insight that since I was born in Germany in my past lifetime as Empress Elisabeth of Austria and was then reborn as a middle class Jewish-American woman during the time of the Holocaust, speaks of karma being fulfilled and lessons being learned. The fact that I had this insightful dream on Christmas Eve validates this interpretation, since in my lifetime as Empress Elisabeth, I was born on the eve of this important holiday.

The dazzling colors, which I saw in my dream, also spoke to me of joy and happiness. This feeling was probably a little prophetic. After lunch on Christmas day, Marvin and I went to the movies to see the newly released movie, *Patch Adams*, starring Robin Williams. This movie about an eccentric medical student who used outrageous humor to help to heal his patients physically, emotionally and psychologically, opened the floodgates of my subconscious mind and allowed spiritually significant insights to come pouring into my conscious mind. Just two weeks before we saw this movie, one of the members of our SOUL group and of Gloria Fleischner's Metaphysics and Parapsychology classes had asked me if I was always as upbeat and happy, as I seemed to be whenever she was around me? My answer to her was, "I have a choice when I wake up every morning of whether I want to be happy or whether I want to be miserable. I opt for happiness every single day of my life." When I think of this choice metaphysically, I understand that this happiness and positive attitude comes from my soul's mission as a connection between God's Universal energy and the physical world. The soul searching that has ultimately produced this book has helped me to understand that my sometimes wacky sense of humor and love of fun have always provided a channel through which my soul could spread love and light into the darker corners of life. I have always lived my life with the knowledge that laughter is the best medicine. When the revealing insights sparked by Robin William's movie stopped flooding into my conscious mind, I was left with the understanding that spreading happiness and joy is a significant part of my spiritual mission.

As has happened so many times before, my mystical mentors wasted no time in validating my insight about how important my positive attitude and sense of humor are in the fulfillment of my soul's sacred mission. As soon as we returned home from the movie theater, I opened our local newspaper to the puzzle section. When I saw that the theme of the Wonderword puzzle was "The Pursuit of Happiness," I knew that my mystical mentors were at it again. The words in the puzzle were a mirror of what I now know to be a fundamental part of my soul's sacred mission. Some of these validating words were harmony, health, laugh, love, luck, peace, smile, soul and goodness.

I was really very happy that 1998 went out on such a positive note. The new year of 1999 was ushered in with the delivery of books, which I had previously ordered, on how to determine one's soul purpose. I found it quite interesting that the authors of these books encouraged their readers to do spiritual research in the experimental laboratory of life. Wasn't that what I was doing? During the last five or six years before I read these books, my soul's purposes had been floating up to the surface of my consciousness. These books were exactly what I needed to finally see these purposes in a sharper light. After doing many of the exercises in these books, I could see things much more clearly. Following these book's suggestions, I wrote out the mission statements of my soul as follows:

❋ To help others to identify the spiritual messages which come from the spirit realm in the form of symbols, signs and synchronicities.

❋ To use humor and playfulness to help people to become lighter and more positive and, therefore, more spiritual.

✳ To help to form more highly evolved groups or communities that would help other souls to become kinder and more charitable.

✳ To help to connect others to God's Universal energy.

✳ To teach others by example, to be kinder, more loving and more optimistic.

✳ To function in some capacity as a Messenger of Peace or an Emissary of Light.

The signposts, which inform me that I am fulfilling my soul's purpose are:

✳ Living with a natural flow of events or synchronicities.

✳ Seeing others benefit from the good things that we do for them.

✳ Feeling that God exists in everything.

✳ Recognizing that things are happening in my life for a purpose.

✳ Feeling more energy and perservence.

✳ More frequent feelings of bliss, euphoria and unconditional love.

The feelings of contentment and of gratitude that this confirmation of the success of my spiritual investigations gave me, were so powerful and so nourishing that I decided to imprint them upon my subconscious mind by doing a meditation. I closed my eyes and took three slow and deep breaths. As soon as I reached the alpha state, I was filled with a wonderful feeling of peace. The beauty of the world filled my heart with overflowing love. A deep feeling of gratitude overwhelmed me for my soul's mission and its sacred journey and for the honor of being able to share this spiritual information with others. When I finished this wondrous meditation, I walked into my *angel room*, which is filled with most of my spiritual possessions and functions as an altar. I sat down and gazed at all of my angels, pyramids and crystals and all of my books and video-tapes, which were neatly lined up on the bookshelves that lined one wall. As I sat there, still in a semi-meditative state, everything in this room became luminous and started to glow with the Light of God. When I finally brought myself back to the normal, everyday state of reality, I recognized that what had just happened was actually a reward for my success as a spiritual detective and for the knowledge, which I was accumulating and sharing, about the workings of the Universe.

When I told my mentor and teacher, Gloria Fleischner, about my most recent spiritual insights and the incredible otherworldly corroboration of their authenticity, which I was experiencing, she told me, "One of your most significant soul missions is the ability to see the connection between things and then to pass this on to others." Gloria's feedback, which I always valued, helped me to finally understand why I had given this book the title, *Discovering Soul Connections*.

Rereading my Lucid Notebook has also helped me to see how important my role as a connector has been in my soul's spiritual evolution. As I did this rereading, I recognized that many of the celestial clues, pointed to my position in the middle of things. This seemed very appropriate to me because a connector is usually in the middle, functioning as a link between two separate things.

The first heavenly hint of my position in the middle, as a connector, came in my recollection that in the human chakra, or spiritual energy system, like the rainbow; green is the color of the middle, or heart chakra. Green seems to be the color that I function by. I have always seemed to be happiest when I am around green things, like grass, trees and plants. This intuitive recognition of my role as a connector between things caused me to coin a word to describe my newly discovered position in the middle. Coining this new word, *middleship*, has led me to understand that people who are considered to be mediums are also in a middle position, connecting to and delivering information from the more spiritual dimension to our physical world. These new insights, that I have arrived at through my spiritual sleuthing, have brought me to the recognition that I have spent my entire life in the middle. I also see that being in the middle has been symbolic of my destiny as a medium of sorts, a medium whose mission has always been to bring in spiritual wisdom and information from the dimension of the infinite, into the finite dimension where all of us now exist.

My insights about *middleship* have helped me to see the many ways that my current lifetime fits into this category. First of all, I am a middle child who was born into a middle class family. I was born on the 14th of September, which is in the middle of the month and as a Virgo, my birthday is also in the middle of the Zodiac. Interestingly, I am the only one of my siblings who was given a middle name. I am of medium height and medium build. My eyes are even green, like the middle color of the rainbow, the human chakra system and the middle column of the Kabbalah's Tree of Life. I now recognize that this middle position was bestowed upon me in order to reinforce my position as a contact or connector between our Earthly physical dimension and the dimension of the spirit. The more that I think about this insight, the more convinced I am that this was what my father's spirit was trying to tell me when he sent me a message in the movie, *Contact*. I am sure that my dad, wherever he may be in the world of the spirit, is feeling pretty good about the fact that I finally caught on to what he was trying to tell me. Figuring out the reason for my *middleship* has caused me to take my mission as a connector or communicator very seriously. I find myself communicating spiritual information wherever I go.

LESSONS FROM CHAPTER X

✳ Each soul is born with a unique mission in life. Every soul has special abilities and talents with which it can make a needed contribution to the world.

✳ Helping others is important because when we share our talents and gifts with them we help them to fulfill their own purposes. By giving, we receive.

* All of us have the drive to find the spiritual meaning in life.

* We have the responsibility of determining what our capabilities are. We also are responsible for making the best possible use of what we have been given.

* Starting a journal will help you to determine what your talents and your soul's purpose are. Paying close attention to dreams and adding them to your journal as soon as possible will help you to eventually discover your soul's mission.

* Your mission in other lifetimes has helped to determine your mission in your present lifetime. Experiencing past life regression will, therefore, help you to discover your soul's purpose. It is imperative that you put what you have learned about past lives into your psychic journal.

* We are all part of God. Our purpose is to express the divine qualities, which we share with God, in an individualized way, in our physical world.

* Reincarnation is God's way of giving us more chances to become less selfish and to connect the divine of the infinite world to the finite world of the physical.

* Our true spiritual nature resides in our subconscious mind. Meditation can help us to connect to this spiritual nature. A connection to our spiritual nature can also be found in dreams and in prayers.

* You can learn a lot about your spiritual purpose by spending quiet time in nature.

* When you help others with no thought of what you will get out of it, your true self reveals itself to you.

* The part of our spiritual nature that we forget about when we reincarnate into the physical world is our spiritual core or our Higher Self. Your Higher Self is directly connected to God and communicates with you in the form of intuition, hunches and feelings.

* When you step aside and observe yourself living your life you may remember your Higher Self and your soul's purpose.

✳ We all reincarnate into a new lifetime with negative karma to overcome. This negative karma comes from the non-spiritual things that we did in past lifetimes. Releasing negative karma and living in a spiritual way will help you to identify and fulfill your spiritual mission.

✳ Making a list of your talents and special abilities will help you to see how you can serve mankind. You can also ask those who are close to you to make up a list of what they see as your talents and capabilities.

✳ You can identify your special talents and abilities by reviewing previous successes that you have had in this lifetime.

✳ Listen to the insights and intuitions that come from your Higher Self because this spiritual part of you is always trying to communicate to you what your mission in life is.

Chapter XI

The Wizard of Oz

Forgiveness and unconditional love are on the same plane of understanding.

After spending several months at my computer, I was convinced that this book was completed. I gave copies of the manuscript to two of my friends for proofreading. Although what I originally thought was a completed book gave me a feeling of accomplishment, an unwelcome feeling that something was missing began to gnaw at me. Awareness that my subconscious mind was sending me little messages was beginning to dawn on me. It was telling me that there were still missing pieces to the spiritual story of my soul. As I tried to figure out what the missing pieces of this puzzle were, I became more and more frustrated. I was living with the very annoying feeling that I had something on the tip of my tongue that I was having a great deal of difficulty spitting out. Something was not right. I started to look around for an answer to my dilemma.

Gloria Fleischner had recently met a woman named Sonya Lugo who besides being a Pastoral Counselor and Minister was a hypnotherapist, a metaphysician and a shaman. Sonya had helped my teacher and mentor both emotionally and metaphysically on several occasions. Gloria was so impressed by Sonya that she opened every one of her classes with enthusiastic raves about the metaphysical marvels that this highly telepathic, clairvoyant and clairaudient woman had recently accomplished. After some of the other members of Gloria's classes and of our SOUL group had paid visits to Sonya, the accolades increased.

Although I intellectually knew that making an appointment to see this highly recommended metaphysician and shaman would unlock some more of my soul's history and its spiritual mission, it took what happened next to convince me that a visit to Sonya Lugo was inevitable. While sorting through miscellaneous papers on my computer desk, I came across a little pamphlet, which I was absolutely sure that I had never seen before. As I read what was in this pamphlet, I realized that the unseen hand of fate had just handed me the synchronicity that I needed to move me in the right spiritual direction. The folded piece of paper in my hand was an advertisement for Inner Dimensional Pathways of Healing, founded by none other than Sonya Lugo. Knowing full well that nothing happens by accident and that this synchronicity was sent to me for a reason, I telephoned and left a message for Sonya Lugo on her answer machine.

As soon as I hung up the phone, I began to have feelings of apprehension. The realization that I was going to expose myself to a total stranger who I was told was extremely psychic and intuitive was the cause of the uneasy feelings that swirled around deep inside of me. Despite my apprehensions, when Sonya returned my phone call, I made an appointment to see her. The scheduled appointment was on a day that was less than two weeks before Marvin and I were due to leave on a trip to Germany, the Czech Republic, Poland, Russia and the Scandinavian countries.

I arrived early for my appointment and awaited Sonya's arrival with a mixture of excitement and apprehension churning in my stomach. When she finally arrived, she unlocked her office and proceeded to light a candle that she explained would usher in the Light of God. We agreed to audio tape the session. As soon as this was done and we both sat down, everything that I had recently discovered about my soul's mission and spiritual journey came tumbling out of my mouth. My obviously strong need for catharsis made it quite difficult for my speaking faculties to keep up with the thoughts that were coursing through my mind.

When I was finally finished with my emotional explanation of what had brought me to her office, Sonya took a few minutes to digest what I had just told her and to determine the course of action that she was going to take in order to help me to accomplish my goal. After a short meditation, Sonya asked me to give her permission to open up my Akashic Records, the records of my immortal soul's journey through all time. She explained to me, "When I read these otherworldly records, I will be able to communicate their contents to you. This will help you to understand the story of your soul's sacred voyage through time with greater clarity. I will also share what I discover about your soul's spiritual mission with you."

While I sat in a state of awe, barely breathing, I watched as Sonya closed her eyes and said a prayer of protection. After she had taken care of all the preliminaries, she began to gather information from my file in the other-dimensional data bank, which contains the history of every soul that has ever incarnated on this planet.

I listened with rapt attention as Sonya shared with me what she was beginning to see. She said, "I can see a legion of guards who are paying homage to you and protecting you in a past lifetime as a Pharaoh, very early in Egypt's history. Gloria Fleischner is a priest and your right hand spiritual consultant in this lifetime. You are clairvoyant and also adept at mental telepathy in this incarnation. You are also aware of the resonance of sound. As a child, you were fascinated by the invisible other world and could see your spirit guides. Then, when these supernatural abilities became overwhelming, the priests helped to close your otherworldly contacts down."

Sonya continued by telling me, "When you finally reached maturity and were capable of handling the more spiritual, invisible realms that surround all of us, you delved into the esoteric mysteries and went through a series of initiations in a pyramid. You did not complete the last initiation, which was an attempt at a near death experience, because you did not want to risk depriving your people of their ruler."

As I listened intently to what this amazing woman was sharing with me, she went on to astound me with her discovery that I had a high head in this lifetime. She continued,

"Having a high head is proof that you were a Son of God in physical manifestation. You were in constant communication with the Almighty." She said, "In this lifetime, like the Native Americans, you could penetrate the consciousness of animals, plants and trees." Sonya finished her report on this lifetime that occurred thousands of years before the birth of Christ by informing me that my mission in this lifetime was to narrow the gap between Heaven and Earth.

I sat mesmerized by what Sonya was seeing in my Akashic records. She continued, "You have been a significant player in Earth's destiny from the beginning of time. Besides being a guardian of the Earth, you are an anchor for the spiritual light, which constantly illuminates our world. This part of your soul's mission creates stability in the world, which only light anchors can achieve. Because you are one of the guardians of this planet, your soul leaves your body while you are sleeping and joins a group of other highly evolved souls and masters on mystical journeys to strife-ridden areas of the world. You do this in order to guide people in power and to try to achieve peace."

My life reading continued with the disclosure that, "You have lived several lifetimes in Atlantis. You were involved in politics during one of these incarnations on this once flourishing continent. In this particular lifetime, you tried in vain to teach a populace that was becoming too technical to stay in touch with their spirituality. In all of your lifetimes in Atlantis, you were involved in some capacity with the crystal filled pyramids. In fact, you have worked around pyramids, at one time or another, all over the world."

Sonya went on to share her newly acquired knowledge about my soul's earliest history with me. This very spiritual and psychic woman told me, "Before your soul came to our earthly physical plane, you lived on another planet. Your Akashic Records also show that you still have extraterrestrial connections."

While I was trying desperately to assimilate and to understand everything that Sonya was telling me about my soul's spiritual journey, this very intuitive woman appeared to be concentrating even harder than before on my other-dimensional records. Out of this increased concentration came the startling fact that I had lived a long ago lifetime, in the water, as a mermaid. She told me that this incarnation came before my lifetimes on the lost continent of Atlantis. The poignant fact that I missed my gills and my fins when I subsequently incarnated into my first lifetime in Atlantis was immediately added to this shocking information.

My life reading ended with the statement that people were attracted to me because of the light, which radiated from my soul. It was suggested that I continue to write and to teach, so that I can help others to find, and to connect to their own spiritual light. Sonya also suggested that I learn to read the tarot cards in order to sharpen my psychic skills.

In conclusion, Sonya added that I had reached the ceiling of my psychic awareness and my ability to bring in knowledge from my Higher Self, and the realm of the infinite. She suggested that I undergo a spiritual initiation, which would raise my cosmic consciousness and would allow me to tap into a higher level of spiritual information and insights. As I listened to Sonya's explanation, I intuitively recognized that this is what had happened to me and what had brought me in for this life reading. We set up an appointment for this initiation for the following week, right before Marvin and I were to leave on our trip to northern Europe.

As we parted, this highly psychic woman told me that I needed to work on opening up my heart chakra more. I told her that I was aware of this and that I was already working on forgiveness, unconditional love and the elimination of judgmental thinking. This would not be an easy job, but I was determined to do it.

When I returned home, my head stuffed with the extraordinary observations that Sonya had discovered in my otherworldly records, I played the tape of the life reading that she had made for me. As I listened, I entered what Sonya had shared with me into my Lucid Notebook. What came to me as I wrote, was that many of the things that Sonya had learned about my soul from my opened Akashic Records were merely a confirmation and an elaboration of what I had picked up myself during my episodes of personal spiritual illumination. During one of these episodes, information from my Higher Self had alerted me to the fact that I had had a spiritual lifetime in Egypt. I had also discovered on my own that I had had at least one incarnation on the once great continent of Atlantis. It had also come through to me prior to my life reading, that pyramids had been very important to me in several previous lifetimes. My Lucid Notebook also contained my prior insights that I was an Emissary of Light, a peacemaker and an anchor for spiritual light. One of the most useful pieces of information that Sonya had gleaned from my Akashic Records was something else that I already accepted as part of my spiritual destiny. She had told me that part of my mission was to teach and to write about my personal spiritual experiences, in order to help others to connect with their own spirituality. The remarkable information that I had received from this life reading was helping me to tie together much of what I had intuited on my own about my soul's spiritual mission and journey through time.

Since the life reading that Sonya had done for me related so powerfully to many of the things that I had intuited on my own, I did not feel that I had to ask the Universe for a formal validation of what I had learned. But despite the fact that I did not ask for confirmation of what Sonya had found in my Akashic Records, a corroboration of everything that she had just told me came to me the following evening. It was the first Wednesday of the month and the appointed time for our SOUL meeting. This meeting was in my friend Ina's house. The guest speaker was Jack Rambow, who was scheduled to do soul readings from the dates of our birth. Most of us, myself included, had never met Jack before and were curious about what he could pick up from just one date and one meeting. He began to give readings to each of us. When Jack finally got to me, I was flabbergasted at how similar his reading was to the one that Sonya had done for me the day before. This highly intuitive man told me, "You are an ancient soul who does not have to reincarnate. You do so in order to teach and to understand human emotions better." He added that I am very spiritually evolved and that I have very highly evolved spirit guides. Since, metaphysically speaking, nothing happens by accident, I recognized that this similar reading, just one day after Sonya's reading, was my mystical mentors' way of validating what I had learned, in the first, more extensive reading.

The day after Jack Rambow's soul reading, I replayed the audiotape of Sonya Lugo's life reading once again, in order to see if I could get any more important insights about how closely it had mirrored what I had learned during my episodes of personal enlightenment. As I listened, I realized that the information about how I tried to bring the realms of Heaven and Earth closer together during my incarnation as an Egyptian Pharaoh was very closely connected to what I had intuited about one of my missions in my present lifetime. I had labeled my attempts at bringing the spirituality of the infinite dimension into our finite realm as *middleship*, because this is where I have placed myself so that I can function as a connector between dimensions.

One of the most significant pieces of information that I received from the life reading that Sonya did for me, was what she told me about my soul's involvement with a highly evolved group of soul's and masters who travel together at night in an attempt to bring peace to our planet. My intuition had led me in the same direction prior to this reading, by letting me know that I was a member of a group of peacemakers called the Emissaries of Light. The difference between these two revelations was that in the one that I had on my own, I would never have imagined that my soul would be doing this work at night, while I slept, with other highly evolved souls and masters. I merely thought of myself as an Emissary of Peace, who worked in the flesh, to try to get people to behave in a kinder and more spiritual way. I do not think that I would ever have discovered the enormity of my work as an Emissary of Light, if I had not met Sonya Lugo.

The day arrived for my initiation with Sonya. I awoke filled with excited anticipation. I found that I was pleased with the fact that this time my apprehensions were minimal.

I, as the student, was certainly ready to be helped by my newfound teacher and mentor, to reach greater heights of cosmic consciousness.

When I arrived at Sonya's home, where the initiation was going to take place, I saw that her living room floor was set up with a series of cushions, which were covered by a sheet. A beautiful large statue of an angel and a wooden eagle with its wings stretching upward surrounded these cushions. Within easy reach, placed by a lit candle, were a Native American drum and a large gong.

After Sonya took me out on her patio and smudged me with sage, she invoked Archangel Michael and asked for his help in this initiation. She said a prayer of protection, which created sacred space around us. She reminded me to set my ego aside and that I should realize that I am merely a channel for God's wisdom.

After all of these essential preparations for my initiation were completed, Sonya asked me to visualize a chalice on a platform in the middle of an other-dimensional temple of light. She then requested that I visualize a great ball of light in this chalice. She asked me to release no longer needed karma from my seven chakras or spiritual energy centers, into this ball of light. My eyes were closed through all of this and I could see waves of color washing across the mental screen of my closed eyes. I could actually feel a vacuum-like, sucking sensation as my chakras were emptied of accumulated debris.

When this part of what Sonya Lugo called the removal of dark crystals was completed, she told me, "We are now going to purify your past lives, by removing no longer needed karma, or accumulated compensation for your past actions, from them as well. Close your eyes and visualize a long hallway with a dot of light at the end of it, that has many doors to your past lives lining its sides." Sonya then beat her drum, while I visualized karma, which was ready to be released from my past lives being sucked out of these inter-dimensional doorways and into the still present ball of light. This was then followed by the visualization of a flood of light, which swept down the hall toward me and that washed into every doorway to a past lifetime in order to purify it. When all of this was accomplished, the purifying flood of light joined with the ball of light in the chalice. Sonya told me, "What just happened was the death of the part of you that no longer serves you." After this inter-dimensional cleansing was completed, we thanked the spiritual beings, the shamans, the spirit guides and Archangel Michael, who had been summoned to help us.

The next part of my initiation required that I stretch out, face down, on the makeshift mattress, which Sonya had put together on the living room floor. I listened carefully as Sonya explained, "Unseen spirit guides and masters will be performing psychic surgery on you in order to remove the old template, or pattern, in your spine. They will then replace it with a new one." After she had finished this explanation, Sonya began to beat the Native American drum. As I listened to the rhythmic beat of the drum, I could actually feel a pressure gradually inching up from the base of my spine toward the nape of my neck. When the pressure finally reached my neck, the drumming abruptly stopped. The other-dimensional, bloodless surgery was finished. The procedure, which had been done to shift my consciousness and to prepare me for the new millennium had been successfully completed.

As Sonya and I expressed our mutual gratitude to the unseen entities that had performed my psychic surgery, I unexpectedly connected to a synchronicity, which was obviously a verification of the necessity of the spiritual procedure that I was undergoing. From the vantage point of the chair that I had moved to after the psychic surgery, I could see a spiral pattern on the sheet that I had been stretched out on just a few minutes before. This spiral pattern was almost identical to the spiral design on the fabric of the outfit that I was wearing. What made this synchronicity even more striking was the fact that when I was stretched out stomach down on this sheet, the two spirals had touched each other. This meaningful coincidence reassured me that this was the place that I was supposed to be at this moment in my spiritual journey.

As soon as Sonya and I had caught our breaths and had taken sips of water, we went into the third and final part of my initiation into a higher cosmic consciousness. Sonya started the next part of the initiation by telling me, " Please envision a sacred temple of initiation again." She then said a prayer, which stated that my spirit was reclaiming dominion over itself. She also commanded that my spiritual helpers and healers make themselves be known. As my spirit guides came forward, I became aware that one of them was a Native American man. When I sensed the presence of this Indian, I understood that this was the guide who had helped me to see the spiritual messages in my immediate environment. After all of my spirit guides had finally presented themselves, Sonya and I expressed our heartfelt thanks for all of the lessons, which I have learned under their guidance. Then we released those who felt that it was time to go to higher realms to continue their own spiritual development. When those who were ready crossed the threshold of light and soared to higher dimensions, Sonya told me that two-thirds of my spirit guides had accepted our invitation and had left.

The final and most exciting part of my initiation came next. Sonya Lugo invoked the Lords of Light. She then invited new spirit guides and helpers to come into my life, in order to illuminate me and to assist in my ascension process. My eyes were closed while Sonya sounded the gong and performed this final segment of my initiation. At this point, something very beautiful happened. As I concentrated on the mental screen, that was formed by my closed eyelids, I could see the back of two beautiful white outstretched wings that seemed to be coming out of flowing, light blue robes. I immediately knew that this was the back of my guardian angel, welcoming my new spirit guides and helpers into my life. When I shared this unbelievably beautiful sight with Sonya, she told me, "You are very strongly connected to the angelic realm."

As my new spirit guides made themselves known, Sonya described some of them to me. "There is a tall slim priestess, wearing a long gown and a headpiece that is like a circle of light. This high priestess is from some extraterrestrial place and reminds me of a Hathor." Later research taught me that a Hathor is an ancient Egyptian Goddess of Joy, Love and Mirth. Learning this confirmed what I had previously intuited on my own, that part of my mission was to bring Universal light to the physical world and to anchor it through humor and joyful activities.

It was obvious to me that Sonya was enjoying the appearance of my new spiritual helpers. She was very enthusiastic as she told me, "Your spirit guides are certainly an eclectic group. There is quite a lot of extraterrestrial consciousness in this group. It seems to me that the guides who came from other planets are here to further the development of our planet."

After describing one more spirit guide to me as a sphinx-like entity, a human body with the face of a lion, Sonya decided to leave the rest of the spirit guide identification up to me. As soon as Sonya suggested that I identify my new mystical mentors, I saw a goddess who was a Mother of the Universe. She was heavy breasted and had very compassionate eyes, which were overflowing with love. I intuitively knew that she had come to me in order to connect me to the feminine goddess energy, which was coming to the earth plane at the beginning of the Age of Aquarius. I knew that this was happening in order to balance the preponderance of male energy that is here at this time. This Goddess of Love, nurturing cooperation, acceptance, togetherness and lack of competition would be helping me by reinforcing these virtues in me, so that I could teach them to others by example.

Sonya ended the session by instructing me to greet and to interview my new spirit guides at home by meditating and asking them to appear to me. She then added, "You are going to be a writer from now on." After a final thank-you to all of my new spirit guides and to Archangel Michael for the honor of their presence, Sonya closed my Akashic Records and I went home.

As soon as I returned home, I did what Sonya had told me to do. I did a meditation and asked my new spirit guides to appear to me. The first one that appeared on the mental screen of my closed eyes was a beautiful Asian woman with long dark hair, who was wearing a long robe with a high pleated collar. I was sure that this was Kwan Yin, the Asian Goddess of Compassion, Nurturing, Love and Healing. Meeting both Kwan Yin and the Mother of the Universe corroborated what Sonya had seen in my Akashic Records and what I intuitively knew, that my soul is part of a larger group of evolved souls and masters who function as earthly peacekeepers.

A subsequent meditation introduced me to a Native American who was wearing an eagle headdress. He was obviously a shaman or a medicine man, and I somehow knew that he was going to help me to heal others and myself. Then a Moses like figure, with white hair and a white beard, holding a staff and wearing a long robe appeared on my mental screen. He had come to help me with my spiritual evolution and ascension. Next came another spirit with a tall hat, who looked like a wizard or a magician, who had come to help me to develop my psychic powers.

My next meditation brought forth another female spirit guide. This time it was a black woman with a gold coil necklace around her long and elegant neck. This obviously Native African lady wore large golden hoop earrings, was bare-chested and wore her hair in a high woven coiffure. I instinctively knew that she was an Earth guide, whose job it was to nurture our planet and all of the souls upon it. I knew that this was a very powerful guide, because I could see beautiful ebbing waves of color on my mental screen as she left me.

I was really beginning to enjoy meeting this eclectic group of otherworldly helpers and I looked forward to the meditations that brought them to me. In my very next meditation I met an Incan or Mayan man with long straight black hair, a serape and a bowler type hat. He introduced himself to me as a South American from Chile or Peru. I thought that he might have once lived in Machu Pichu, a spiritual spot in Peru that I long to visit someday. It was clear to me that he had come to me to bring some of the magic and spirituality of this sacred spot in the Andes into my life.

Meeting so many of my fascinating new spirit guides was an exhilarating experience. Unfortunately, I had to stop my meditations in order to pack for our upcoming trip to northern Europe. I went to bed early on the night before we were scheduled to leave on our European vacation. Sleep eluded me. As I lay tossing and turning on my bed, not feeling very well and wondering why, one of my newly acquired spirit helpers came to my rescue. The little Native American with the eagle headdress came floating into my mind's eye. This helpful little shaman communicated to me telepathically that there was a certain food that I had to give up if I wanted to feel better. I expressed my gratitude for his swift response to my distress and fell asleep in a state of utter amazement. I couldn't believe that my new guides were on the job already.

The following morning, we boarded a jet plane at Fort Lauderdale Airport and took off for Europe. When we reached Prague in the Czech Republic, we met out local guide and started on a walking tour of this beautiful city. As we walked across a pedestrian bridge and just before we reached the other side, I was stopped dead in my tracks by something that seized my attention and would not let it go. Rising up from the railing of this bridge was a huge metal crucifix with a halo of Hebrew letters surrounding the hanging body of Christ. I asked Marvin to take a picture of this singular work of art because it seemed to be stirring up emotions and memories from deep within my being. When we returned to our hotel that evening, the very first thing that I did was to enter this unique experience into my Lucid Notebook. When we finally determined that the halo of Hebrew letters translated to "Holy, Holy, Holy, Army of God," I intuitively knew that there was a message for me in this distinctive work of art. It would not be too long before I realized what this message was.

Since I did not immediately understand what the message in this singular experience on the bridge was, I did not ask the Universe for a corroborating synchronicity. But a synchronicity that I did not ask for came in anyway, getting my right brain ready for some more spiritual sleuthing. After our walking tour of Prague, we ate lunch and then shopped. Our shopping excursion brought us into a crystal shop where I purchased a beautiful crystal pyramid within a pyramid, to add to my growing collection at home. After we ate dinner at our hotel, we went to a Czech folklore show. When we arrived at the hotel where this show was being held, my mouth dropped open. Of all of the hotels in this cosmopolitan metropolis, the one that our tour bus took us to was the Pyramid Hotel. The appearance of two totally unrelated pyramids in the space of a few hours became the meaningful coincidence that put me on the alert. This dramatic synchronicity gave me a familiar feeling of having something on the tip of my tongue that I just couldn't spit out. The Universe was trying to tell me something. What was it?

My mystical mentors continued to prod me when we reached Moscow. Marvin and I signed up for what turned out to be a one ring, one tent Russian Circus. Perhaps it was the tent, so much like a pyramid that was pointing toward the realm of God that caused what happened next. As I watched the Russian families, so much like our own, enjoying the acrobats, dancers, clowns and animal acts, I began to experience a feeling of deep unconditional love for all of humanity. This feeling was so intense that a waterfall of tears cascaded down from my eyes and landed all over my cheeks. This overwhelming emotion felt very much like the feeling that I had experienced during my first Reiki healing under a pyramid. This experience was so powerful that it sent me reeling. As I slowly recovered from its impact, I recognized that the mystical moment that I had just experienced was somehow related to the crucifix with the halo of Hebrew letters that I had seen in Prague just a few days prior to this.

When we returned to our hotel after attending the Moscow Circus, I opened my Lucid Notebook and did the best possible job that I could of putting the epiphany that I had just undergone into words. I felt a compulsion to open one of the spiritual lesson books to resume where I had left off the night before. After reading a few pages, I realized why I had felt compelled to read this particular section of this book. It explained exactly how I had gotten to the point of personal spiritual illumination that I found myself in at this particular time. The more I read, the stronger my understanding was of how and why this illumination had occurred. I found out that the meditations and the conscious breathing exercises that I had been doing over the past few years had caused my kundalini, or spiritual energy, which was coiled at the base of my spine, to rise and to travel upward toward my brain. At the same time that this was happening, the humanitarian love that I was feeling, the acts of service to humanity that I was involved in, and my devotion to esoteric and mystical studies and meditation, stimulated the secretion of a spiritual oil in my body.

The book went on to explain that this sacred oil activated both the pineal and the pituitary glands in my brain, which stimulated the excretion of a liquid called the brain dew. The subsequent union of the spiritual oil with the brain dew illuminated my consciousness, raised my vibrations and intensified my auric emanations. As I read this, I recognized that this entire process was responsible for opening my third eye, the chakra of illumination, in the middle of my forehead. All of the epiphanies and revelations about my immortal soul's sacred journey through time and its mission on this planet came in at this time. The disclosures of the symbols and signs by which my soul could be identified and by which I could know it, came in at this time as well. It became quite clear to me that all of this had happened because I had connected to my Higher Self and to my spirit guides in the more etheric dimensions. I had also connected to my Akashic Records. These connections had brought me information that I could never have obtained through my five physical senses. As I wrote all of this in my Lucid Notebook, a feeling of exhilaration and completion ran up and down my spine. More pieces of my sacred puzzle were falling into place and the total picture of my immortal soul was beginning to reveal itself to me.

My Higher Self or my mystical mentors, good teachers that they are, sent me a dream the next day that verified all of the insights about how I had attained the spiritual illumination that I had had the night before. About an hour after we had boarded our tour bus and taken off on the next part of our trip, I fell asleep and started to dream. I dreamt that the bus was going straight up. A few minutes later, when I awoke and regained my bearings, I realized what this dream was all about. I intuitively knew that my Higher Self had communicated with me in this dream. It had reinforced my knowledge that I was in a state of spiritual ascension. It was also congratulating me on finally discovering why and how my spiritual ascension and illumination had come about.

The final and the most spiritually illuminating day of our tour was spent in Frankfort, Germany right before we took off on our flight back to the United States. I still do not know what triggered the insights that came tumbling into my consciousness at this time. Perhaps it was merely being in Germany, where I had been born in my incarnation as Empress Elisabeth and where I had made a conscious decision to send out unconditional love, that brought this material into my awareness. Whatever the reason, all of the insights, disclosures and messages that had surfaced to the conscious part of my mind during the last few years finally made sense to me.

From out of nowhere came the insight, the deep inner knowing, that my soul came into the body of a Jewish American woman in 1938, as an Emissary of Light, with the mission of bringing and anchoring spiritual light during one of the most horrendous times in Jewish history. As I digested this insight, it also became quite clear to me that what

Sonya Lugo saw when she opened my Akashic Records was most definitely true. I was brought to the lucid awareness that my soul really did leave my body while I slept, and traveled with other evolved souls and masters to war torn Europe during World War II. We did this in order to bring whatever spiritual light we could into a spiritually black abyss. This insight helped me to understand why, although I was quite young during World War II, I had such vivid nightmares of synagogues being destroyed by leaping flames. I also now understood the message in the crucifix surrounded by Hebrew letters that I had been transfixed by in Prague. The Hebrew letters spelling out, "Holy, Holy, Holy, Army of God," referred to the group of peace seeking souls and masters that my soul was with when it left my body during sleep. At this point, another startling intuition came coursing across my consciousness. I had a powerful recognition of the fact that my soul had actually seen this spiritual work of art on a bridge in Prague, when it had traveled to Europe during World War II.

A subsequent flood of memories verified this impressive insight. The synchronicity of Marvin and I both having had near death experiences during October 1941, right in the middle of the Holocaust, was now seen as a clue to this important soul mission. Another clue to my soul's part in a spiritual peace-seeking mission during World War II had come to me during our last trip to Israel in 1995. I now understood why Marvin and I had selected a day at random, which turned out to be Holocaust Memorial Day, for a trip to Safed, one of the holiest spots in Israel. The last memory that validated my insight about my soul's mission during the holocaust was from the movie, *Contact*, the movie in which my father's spirit came through to me. In this movie, the first communication from space to Earth, was Hitler's speech during the 1936 Olympics in Germany. I was overjoyed that I had finally reached a point of enlightenment and illumination that had connected me to an understanding of personal spiritual information that had previously been but a whisper in the back of my mind.

These new insights clarified another significant previous insight. I was now even more sure than ever that my soul, along with the rest of the evolved group that it was part of, had definitely been influential in convincing Anwar Sadat to sign a peace treaty with Israel on March 26, 1979. As my memories stretched back to the time that the art exhibit that commemorated this auspicious event mesmerized me, I was suddenly filled with another inner knowing. I was completely convinced that the number 26, the holiest number in the Kabbalah, was not just my most powerful spiritual symbol. I now knew that this sacred number was also the emblem of the entire group of spiritual souls and masters, the group that my soul travels with, and which I call the Emissaries of Light.

As I entered these new insights into my Lucid Notebook, I was filled with a sensation of deep reverence. I was also filled with a gratitude that came from the knowledge that my spiritual evolution had progressed enough to allow my Higher Self to release this sacred information into my conscious mind. But, skeptic that I am, I still asked my mystical mentors for a confirmation of these insights, preferably in the form of a synchronicity.

The meaningful coincidence, which I asked for came the very next day. When I awoke the following morning, I realized that it was cooler than the day before. This change in temperature made me decide to wear my turquoise pants, which were a little heavier than the other clothing that I had brought with me on this trip. The jacket that went with these pants was also turquoise and was embellished with golden studs. After breakfast, we boarded our tour bus and took off for Frankfort. The first sightseeing stop on our itinerary was the San Souci Palace, located between Berlin and Frankfort. Eager to stretch our legs, we all piled off the bus and started to walk up the hill that led us to the palace gardens. About five minutes after I left the bus, I stopped in my tracks. What I saw before my eyes was the confirmation that I had requested from my mystical mentors the night before. The palace grounds were covered with decorative metal work and gazebos, which were not only exactly the same color as my pants outfit, but were also adorned with golden studs. The similarity was so dramatic that other tourists remarked as they passed by and some even laughingly took my photograph in front of the matching backdrop. I chuckled to myself as I made a mental note to add this remarkable confirmation to my Lucid Notebook. As usual, my heavenly helpers had not disappointed me. The verification that my insights were true had come in as requested on the wings of a double S, another one my spiritual symbols.

On the flight back to the United States I spent a considerable amount of time digesting and assimilating the important insights that I had connected to on our trip. I was finally coming face to face with my immortal soul and learning more about its history and sacred meaning. There was no turning back. I sat in my seat in space, hurtling toward the resumption of my present life, and vowed to myself that I would continue to delve beneath my dense suit of flesh, in an attempt to have as full a knowledge as possible of the sacred being within.

LESSONS FROM CHAPTER XI

* One of the first things that you can do in order to reach enlightenment, or awareness of your soul, is to start to read books on spirituality and metaphysics. Attending seminars and taking classes in these subjects will also help.

* Starting a psychic journal and recording any paranormal experiences, dreams, insights and intuitions will also help. When you put these things in writing, your Higher Self and your spirit guides know that you are serious and will send you more.

* Start a collection of spiritual objects such as angels, or pyramids, or crystals. When you start such a collection your heavenly helpers see that you are a serious seeker of spiritual enlightenment.

✻ One of the most important things that you can do in order to gain personal spiritual enlightenment is to meditate. When we meditate, we relax our bodies and quiet our minds. As we clear away the noise and the distractions that are constantly going on in our minds, it is easier for us to hear communications from our Higher Selves and our mystical mentors.

✻ Meditation puts us in an alpha state and allows our souls to talk to us. In order to meditate, sit in a comfortable chair, close your eyes and begin to inhale and exhale slowly and deeply. As soon as your breathing slips into a slow and steady rhythm, try to concentrate all of your thoughts on one idea. Doing this will help you to slip into an alpha state, shut out the outside world and to connect your awareness to your Higher Self, that part of your spirit that remained behind in the non-physical dimension.

✻ Another path to spiritual enlightenment is the path of service to others. This service can be in the form of fund-raising, monetary charity, volunteerism or simple acts of random kindness.

✻ We speed our way to soul enlightenment when we send positive energy to others and out into the Universe. The most powerful form of positive energy that we can send out is unconditional love. Forgiveness is another powerful form of positive energy.

✻ When you express gratitude for your blessings, whether spiritual or material, you also help to propel yourself up the path toward soul enlightenment. God, your Higher Self and the Universe respond well to the expression of gratitude. Try making a mental list everyday of what you are grateful for. Keeping a gratitude journal helps too.

CHAPTER XII

The Wizard Within

*The insults of past lifetimes adhere to our etheric bodies
and can affect us in our present lifetimes.*

A powerful mystical message was waiting for me on our
return to the United States from our northern
European trip. As I sifted through the pile of accumulated
mail that our letter carrier had dropped off at our house, I
discovered that the state of Florida had sent me a new
license plate for my car. At first I was unaware of the fact
that there was a message in the six digits on this plate.
Marvin picked up the first part of this obvious communication from another dimension, by telling me that my ubiquitous spiritual number, twenty-six, was contained within
these digits in the form of XX, the Roman equivalent of
twenty, and the number 6. This observation alerted me to
the fact that there actually was a message for me in this
license plate. Before the week was over, I had deciphered
part of the message. Interspersed between the XX and the 6
were three letters, AOL. This discovery set off an alarm bell
in my head. As far as I was concerned AOL was synonymous
with Web as a symbol for the Internet, the most powerful
technical connection between people in the world today. I
took this message in a license plate as seriously as I had
taken the message *WEB* that had come to me through my
automatic writing. These six digits made it clear to me that
I was destined to use the Internet to share the spiritual wisdom that I was connecting to with the entire planet.

Sonya Lugo called shortly after we had settled back into
our normal routine, to tell me that she was starting a class

in Tarot card reading. She suggested that I take this course in order to strengthen my already sharp psychic abilities. Since I knew that strengthening my intuitive capacities would help me to further connect to my soul, I followed her suggestion and signed up for this class. My psychic and spiritual progress was uppermost in my mind and I welcomed any means that could foster this progress.

About a week before the first session of this highly anticipated course, I went to a metaphysical shop and purchased what Sonya had recommended, a Voyager Tarot deck. As soon as I returned home with my new purchase, I opened the box and began to study the rich imagery on each card in the deck. When I reached the card called the Star, which had a picture of Kwan Yin, the Asian Goddess of Love, Nurturing and Mercy on it, I stopped going through the cards. Kwan Yin was portrayed on this card as a statue of a beautiful Asian woman dressed in robes, accented by a pleated collar that framed her face. This representation was the exact duplicate of how Kwan Yin had presented herself to me after my initiation, when I asked to meet my new spirit guides. The synchronicity of this occurrence was intensified when I opened to the page in the Tarot book that explained the significance of this card. Everything about this card and its description seemed to refer to me. The number on the Star-Kwan Yin card was 17, which adds up to 8 in numerology and equates to my birth number and to the sum of 2 and 6, my two mystical guiding numbers. These meaningful coincidences alerted me to the fact that I had to take the message within the explanation of this card very seriously. This message told me to shine like a star. I remembered that during my initiation, Sonya had told me that I was shining like a star. I was told to receive inspiration from the heavens and then to become a guiding light to others, a way-shower. Finally, I was told to radiate my light into the darkness to nourish and nurture the dry, barren and needy. I entered this intuitively accessed message into my Lucid Notebook and then thanked my mystical mentors and God for this cosmic confirmation that I was truly on the right path.

Sonya's Pathway of the Metaphysician classes started a few days after our first Tarot class. Our teacher explained to us that we would be doing exercises that would help us to release psychic debris, which had accumulated over many lifetimes and which was interfering with our psychic and spiritual development. We were assured that when this debris was removed, we would all become more psychic and would also become attuned to higher spiritual vibrations. I was thrilled to be in a situation that would help me to detoxify inner dimensionally. Even Sonya's warning that this purification process could cause dizziness, headaches and nausea could not separate me from my desire to have this experience. I intuitively knew that this spiritual cleansing was necessary so that I could release the mystical poisons that had stuck to me through many incarnations. My Higher Self was telling me that this painful procedure would ultimately help to bring me greater knowledge of my soul and its spiritual essence.

The very first exercise that we experienced was very similar to my initiation experience with Sonya. We cleared out old, unneeded karma from our past lives. Then we were instructed to visualize our souls stepping out of our bodies and scanning for holes in our auras, the spiritual energy fields emanating from our suits of flesh. It was explained that these holes were created by physical, emotional, and mental trauma in our present and past lives. The first auric hole, which I sensed rather than saw, was in the middle of my back. As soon as I became aware of this hole in my aura, my intuition told me that it had been created during my past lifetime as a young boy in Ireland, who tended to the horses and wagons of the travelers who stayed at his parent's roadside inn. As soon as I connected to the reason for this insult in my aura, a scene of myself as this young boy being hit by a runaway wagon flashed before my eyes. The next auric hole, which caught my attention, was located in my chest, between my breasts. As soon as my awareness centered on this gaping hole, I intuitively connected this insult to my assassination by dagger in my past lifetime as Empress Elisabeth of Austria.

The last auric hole that I pointed to was on my lower left side. Since I had absolutely no idea of what had caused this insult to my aura I sat in silence, with a look of what must have been consternation on my face. Sonya immediately dispelled my confusion by telling me that I was pointing to my left ovary. She enlightened me by adding that I was pregnant in a past lifetime and, as a form of torture, my stomach was cut open and the baby was removed. A series of light bulbs were turned on in my head as Sonya spoke. The blinding light that this newly acquired knowledge had produced in my conscious mind brought me to a lucid understanding of how this terrible past life trauma had influenced my present incarnation. I now understood, with utmost clarity, why I have had three miscarriages, a fertility problem, and frequent hemorrhaging and menstrual irregularity in my present lifetime. I added this startling revelation to the entries in my Lucid Notebook. This entry was followed by a description of how excited I became when I recognized how strong the impact of a past life could be on one's present lifetime.

After we had sealed up all of our auric holes with divine fire, Sonya made it quite clear to us that the work that we were doing was detoxifying us spiritually and that this purification would open interdimensional doorways. These new openings between realities would help us to become more intuitive and to communicate more easily with the invisible spiritual dimension where we all abide between lives.

Less than a week after this class, Sonya's words became reality. An unexpected storm, Hurricane Irene, came howling down upon us and knocked out our electric power. When night fell, our house was filled with glowing candles breaking the complete darkness of a total power outage. The fierce sounds of the hurricane and my fear of all of the untended candles kept me from the sweet surrender of peaceful sleep. I quietly crept out of bed and walked into the front bedroom to try to see what the powerful hurricane was doing to our street. As soon as I passed the threshold of our guestroom, I was hit by a strong odor that reminded me of what my father smelled like when he came home from the butcher shop where he handled raw meat. This assault on my nostrils sent me scurrying back to my bedroom with the certain knowledge that my father's spirit had come to visit us in order to protect us from the violent storm. Within minutes of getting back into bed, I was up and around again. My curiosity had overcome my fear. I walked into the kitchen to get a drink of water. As I stood, glass in hand, I looked down toward our guestroom. For the very first time since his death, I could see the outline of my father's spirit body. As I again fled back to the safety of my bed and closed my eyes, my last thought before I fell asleep was that Sonya was right. My soul was being relieved of the layers of interference, which kept it from connecting to the other side. I could almost see my Higher Self breathing a sigh of relief as I finally drifted off into the oblivion of restful sleep.

When the morning finally came, the hurricane had stopped releasing its wrath upon us. Marvin and I walked outside to see if any damage had been done to our property. As we walked around, we realized that ours was the only house on the block that had not been touched by Hurricane Irene's fury. Large trees had been toppled like bowling pins up and down the street, while only a small branch lay on our back lawn. As I glanced at the damage that the storm had done on our street and the pre-hurricane wholeness of our property, I recognized what my father's spirit had accomplished while we slept. I thanked my father and God for this little miracle and for the larger miracle of being able to see my father's spirit.

As I entered all of this into my Lucid Notebook, I received an enlightening insight. It dawned on me that hurricanes were one of my important spiritual symbols. I was born right before a hurricane in 1938. Then in 1979, which adds up to twenty-six, a hurricane ushered in a time of great spiritual cleansing and initiation. As I added this insight into my journal, I chuckled to myself when I realized that hurricane even has a double letter in it, another one of my spiritual symbols.

Additional proof that clearing away psychic debris could raise ones spiritual vibrations came within days of my Hurricane Irene experience. This outstanding example of how my spiritual vibrations were speeding up occurred while I was in the bathtub, soaking in one of the salt baths that Sonya had recommended as a means of further purging psychic debris. As I luxuriated in this therapeutic bath, a softly glowing candle helped me to enter a peaceful meditative state. When I finally felt that I was deep enough within myself, I began saying healing prayers and sending love to those who needed it. When I opened my eyes after about ten or fifteen minutes of pumping out love from my heart chakra, I was startled by the observation that the clear glass shower stall right in front of the bathtub had turned bright green. As I stared at this miraculous apparition, I swiftly became aware that this green hue was a physical representation of all of the love that had just left my heart chakra to be sent out to those in need of it. I lay silent in the tub for several minutes as I digested and assimilated the important ramifications of this supernatural occurrence. As the green on the shower stall gradually faded out and the glass returned to its original colorless condition, I was struck by the recognition that we are all, indeed, very powerful spiritual beings and that all of our souls have wondrous and magical capabilities.

Green, which is in the middle of the rainbow and is the color of our middle, or heart, chakra made me think of my intuited position in the middle, as a connector, contact or communicator. Was the magical appearance of the color green whenever I said my healing prayers and sent love to those in need, a reminder of my soul's sacred mission as a link between Universal Spiritual Energy and information and the physical dimension? When I gave this question some thought I recognized that this was definitely one of the messages inherent in this mystically colorful apparition. My Higher Self and my mystical mentors were also reminding me that green is the true color of love and that love is always in the middle. It is the glue that holds everything in the

Universe together. Before I climbed out of the tub and left my metaphysical musings behind me, I had the most beautiful insight that I have ever had. I saw with cosmic clarity that love spelled backward is *evol*, which is the beginning of the word evolution. Love helps us to evolve.

I started to teach Metaphysics and Parapsychology in our community's clubhouse three weeks after my experiences during Hurricane Irene. The eighty-two people in my class received my story of how my father's spirit had come to protect us during the hurricane with interest and excitement. This interest increased when I shared with them that I had seen the outline of my father's spirit for the very first time during the night of the hurricane. When I returned home from teaching this class and opened the local newspaper to the puzzle section, I was more than astounded to come face to face with my father's confirmation that he had actually been with me on the night of the storm. The theme of the Wonderword puzzle was *Schweitzer*, my father's last name and my maiden name. My heavenly helpers were at it again. A spiritual scribe had reached down from the heavens and had left me a written sign that I was on the right spiritual path and that I should continue on my sacred itinerary.

Very shortly after I started teaching Metaphysics and Parapsychology, I took the second section of Sonya's Pathways of the Metaphysician course. Sonya taught us how to open up our Akashic Records, which are very much like our own personal spiritual autobiographies. As soon as my soul's records through time and space were opened up, I saw myself on top of a hill by a large sonar dish, which was pointed at the sky. When I reported this to the group, I added that this reminded me of Jodie Foster's role in the movie *Contact*. Sonya's reaction to this was that this might be a future life progression or the possibility that I might be sonar astronomer in a parallel life, one that I was doing at the same time that I was experiencing my present incarnation as Barbara Yudell. I also saw myself zooming into space and back. I was a volunteer from another galaxy who was in a sort of Cosmic Peace Corps, here to help with the evolution of the planet Earth. This picture dissolved into a picture of me as a Native American woman and then to a lifetime as a cavewoman who was drawing simple pictures on the wall of a cave. Simultaneous with the appearance of myself as a cavewoman came the deep inner knowledge that I was drawing these pictures in order to show others that there was more to life than just the physical.

After sharing what I had just accessed about two of my past lives with the rest of the group, I followed Sonya's suggestion that I go inside of myself again while visualizing myself holding the history book of my soul tightly against my chest. I was astounded by the results that I achieved. My entire being was flooded with a sparkling ethereal white light that brought the words love, joy, peace and laughter in with it. The light brought a reinforcement of the awareness that I am a connector, one who shares with others the knowledge she has gathered about spirituality and how our earthly lives can be improved. When I finally came back to waking reality and told Sonya what had come in she confirmed what I had just accessed and called me a transmitter.

So much startling information about my soul's history and purpose was flooding in at this time that I found myself slightly off balance. The key words that kept coming up when I sought information about my immortal self were middle, contact, connector, communicator and transmitter. All of this helped me to recognize that my mystical mentors and my Higher Self had been trying to communicate this important part of my soul's purpose to me for a very long time. This knowledge had come through when my SOUL group had done automatic writing and the word *WEB* had come up. Then there was the message from my father in the movie *Contact* and finally the AOL XX6 in my new license plate. Then the light that I had just encountered when I went deep inside of myself actually came out and told me that I was a connector, one whose most important mission in life was to be a communicating link between heaven and Earth. Finally, Sonya had confirmed all of this by calling me a transmitter. As if all of this was not enough to finally make me see what I could not see for so long, another corroboration of the veracity of this important insight came the very next day. I turned on my television set and before I could even use the remote control to channel surf, a character in the show that I had randomly tuned in to said the word Schweitzer, my maiden name and, therefore my dead father's surname. The message came in loud and clear because experience had taught me that this name was one of the ways in which my father communicated with me. He was obviously telling me that everything that I had just learned about my soul's most significant purpose was indeed true. I was a communicator, a middle link connecting others to information, spiritual or otherwise, which could be instrumental in improving their lives.

A few days after this extremely enlightening class, I had a very empowering dream where I found myself trapped in something that looked very much like a submarine. My solitary struggle did absolutely nothing to release me from this restrictive atmosphere. It took a powerful group effort to finally help me to escape and to reach the light of day. As soon as I awoke and put a description of this dream into my Lucid Notebook, the message that it brought me virtually jumped out at me. This dream was showing me that the group exercises in Sonya's classes were helping me to connect to an understanding of who I really am under my dense suit of flesh. As soon as this insight came to me, I offered a prayer of gratitude to God and to the Universe for bringing me the help that I needed in order to continue my voyage into my personal spiritual unknown.

During Sonya's next class, after creating sacred space and doing a healing meditation, Sonya instructed us to open our Akashic Records again. Since I was still suffering from menopausal hot flashes, I wasn't surprised when I had one of these unwelcome reactions right before we were instructed to go inside of ourselves, in order to read what was in our autobiographical soul records. There was something different about this particular hot flash. It seemed to be stronger than what I usually experience during the day. The timing and the severity of this hot sensation convinced me that I had better investigate this in order to see if there was some past life connection to the stubbornness of my menopausal symptoms.

My intuition was right. As soon as I closed my eyes, I saw myself about to be burned at the stake in ancient Greece for practicing and studying the spiritual and the metaphysical, the same things that I am studying and writing about in my present lifetime. The image of my fiery demise in this past lifetime was so clear that I could see exactly what I was wearing and what the surrounding environment looked like. I told the group, "I am wearing a long white Grecian dress, which is belted at the waist with a gold rope. The platform that I am standing on and where the fire is soon to be ignited is framed by a white marble columned building." The past life connection to what I was suffering in my present lifetime was strengthened in my mind by the second, even stronger hot flash that greeted me as soon as I came out of my trance. When I shared this unusual occurrence with the rest of the class, the response that came back to me was that I probably have lived more than one lifetime in which I was burned to death at the stake. This feedback helped me to understand why I had come to the study of esoteric spirituality later in life. It was possible that the fear that I would again be burned at the stake if I studied spirituality might have functioned as a deterrent to an earlier exploration of this field.

My curiosity had been so piqued by what I had discovered in class, that I decided to do another meditation as soon as I returned home. When I went inside of myself at this time and opened up my Akashic Records, I found myself in another lifetime, right before I was to undergo a fiery death. I saw myself as a gypsy woman who was also going to be burned at the stake for practicing the mysteries. I was a spiritual healer. A baby who I had attempted to heal had died, and I was being blamed for this tragedy. My Pathways of the Metaphysician class was right. I had been burned at the stake in more than one lifetime. Were there any other lifetimes in which I met a fiery death? Only time would tell.

As I continued to delve into my past lives in order to understand my immortal soul's journey and purpose, I had another very strange dream. I dreamed that all of my jewelry was stolen, except for a diamond pendant that I frequently wear around my neck. The meaning of this dream eluded me for a long time. Then one day I recognized that this diamond pendant was worn at my throat chakra and that this was the spiritual energy center for communication. When this new understanding entered my consciousness, I was struck by the fact that my Higher Self considered my soul's mission as a communicator so important that it had chosen to remind me of this in a dream. When I entered a description of this dream into my Lucid Notebook I made a special note that this was probably one of the most important missions that my soul had contracted to work at when it came back into physical form.

Three days later a dream with another message of validation came to me. This dream was so real that I actually felt that I was awake. In this nighttime vision, somebody's body was being burned at a funeral. The intensity of the flames and the acrid odor of burning flesh awakened me. My immediate reaction to this dream was that this was a confirmation that I had been burned at the stake during past incarnations. My Higher Self was certainly on a roll. It was depositing past life information and confirmations of my spiritual insights into my conscious mind at an increasingly accelerated rate.

It continued to do so at a past life regression seminar that I had invited my metaphysics class to a few days later. As soon as the past life regression videotape started, I drifted backwards in time until I stopped in the Ireland of 1795. I saw myself in this lifetime, as I had once or twice before, as a young boy with long blonde hair that was tied back in a ponytail. I spent most of my time taking care of the horses and wagons that belonged to the guests who were staying in my parents' roadside inn. Most of my recreational time was spent out of doors too, because of my intense love of animals and of nature. Before the past life regression videotape had come to a conclusion I saw myself being killed at an early age, when a runaway wagon slammed into my back. My son, Jay, who was my sister in this lifetime, died with me. After my class left, I added this vivid past life regression into my Lucid Notebook. I concluded this entry by speculating about its possible connection to a trip that Marvin and I were planning on taking to the British Isles and Ireland within a few months. This speculation was followed by the postscript that "only time would tell." If I had learned anything on this fascinating spiritual journey that I felt so blessed to be on, I had learned that you couldn't rush the progression of spiritual enlightenment and evolution.

The floodgates that separated my subconscious mind from my conscious mind lifted and a past life regression that was a repeat of one that I had recently had came pouring into my conscious mind during one of Gloria's metaphysics classes. When Gloria led us in a meditation that opened up our Akashic Records, I saw myself again as a woman, a gypsy soothsayer and spiritual healer. Within seconds of this repeat glimpse of myself in this long ago lifetime, I again learned that a baby that I had been trying to help with hands on healing had died and that I had been blamed for it. I could actually feel the fear as I was tied up to a stake and a fire was lit around me. Having this regression twice in the space of just a few days made me pay attention. I had learned that this happened when your Higher Self felt that there was an important message for you in that particular lifetime. When I returned home and added this past life regression in to my Lucid Notebook, its message hit me loud and clear. My Higher Self was trying to tell me that times had changed and that I no longer had to fear retribution for studying and for exploring my more mystical affinities and abilities.

My spiritual journey was becoming more and more exciting. Finding out where my soul had been in past lifetimes was broadening my understanding of who I really was under my dense suit of flesh. The more that I learned, the more I wanted to know. My desire for personal spiritual knowledge was becoming almost insatiable. This strong need for enlightenment led me to another individual session with Sonya.

As soon as Sonya said her prayers and helped me to reach a hypnotic state, the doors to another lifetime opened up. I found myself running across a lush meadow. Before long I stopped short. I found myself at the edge of a cliff. When I looked down, I realized that I was looking into a volcano. Fear was bubbling around in my stomach like the hot, molten lava that I saw beneath me. Then I stepped outside of my body and saw myself as I stood and stared down at the fiery inferno inside of the volcano. I was a beautiful young Hawaiian maiden who was about to be thrown into this flaming pit by a group of fierce looking Hawaiian men, a chief and his cohorts. These men were wearing official looking robes and headdresses and seemed to be very angry with me. They were ready to sacrifice me to an equally angry Pele, the Goddess of the Volcano. As I watched this terrifying scene, I immediately understood that I had been chosen to be a priestess and that this meant that I was supposed to remain celibate. But since I was young and hot blooded, I had followed some of the other women down to the beach and had had sex with the light skinned sailors who had arrived on our island. I was obviously pregnant, which was proof positive to these powerful Hawaiian men that I had broken a very strong taboo and had to be sacrificed in order to appease Pele.

As I felt myself hovering over the volcano, fearfully waiting to be thrown in, I could hear Sonya's voice in the distance, telling me that we were going to reframe what had happened to me in this lifetime and, therefore, change it inner-dimensionally. She explained that this would help me to release the psychic interference that this traumatic past life had produced within me. When she told me to persuade the hostile group of men not to throw me into the volcano, I made a sincere attempt to do just that. This did not work. There was a great deal of terror in my voice when I told

Sonya that this powerful Hawaiian group would not listen to me. They had their minds set on throwing me into the volcano, and that was that. Sonya did not like this news. She told me that we would create a miracle together. She told me that somehow I would be saved from this fiery death. As she was saying these reassuring words, a beautiful large white bird came swooping down from the sky and flew directly under me as I was being thrown into the volcano. I miraculously landed on its huge back and flew with it to a nearby beach, where it gently deposited me on the sand. As soon as I found myself safely on the ground, I took off my clothes and went directly into the ocean in order to purify myself.

Sonya told me that I was now a priestess. She then instructed me to put on my ceremonial robes. When this was accomplished, she helped me to get back to the men who had wanted to sacrifice me to Pele. This powerful group that had almost killed me, actually bowed down in respect as I walked up to them. The chief apologized for the group. I was told that they were wrong. Pele did not want a sacrifice. Sonya then suggested that I shift the scene to the birth of my baby. Doing this brought me the awareness that this baby was spiritual and wise and would help me to spread goodness and wisdom. The reframing had been accomplished. Sonya had helped me to create an innerdimensional miracle. I was sure that this miraculous experience would help to heal some of the trauma that my soul had experienced in this long ago Hawaiian lifetime. I was sure that this would eliminate some of the interference that was holding me back from truly knowing my sacred self.

At this point, Sonya asked me to open the door to another past lifetime. The door that I chose was blue. When I opened it I found myself on the shore of a very large lake. I was a Native American woman. A question came into my mind. Had I returned to my lifetime as Blue Rose? I received an immediate response. The answer was no. This was another Native American lifetime, a lifetime that I lived a few hundred years after my lifetime as Blue Rose.

As I surveyed the scene, I saw that I was wearing a deer-skin dress and moccasins. There was a necklace of colorful stones around my neck and in the long black braids that tumbled down my back. I had a papoose on my back and was drawing pictures in the sand. I seemed to be preoccupied, and wasn't paying attention to what was going on around me. While I was daydreaming, a canoe filled with ferocious looking braves from another tribe landed on the shore and killed my baby and me. They slit my throat and took my scalp. As I died, a feeling of remorse and guilt came over me. I tortured myself with the thought that if I had only been paying attention to what was going on around me, I could possibly have run back to my village to warn my tribe about the enemy tribe that had come to annihilate them.

Sonya stepped in at this point and asked me to rethink this remorse and guilt. When I followed these instructions I understood that it would not have done any good to warn the tribe about these attacking marauders. Our braves were out on a hunting trip and there was no one left in the village to protect it. I also recognized that the elders of the tribe had brought on this terrible tragedy. We were a tribe that moved frequently. The area where we now lived was beautiful, fertile and lush, but we had put down our roots before we had made sure that this land was available for settlement. We were finding out the hard way that this land belonged to another, not very friendly, tribe.

When I had finished describing this sadly shortened lifetime that I saw before me, Sonya told me that she was going to create another miracle and, therefore, remove the trauma from this lifetime. She stepped into my past incarnation and convinced the braves that there was no reason to be hostile and to kill my baby, my tribe, and me. She told them that there was more than enough land for all of us and that we could all live in peace and harmony. She went on to convince them to be more loving and sharing and to welcome us into an extended Native American family. I sat with my eyes closed, marveling at the way in which Sonya was making these formerly ferocious braves into loving and docile men. I followed Sonya's lead and visualized a much more peaceful and loving scene. When I had accomplished this, I saw that these braves had not killed my baby and me. I followed them as they walked into my village and sat down around the ceremonial fire burning in the middle of the circle of teepees. After my baby and I had settled down beside them, we were all served food and had a marvelous time, eating, talking and laughing. It was all very serene and spiritual. Sonya had helped these former killers to understand that we are all connected and that when we hurt others we actually hurt ourselves. Sonya had miraculously helped me to create heaven on Earth. I could feel my soul breathing a sigh of relief, as more interfering trauma from a past lifetime was removed.

More information about my soul's spiritual itinerary came in at Sonya's very next class. The only difference was that this time I found out where my soul was heading in the future. My metaphysical reading and classes had brought me the understanding that accessing a future life was possible because in the non-physical dimension everything happens at the same time. Despite this knowledge, I still seriously doubted that I would be able to access a future incarnation. I was wrong. When I closed my eyes and rode my power animal, the giraffe, right through a luminous star in a visualized nighttime sky, I found myself, to my surprised delight, smack in the middle of a future life. I saw myself as a female sonar astronomer, working as an administrator for a company that has already contacted other civilizations in the Universe. The name of the company that I work for is *E.T.C*, or Extraterrestrial Communications. My job entails coordinating the communications that are coming in from outer space. I am married to a man who works for the same company and I have one child and one dog.

As soon as I came out of the meditative state that had allowed me to access this future life, a tremendously important insight hit me smack between the eyes. The message that my father had sent me via Jodie Foster in the movie *Contact* had another totally different meaning. I now saw, with total clarity that my father's spirit wanted me to know that not only was I a communicator in my present lifetime, but also that communication was a theme that I would carry over into my future incarnations. Wasn't the task of picking up, deciphering and disseminating radio transmissions from outer space the epitome of communication?

My excitement at actually having accessed a future lifetime was intensified when we went inside once again and programmed our subconscious minds to take us to yet another future lifetime. This time I found myself in a futuristic city where people traveled in flying vehicles rather than the land transportation that I have become accustomed to in my present lifetime. As I looked around this city of strangely shaped buildings and heliports, I noticed that every street corner was equipped with a large television screen that enabled pedestrians to get important spiritual and mundane information. The commentator on these screens was enthusiastically sharing important insights and information with several people gathered on the street in front of these gigantic television monitors. As soon as I brought my attention to what the commentator was sharing with the crowd, I recognized that the woman on the television screen was I, in a future lifetime. This discovery startled me for an instant. The surprise was short lived. Immediately after my attention came back to the present, the logic of this future lifetime made sense to me. A television commentator was a communicator of the highest order. A career such as this one certainly fit into my soul's spiritual job description.

The third lifetime I accessed during this class was more ambiguous than the first two. While there was no doubt in my mind that the first two lifetimes that I had found myself in were future incarnations, the third one that I had, could have been either a future lifetime or a past incarnation. I saw myself as a Buddhist monk in a Tibet not under Chinese rule. I wore the traditional robes and my head was shaven. Most of this simple lifetime was spent in the garden, growing fruits and vegetables that would feed the monks in the monastery, and in the kitchen where I turned the products of my garden into tasty and nutritious dishes. When I was not doing these very important jobs, I found myself functioning as one of the Dalai Lama's advisors and confidants. When I came out of my hypnotic trance and shared this lifetime with the class, I was told that when we try to do future life progressions, sometimes a past lifetime would squeeze through the floodgates that connected the subconscious mind to the conscious mind. I accepted this explanation. In the light of wide-awake reality, when this highly spiritual lifetime occurred did not seem important. Whether it had occurred in the past or was going to occur in the future was of no significance. It just made me happy to know that I would experience what it was like to be a loving and kind human being in the highly spiritual atmosphere of the Dalai Lama's Tibet.

Seeing myself as a Tibetan monk brought back the memory of the flashing *"RA"* on the Radisson Hotel's neon sign and the large group of Buddhist holy men who joined us on the Jungle Queen boat ride. This past experience took on a totally different meaning in light of the visit to another lifetime that I had just undergone. I could now see what this experience on the Jungle Queen was trying to accomplish. My heavenly helpers were desperately trying to communicate to me that I had had a lifetime as a Tibetan monk in my repertoire of lives. My mystical mentors knew that this knowledge would add a great deal of richness to my soul's spiritual story.

Things were happening fast. Knowledge about my soul's spiritual journey and its mission on our earth plane, for which I had been thirsting for such a long time, was streaming into my conscious mind. I could not help but find all of this very exciting. But, what happened next was even more exciting.

Sonya and her entire Pathways of the Metaphysician class were seated in a circle during one of our class sessions. After our teacher did an opening meditation and an explanation of the day's work, we all went inside of ourselves and opened up our Akashic Records. As soon as I opened up my individual records, I seemed to be consumed in flames.

With fear choking at my throat, I immediately shared my fiery distress with Sonya and the rest of the class. I told them that a town was burning down around me. The air was filled with terrified screaming as the townspeople ran in all directions. Sonya's immediate reply was that I was reliving a past lifetime in Pompeii at the time of the eruption of Mount Vesuvius. When I came out of the trance that had allowed me to access a past lifetime in Pompeii, the class questioned me. When I was asked if I had ever visited Pompeii, I answered, "Yes, I've been there twice. Even though I did not have any dramatic spontaneous past life regressions when I was there, I found it fascinating. Now that I think about it, Pompeii did have a strange feeling of familiarity to it."

After our lunch break, Sonya explained that we were all going to be rewired. We did an exercise that allowed all of the damaged aspects of ourselves, the parts of us that had been wounded through countless lifetimes, to come forward and to walk into the light. As all of these casualties of the war-like side of reincarnation stepped forward, I had the most surprising and awesome reaction. I felt absolutely no pain at seeing the entire trauma that my soul had experienced through the ages. Instead I felt like a compassionate historian reporting on what was to me a virtual reality. None of the trauma and pain that I was seeing was real. The only thing that was real was my immortal soul. Everything else was like an epic film on the movie screen of time. The only importance that these painful experiences held for me was that they were important lessons that my soul had to learn. I peacefully reported to Sonya and the class that my sacred self would no longer be tortured by these traumas.

As if this experience was not amazing enough, something even more unbelievable happened next. An enchantingly beautiful, serene and ancient face in the form of an ethereal mask came floating before my closed eyes. When I described this mask to the class I added, "This mask seems to express total contentment and omniscience. It seems to epitomize an ineffable quality of peace, wisdom and unending unconditional love." As I finished this description, I could hear Sonya chuckling. She could hardly control her glee as she told me that this mask was actually my immortal soul. I had finally come face to face with my sacred self. It is difficult to explain the feelings of completion and accomplishment that this unexpected meeting produced within me. A tremendous feeling of gratitude followed. I thanked God, my spirit guides and all of my mystical mentors for helping me to arrive at this hallowed place. My vibrations, which had been speeding up for a very long time, had finally raised me to a place that was spiritually high enough for my soul to come forward and introduce itself to me. The feelings of joy and spiritual attainment that this experience connected me to will sustain me for a very long time.

Even though I knew that my spiritual journey was continuous and that there was much more that I could still discover about my immortal soul, I had finally reached a point of satisfaction. I had uncovered a plethora of information about where my soul had been and would be on the stage of continuous physical life. I had also been fortunate enough to have deciphered my soul's most important missions on the earth plane, especially the ongoing mission as a communicator of interdimensional knowledge. I had even met many of my spirit guides and mystical mentors. And, last but certainly not least, I had been blessed with the knowledge of many of the signs and symbols that identify and guide my sacred self. Although I know that my spiritual sleuthing is not done, I am truly satisfied with what I have connected to so far. Having traveled so far and learned so much, I can only wish others the same success and feelings of accomplishment that my ongoing spiritual journey has brought to me.

LESSONS FROM CHAPTER XII

✳ Meditation helps you to receive intuitive spiritual guidance because it puts you into a state where your mind is relaxed and is less distracted by physical things.

✳ When you still your mind you cut down on static. This allows guidance from your spirit guides and from your Higher Self to come through.

✳ In order to meditate properly, seat yourself in a comfortable straight back chair in a quiet place. It is better to meditate with your eyes closed.

✳ Take three slow and deep breaths. It is better to breathe in through your nose and out through your mouth. Concentrate on this breathing process.

✳ Try to visualize your ideal place of relaxation. Make this a beautiful light filled scene. Bring the white light of this scene into every cell of your body. Then imagine that you are glowing with the same white light that this idyllic scene is filled with.

✳ Make sure that you pay attention to your breathing. While shutting out everything else around you, inhale this wonderful white light full of love and wisdom. Try to imagine that this white light is connecting you to a Higher Source and your Higher Self.

✳ Your meditation will benefit from the repetition of a special spiritual word such as "peace," "love," or "joy."

✳ Always ask for a message when you meditate. When you pray you are asking for help. When you meditate be sure to listen to messages that are sent to you from a Higher Source.

✳ Always end your meditations with a sincere thank-you. Your heavenly helpers always respond well to a show of gratitude.

Epilogue

We are always connected to those we love and who love us. Death can never separate us.

When I had completed the writing of this book and was beginning to prepare it for publication, it occurred to me that the number twenty-six was manifesting itself into my life again. I recognized that I had unconsciously pushed the book to completion so that it would be published during the year of my 62nd birthday and the 26th anniversary of my father's death. After I added these startling synchronicities to the other entries in my Lucid Notebook, I spent some time meditating about their significance. Looking inward helped me to understand that this mystical time schedule had been set for me by my Higher Self in collaboration with my father's spirit. This recognition wiped away any lingering doubt that I may have had about sharing the soul enlightening experiences contained in this book with the world.

As time went by and I got myself involved in the self-publishing of *Discovering Soul Connections*, another profound insight found its way into my consciousness. I was awakened one morning by this unexpected insight. My book was not complete. Something else, possibly relating to my father's spirit was going to happen. Questions about what this momentous something was going to be began to whirl around in my mind. It did not take long for me to receive the answer that I was so eagerly awaiting.

Marvin and I were excited about the upcoming birth of our first grandchild. When we were told that the baby would be a boy and that he was going to be named after my father,

I immediately knew that my father's soul was going to reincarnate into Ethan Frederic. I entered this revelation into my Lucid Notebook and decided that it would be my little secret. About two or three days after I made this astounding spiritual discovery, my son, Jay, the father of this child, asked me a surprising question. He asked me if I had any idea whose soul would be entering his first child's body. Without any hesitation, I blurted out, "I am absolutely convinced that my father's soul will be coming into Ethan." The conversation ended with this disclosure and life went on.

For two weeks before the birth of this special child, the occurrence of synchronicities and the incidence of twenty-sixes increased. Also, electric lights flickered wherever I went. As the frequency of these mystical events intensified, I became more and more convinced that this was my father's way of letting me know that he was about to reincarnate into my very first grandson. When Marvin and I walked into the hospital on the day that Ethan's birth was going to be induced, we stopped at the reception desk in the lobby. As we stood there, waiting for admittance into the birthing room, I finally told Marvin, "I intuitively know that my father's soul is coming back into the physical world in Ethan's body." As I told him about the flickering lights and what they meant, the light bulb above our heads blinked on and off. If this wasn't enough to convince me that my intuition was right, that my father's soul was ready to come back into the physical world, into the body of my first grandchild, what happened next was all the proof that I needed.

I walked into the birthing room and sat down on the sofa, camera in my shaking hand, to wait for the process of inducing labor to reach the desired results. As soon as I sat down, the fluorescent lights above the birthing bed began to flicker in a wild and uncontrollable way. I wasn't ready to share the intuitively obtained truth that my father's soul was alerting me of his upcoming descent into Ethan Frederic's body, but the lights were flickering so riotously that I had to say something. I said, "Oh, those dancing lights are just my father's way of expressing his delight at the upcoming birth of my first grandchild and the first great-grandchild to be named after him." Jay seemed to accept this. He told me with a nervous smile that the lights had been completely quiet until I walked into the room. This information did not surprise me at all.

I rested my head on the back of the sofa and closed my eyes in an attempt to control the overwhelming excitement that was bubbling up inside of me and was threatening to shatter my composure. I knew that I had to shut out the exuberantly dancing lights, which I now knew beyond a doubt were my father's way of letting me know that he was coming back into physical form. There would be time to celebrate this rebirth later on. I could not and would not share my unexpected joy with the parents of the blessed little baby who was coming into the world to complete their union at this time. It was not fair to allow my personal joy at my father's return to the flesh to eclipse their happiness.

A short time before Ethan Frederic was born, the lights over the birthing bed stopped blinking. When Ethan's head pushed through the birth canal and greeted the harsh light of the physical world with a stabbing cry of pain, I knew that my father's soul had made the transition that I was so eagerly anticipating. I quickly made a note that Ethan came in on the number seven. He weighed seven pounds and seven ounces when he was born at 2:57 in the afternoon. He was born in the seventh month of the year.

The rest of the day went by in a blur of excitement. When my head hit the pillow that night, my eyes would just not stay shut. Sleep eluded me. Spiritual insights and under-standings were whirling around in my mind. I lay in my bed and allowed the new pieces of the spiritual puzzle that had motivated the writing of this book, to finally fall into place. My father had returned to the physical dimension at this time because his other-dimensional work was done. He had succeeded in helping me to gain spiritual enlightenment and to share what I had learned with the world.

Before I finally drifted off to sleep, I had another insight that proved that my most recent intuition was right. My

insight was that my father's spiritual number was also seven. He was born on November 7th and was one of seven children. Some quick mental arithmetic brought me the knowledge that his birth number was also seven. This was proof positive to me that Ethan Frederic and Fred Schweitzer share the same soul.

This corroboration of the veracity of my insight about my father and Ethan Frederic motivated me to utter a prayer of thanks for the privilege of having attained spiritual awareness. There was no going back. This awareness was the soul connection that I had so fervently sought for so long. I had finally learned the most important spiritual lesson of all; we are always connected to those we love and who love us. Death can never separate us. The connection between dimensions is incredibly strong when love is involved. I also learned that we are all most definitely powerful spiritual beings, even when we incarnate into the dense world of the flesh. Nothing can ever keep us from connecting to our innate spiritual nature when we are ready to do just that. The connections are always there. All that we ever have to do is to take advantage of them.